To Verena
Who Shared it All

584   C. Jacques

With all my love
            Carol

Christmas 1974
        Durban

A Desk in Rome

Patrick Smith

A DESK IN
ROME

❧

COLLINS

ST JAMES'S PLACE, LONDON

1974

William Collins Sons & Co Ltd
London · Glasgow · Sydney · Auckland
Toronto · Johannesburg

First published 1974
© Patrick Smith 1974

ISBN 0 00 211043 1

Set in Monotype Baskerville
Made and printed in Great Britain
William Collins Sons & Co Ltd Glasgow

Contents

Author's Note

Much of this book is inevitably devoted to the intriguing activities of the Roman Catholic Church. Rome without the Vatican would be *Hamlet* without the Prince. Although Italy is a republic, a triple-crowned monarch lives in its midst, and exerts enormous influence on its affairs.

The collective anonymity of the British Broadcasting Corporation made it possible for me to spend most of my working life abroad, and Rome, where I spent almost half of that eventful time, was a wonderful final port of call. My thanks and acknowledgements are due first of all to the BBC for much of what I have written in the following pages. So many friends both in and outside the Corporation have helped and encouraged me that it would be invidious to name them. Without their succour I would have achieved nothing and to them go my heartfelt thanks.

P. S.

Prelude

Some of our happiest times in life are spent at the tables of our friends. It is then that we are most at ease, enjoying good food and drink and good talk. Yet there are pitfalls even on such relaxed occasions. It was over the dinner table of Milton Waldman that this book had its origin. There was the flattering request to write something of my life and work, which I accepted in the bonhomie of the moment. Yet once I set about rummaging in the ragbag of memory I became appalled. There were thousands of despatches and broadcasts, scores of well-thumbed notebooks to which I was adding steadily. There were on my shelves already dozens of superb books written by friends, who seemingly poured out their literary talents with consummate ease, and who seemed to have said everything already. It seemed an impossible task for a working journalist.

However, once I had left Italy a perspective slowly began to emerge from the crowded events and the welter of people encountered in the busy years spent reporting from Rome. Almost half my working life had been based there, though news is a fickle master and had sent me off in all directions; to North Africa, to the Middle East, to many of the Mediterranean islands, to vast tracts of Europe itself, including Russia. All roads led from Rome as well as back again. I swung through all points of the compass, but Rome remained the pivot of the magnetic needle.

Like so many things in life, I became a BBC foreign correspondent by chance. At the outset of the war I had been taken on as one of a small group engaged in building up our wartime broadcasts to Europe. In those early, formative days of the BBC European Service we had to turn our hands to many things. We broadcast talks in a number of languages, putting the British point of view on some of Goebbels's grosser lies; checked translations from English into the languages we knew, and found others who could do it for the rarer tongues; saw that contributors, well-rehearsed if possible, got to the microphone on time; worked on long-term directives and programme plans; took one's turn at firewatching in the Blitz and subsequent bombing raids; and somehow tried to keep going family life. As Hitler's panzers overran most of Europe, the stream of exiles grew to a flood: there were crowned monarchs, such as Queen Wilhelmina and King Haakon, doughty politicians, such as President Benes and General Sikorski and many others, such as a young, fresh-faced captain in Norwegian uniform, Willi Brandt, who were to become significant in the history of post-war Europe.

One evening in June 1940, while I was on duty in Broadcasting House, a call came from the Foreign Office informing us that a French officer had just come over, following the capitulation of France, and was to broadcast. Would we please 'vet' his script before allowing him on the air? The Foreign Office man could not quite recall the officer's name – 'Gaulle', or some such – it could be a pseudonym. This request to look over scripts of foreign speakers was part of a loose security check; we were supposed to be able to spot whether the talks contained any code messages. There was a switch-censor's key in every studio which could cut the speaker off, though I doubt if it was ever used. It is still part of standard equipment today as a 'cough switch', allowing the broadcaster to clear his throat unheard.

I doubt if any of us at the time realized that this was to mark a memorable turning point in French history. All I remember was that it was a depressingly wet night, and I regretted that I had not been able to get off early to drive back to my wife in Essex, who was expecting our first child.

Observing protocol we asked for the keys of the drawing-room behind the statue by Gill which stands in the entrance hall of Broadcasting House. We went down, opened the hospitality sideboard, and waited by the reception desk for the speaker to arrive. He was a tall figure in uniform accompanied by a young lieutenant wearing thick-lensed glasses, called Maurice Schumann. They made themselves comfortable in the drawing-room whilst we tried to summon the Director-General, who had left. Drinks were offered and refused. An awkward wait ensued until we managed to run to earth the Deputy Director-General, Sir Stephen Tallents, whom we caught just leaving for dinner. He was not particularly pleased, but came round within a short time. At our request de Gaulle handed over his script, so that we could see roughly how long it would take and make the necessary cuts in the bulletin which preceded it. It ran to some two and a half pages, and certainly contained no code messages as far as I could judge. It was a patriotic cry from the heart of a soldier politician, furious at the defeat of his country, refusing to accept the humiliating armistice terms of Compiègne. We were highly relieved when Sir Stephen arrived and took our unexpected guest to his office on the third floor. Again de Gaulle was offered a drink, and again refused. There was some polite desultory talk. I looked at my watch, seeing that Sir Stephen was obviously anxious to get to his dinner appointment, and suggested we should go up to the studio.

The studios are situated in a kind of tower in the centre of Broadcasting House, protected from extraneous noises by a narrow corridor which divides them from the outer shell of offices. With de Gaulle following, we had to make our way through a series of double doors to reach the studio where the French news broadcast was in progress. I opened the door to allow the General to pass through. As he edged past, the buckle of his Sam Browne belt caught on to my waistcoat button. I still have a vivid memory of that great nose flanked by two unsmiling eyes bearing down on me as he carefully unhooked himself. The same thing happened at the second set of narrow doors. Again, without the flicker of a smile, he unhooked himself, saying, '*Je vous suis, monsieur.*' So I led the way to the third set of doors without further contretemps, and ushered him into the studio.

The two evening newsreaders, Louis Cauzique (who used to do *petit point* between bulletins when he had finished translating them) and Maurice Thierry were sitting on either side of a double lectern, over which a microphone was suspended from the ceiling. They read alternate items. As Cauzique finished the penultimate story he moved away to give de Gaulle his chair. The General placed his *kepi* on the table, arranged his papers on the reading rack and waited for his cue. Opposite was Thierry, his shirtsleeves hoisted up with those expanding silver armbands one rarely sees nowadays. He perfumed the studio with cognac, for, as a self-respecting Frenchman, he had been drowning his sorrows on this tragic day in their history. Suddenly he caught sight of the French *kepi* with its two stars on the table opposite him, and, looking up from his script, saw the gaunt, erect figure of Charles de Gaulle. Silent tears began to roll down Thierry's puffy cheeks. I could well understand his emotion, seeing a French officer at that of all moments. Rather unsteadily, but with enormous dignity, Thierry half rose from his seat and bowed towards the General. In doing so he banged his forehead against the suspended microphone. It started to swing gently about eighteen inches in either direction on its long cable. The General did not bat an eyelid but got on with his speech, while the engineers at their mixer in the control studio on the other side of the glass panel kept twisting their volume potentiometers in time with the swinging microphone to keep the level of the voice as steady as possible.

De Gaulle finished his memorable broadcast, and then shook hands all round. We escorted him out of the studio, allowing him precedence this time, and showed him into a waiting car. Just before they left, Maurice Schumann said to me, 'You know, the General – he is a tank.' Then they drove off into the blackout. Certainly de Gaulle had remained completely unruffled throughout; his powers of single-minded concentration at his appointment with destiny were apparent. Probably he did not even notice the swinging microphone, or, if he did, perhaps thought it was part of the BBC's anti-jamming technique. This historic first message, in the confusion of the moment, was not recorded from transmission. We learned afterwards that de Gaulle had been furious about this lapse, and had gone off to a private studio to record his words for posterity. Today it is in the French government's archives, together with an account of my description of the scene, which was obligingly and stylishly translated by a French colleague to whom I told the story many years later in North Africa after de Gaulle had resumed power. They are still occasionally aired at appropriate anniversaries.

It was thus because of my wartime duties in the European Service of the BBC that I fell into broadcasting journalism. It was to lead me eventually to Rome through devious stages which included a short spell as a temporary lieutenant-colonel interrogating German prisoners of war at Compiègne and finally as a war correspondent with the Eighth Army in Italy. I remember collecting my accreditation from the War Office in Whitehall and then going across with a fistful of clothing coupons to a nearby tailors to be fitted out with service dress and other accoutrements required for the assignment. Proud in my new uniform – for like many other young men on civilian duty I had something of an inhibition about not being in the forces – I made the mistake of walking back to Broadcasting House through Horse Guards Parade. I received a smart salute from a sword-clanking trooper, which startled me so much that I almost raised my hat, but, remembering just in time that I, too, was in uniform, saluted back as best I knew.

After saying good-bye to my wife and children, I spent the night in Broadcasting House on a truckle bed, rose before dawn and walked down to St James's Street where I was to catch a bus to take me to the RAF station at Lyneham. I walked briskly along the deserted streets of the West End and was surprised to be accosted by a not-so-young lady of the town on a corner of Piccadilly, to whom I explained that I was on my way to the war. '*Bonne chance, chéri*,' she said with a sad smile, and turned away. When I checked in at the RAF office I found that, for unspecified reasons, the plane was not leaving that day. So the next day the same process was gone through. For the second time I encountered the same lady on the same corner, to whom I explained rather sheepishly that the plane had been delayed, but that I would be off within the hour. Once more the plane was grounded.

For the third and last time, the following morning I set forth yet again from my bunk in Broadcasting House. As I approached the Piccadilly corner I felt sure my acquaintance would be on duty. She was, but this time when she caught sight of me, obviously thinking that I had already had my night on the tiles, she spat on the pavement in disgust, turned contemptuously on her heel and went away before I could explain. That morning the plane was ready, and I flew to Naples in time to report on the closing stages of the Italian campaign. Little did I know at the time that I was to return to Italy years later, in vastly changed circumstances, to spend almost all the rest of my working life there.

CHAPTER ONE

How to Become a Saint

It seemed something of a miracle to be back in Rome early in 1958, for my assignments after the war had been taking me farther and farther away from Europe, landing me finally in Cape Town with little between me and the South Pole. I pinched myself as I took a sentimental stroll down Rome's Bond Street – the via Condotti – with its smart jewellers, its ancient Caffè Greco, its high fashion leather merchants and outfitters. I turned through a courtyard of a rambling palazzo, which belonged to the diminutive Duke of Caffarelli, past Battistoni's elegant shirt shop, and took a creaking lift to the top floor to the office I was to work in for the first few years. I sat down at a dusty desk, looked at the incoming post and then began the task of reading through the morning papers. Newsprint in Italy has a distinctive smell, and I recalled my earlier days in Rome, when the *Messaggero* and other papers had made their first post-war appearance. They still had the same smell.

After spending an hour or so alone with the morning press I began to wonder who my first visitor would be. Soon there came a knock on the door, and in walked a tall, ruddy-complexioned Dominican friar. With an unmistakable Irish accent he introduced himself as Father Romuald Dodd of the church of San Clemente, near the Colosseum.

'I am very glad to welcome you to Rome,' he said, shaking my hand warmly. 'I knew your predecessor, and thought I would just look in to greet you and see if there was anything I could do for you.'

Over coffee he told me of the church where he lived and studied, one of the most impressive in Rome. In the depths of its foundations – it is built on the site of a Roman senator's house – a stream still gushes under the ruins of an ancient Mithraic temple. On the lower floor are remnants of the early church, constructed when the ground level of the city was appreciably lower than it is today, where, apart from colourfully naive frescoes, there are buried Saints Cyril and Methodius, who brought Christianity to Eastern Europe. The present church, built on top of this, is also several centuries old and has magnificent tessellated floors and glowing mosaics surmounted by a massive, gilt-coffered ceiling, resplendent with the coats of arms of popes and cardinals of long ago. Fr Dodd told me that some of his fellow monks actually prayed that this golden baroque ceiling might harmlessly fall down one day, so that the more ancient mosaic apse, which it partly cut off, might be seen in its full glory.

'Father Dodd,' I said, 'I am sure you know a great deal about Rome which will be most helpful to me. What is your special field?'

His swift answer took me rather aback. 'Miracles,' he said. 'If you ever have difficulty over the reporting of miracles – and they do happen, you know – just get in touch with me, and I will put you in the picture.'

Of course I had read and heard of the blood of Naples's patron saint, Januarius, liquefying three times a year, and how the Neapolitans believed it to be a good sign if the liquefaction was accomplished quickly and feared an eruption of Vesuvius if it took too long. I had also read of Padre Pio and his stigmata. I have still a very open mind about miracles, but, being a journalist, have always had a sneaking regard for Doubting Thomas.

'What sort of miracles do you have in mind?' I asked.

Father Dodd paused a moment, pursed his lips and then replied, 'These miracles can be very difficult to assess. The Pope, you know, sent out a confidential instruction to all bishops in Italy not so long ago saying in effect: "I don't want any more miracles. There have been far too many reports of such wonders. I want you to deal very severely with them and not allow them to be made public unless they have been absolutely authenticated. We know all about leaking pipes dripping on to statues and the word going round that a statue is weeping or bleeding. We don't want any more of that." However,' continued Father Dodd, 'in spite of the Pope's admonition, there was a case recently which I knew of at first hand. Have you ever heard of the weeping Madonna of Syracuse?'

I confessed my ignorance.

'Well, in Sicily, in the port of Syracuse,' the monk went on, 'there was a ceramic representation of the Madonna hanging on a wall of the church. It was not of great artistic merit, just one of those run-of-the-mill plaques of the della Robbia type you can buy in any religious articles shop. One day this particular one started weeping – and there were no leaky pipes anywhere near it. The faithful in the church soon spotted it. There were murmurs of "It's a miracle", and soon great crowds thronged inside to see the weeping Madonna. The Bishop had had his instructions from the Pope, and tried to hush the whole thing up. Yet this was something he could not conceal, so he had a hasty conference with the Mayor. The Mayor said, "You are causing a public disturbance and I must send for the carabinieri." So the police were posted round the church to control the crowds. The Madonna was then reverently unhooked from the wall, still weeping. The plaque was dried thoroughly, and taken to police head-quarters for further investigation.'

Father Dodd paused for a moment and then resumed his tale.

'And do you know what? As one of the carabinieri was taking it along very gingerly in his hands, this simple tile of the Madonna started to weep again. The poor fellow nearly dropped it, he was so frightened. The plaque was wiped a second time, put into a dry airy room and left. The next morning it was weeping again. Inquiries were made at the factory where this particular tile had been made and tests were carried out on samples of the clay used in its composition. From all these investigations nothing unusual emerged.

'Well,' concluded my Dominican visitor, 'they have not put the Madonna back in its place on the church wall, so I suppose it is still weeping in a dark cupboard hidden from sight. Now that is a miracle for you, if you like.'

I agreed this was most remarkable, and promised to look into any reported miracles with great care. What I did not tell Father Dodd was that, shortly before he came in, I had been leafing through the office inventory and had found listed in it, 'one pair of binoculars, for seeing miracles with'.

In the days that followed I quickly became engrossed with the Italian political scene, and Father Dodd's offer of help receded in my mind. However, it was recalled when some two months later there came reports from Terni, a rather straggly town some sixty miles to the north of Rome, that two children were claiming to have seen a vision of the Madonna who had purportedly said to them, 'Come back again next Friday and I will give you an important message, not only for the people of Terni, but for the world beyond.' The Italian press were quickly on to the story, investigating every angle. Under close questioning both the children, not yet in their teens, stuck to what they had said. Journalists converged on Terni, and even television was alerted, though I could not make out how they proposed to film a vision.

In Rome the weather was at its worst, with torrential rain lashing the streets. On Thursday morning, the day before the vision was promised, Peter Nichols of *The Times* rang.

'Are you going up to Terni tomorrow?' he asked. 'If so, we might go together.'

I told him that I was still thinking about it and would let him know in an hour or so. I sat at my desk, looked out of the window and saw the rain pouring down. I telephoned Fr Dodd, but he was not in. Finally I rang back my colleague and said,

'I shan't be coming to Terni. I don't believe there will be a vision and, anyway, it's raining too hard to go on a wild goose chase. Besides,' I added, 'as you know, I've only just come to Rome. Should there be a vision, the BBC is bound to say, poor old Patrick, he's only been in Rome two months and he has already seen a vision of the Virgin Mary. What can have come over him?'

So I did not go. There was no vision, only a cruel hoax. The incident was tellingly recreated by Fellini, who was at the time making his remarkable film *La Dolce Vita*. In it is a scene of the two children running hither and thither, nudging each other with glee as they giggle mischievously at the duped crowds, including sick on stretchers, waiting for a sign from heaven. It was a terrifyingly cruel scene. Yet I have met people who have assured me that they saw the miracle of Fatima, when the Madonna appeared to shepherd children six times in Portugal in 1917. Perhaps only people of very deep and simple faith can perceive miracles, which I am sure can occur, though it has not been my good fortune to be present at one. The nearest I came to such an event was in the grounds of the Convento Pozzuolo, the summer residence of the Venerable English College, the ancient English Roman Catholic seminary. It overlooks Lake Albano and provides a cool retreat from the summer heat of Rome. I had gone there to see a cricket match, of all unlikely things, thinking it would make a light-hearted topic for a broadcast. Sitting next to me watching the game was a priest in his fifties dressed in rusty black. He told me that he had been a student at the college when a young man, and was at present working in a parish in the north of England. Since the time he had completed his studies and had been ordained he had never been able to afford to return to Rome.

'How have you managed it at last?' I asked. 'Did your parishioners pass the hat round?'

'No,' said the tired-looking clergyman, 'but I suppose it was a bit of a miracle that I am here. You see, I sometimes go to the races for a flutter, though I have never more than a few shillings to spare for the horses. A few weeks ago I went, as usual, put a few bob on a horse I fancied and collected my ticket from the Tote. It came in last. I was about to throw my ticket away when I saw that the number on it was not of the horse I had backed but of the winner, an outsider. Now you can't argue with a machine, so back I went and collected fifty pounds. For me that was a miracle, and that is how I come to be here. . . Oh, good shot, sir! Of course it could have been a mistake, or perhaps it was all a matter of pre-destination. You never can be sure, can you?'

Miracles and saints often go hand in hand, and, though I never had occasion to report a miracle, I often wrote about saints. Shortly after my arrival in Rome in 1958 Pope Pius XII had proclaimed St Clare the patron saint of television. A special Vatican decree explained the reason for this decision making the foundress of the 'Poor Clares', a Franciscan order of nuns, the heavenly patroness of television workers throughout the world. The decree, solemnly issued by the Congregation of Rites, recorded that in 1252 St Clare was lying in her sickbed in San Damiano near Assisi, and had seen St Francis and his fellow monks celebrating midnight Mass at Christmas in the Porziuncula, their tiny chapel some miles away. This chapel, incidentally, is now sur-mounted by a garish white church which completely dwarfs the beautiful tabernacle where the faithful still come in their thousands to pray. Not only did St Clare see them celebrating Mass, she heard their chanting too, so her nomination was indeed apposite.

St Clare was born in Assisi in 1193, and knew St Francis well when he was a rich young man, before he took his vows of poverty. She joined him in his noble work when she was only eighteen, followed by her sister Agnes. Together they founded the first convent for Franciscan nuns at San Damiano. St Clare never left the convent again, except once, when she met St Francis and talked to him of

God. She died in 1253, the year after her vision, and was canonised two years later. Her skeletal body in its rough habit can be seen in its place of honour beneath the high altar of the church of the convent. I shall always remember Santa Chiara, to give her her proper Italian name, because she was the first saint I spoke about after I arrived in Rome.

Having thus dealt with my first saint in the news, I delved more deeply into the whole problem of sainthood and how it is proclaimed. I discovered, for example, that Pope Pius XII, since he ascended the pontifical throne in 1939, just before the outbreak of the Second World War, had declared at least 150 new patron saints. Heading the list was the Virgin Mary, who had been declared patroness of no fewer than eighty-three countries in four out of the five continents of the world. She is still far and away the most popular of saints, being on the threshold as it were of the Trinity. Pope Pius was much enamoured of her, and, it is said, once had a vision of the Madonna while meditating in his private library in the Vatican. Apart from her saintly protection of many countries, the Virgin Mary is patroness of such groups as Italian cyclists, sportsmen in Belgium generally and Spanish speleologists. Everyone has heard of the Madonna of Lourdes, who appeared in a vision to the peasant girl Bernadette Soubirous, the Madonna of Fatima with her prophecies and the famed Polish Madonna of Czestechowa; in fact it sometimes appears that Roman Catholic countries vie with one another in claiming the Madonna as their particular patroness.

There are, of course, a host of other patron saints. The Archangel Gabriel, who appeared to the Virgin Mary, is appropriately the patron saint of postal and telecommunication workers. A British publication dealing with Roman Catholic aspects of broadcasting, simply called *Annunciation*, commemorates this fact. St Matthew, who obviously knew about business through gathering taxes, is the patron saint of merchants. Long before Pope Pius appointed him, merchants would begin their accounts with the flourish 'In the name of God and of profit', and even Dr Livingstone said he opened up Africa 'in the name of commerce and Christianity'. So the link between religion and money-making is very ancient. Journalists have St Cassian as their patron saint, though few know that this third century schoolmaster who refused to make sacrifices to the gods was stripped naked and stabbed to death by 200 of his pupils with their pens.

The Vatican Congregation of Rites deals with these matters, and is at present considering whether St Joseph of Cupertino, who died in 1663 after a wondrous life in his monastery, should be declared the patron saint of space travellers. Early records claim that he walked on air on no less than 70 different occasions. This gift of levitation was something of an embarrassment to his fellow monks, who sometimes had to hold him down to prevent his hovering over the high altar during Mass. During the last war he was chosen patron of many Roman Catholic airmen. He is also revered in Italy for quite another reason. Apparently he was of no special academic brilliance, but when it came to his entrance examination for the order he was asked only those questions on which he had previously mugged up, and so passed without difficulty into the Franciscans.

Apart from proclaiming new patron saints, the Roman Catholic Church has its own honours list, and patiently examines the claims put forward on behalf of those who may, at some later date, be proclaimed saints in the Christian calendar. In recent years the causes of both Pope Pius XII and of Pope John XXIII have gone forward. From my own personal contact with Pope John, I would say that he was, like St Francis, a saint in his own lifetime and needs no formal endorsement. Pope Pius, with his ambivalent attitude towards the Nazis, is quite a different case.

It is a long and complicated process which leads to the proclamation of a new saint. Sometimes the process is spread over centuries and can be very costly. There are two stages:

first beatification, when the person concerned earns the title 'Blessed'. To complete this first step the candidate must have shown heroic virtue illustrated by at least two miracles, or he must have been martyred. Miracles have to be established by witnesses, generally the candidate's compatriots. Initial inquiries are made by the local bishop, and if he is satisfied he refers the case to Rome. If the cause is considered worthy, the 'apostolic process' begins, and the case is taken up by the Congregation of Rites. This Vatican body was set up in the sixteenth century to supervise all that concerns public worship. Its members subject the life, writings and alleged miracles to most searching scrutiny; it is here that the Promoter of the Faith (more popularly known as the Devil's Advocate) submits the cause to severe tests. The proposed candidate is measured against the three theological virtues of faith, hope and charity and the four cardinal virtues of prudence, justice, courage and temperance. All the evidence is most carefully sifted to make sure, for example, that there can be no natural explanation of the miracles reported. His task, in a word, is to make as certain as is humanly possible that no one unworthy receives the highest honour which the Church can bestow. It is a long process, and many fail.

The pope is the final arbiter of beatification, though his decision at this stage is not held to be infallible. I attended more than one beatification ceremony in St Peter's. The brief putting forward the candidate's claims is read out, the *Te Deum* is sung and the picture of the newly beatified person is unveiled above the altar. In pictures and statues the beatified is allowed to be portrayed with rays of light round his head, but no full halo. That is reserved for the saints.

The step from beatification to canonization involves further lengthy scrutiny, and often is not even undertaken. If this final process is initiated, it must be proved that two further miracles have been wrought through the intercession of the beatified. Tests of these miracles are extremely rigorous.

The whole cause is minutely examined at three further meetings of the Sacred Congregation of Rites. The pope presides at the final meeting before canonization is finally approved. The canonization ceremony is an occasion of solemn splendour at which the pope inscribes the name of the new saint in the canon or list of saints already proclaimed. Three times the postulator of the cause asks the pope to inscribe the name of the saint-elect in the register of saints. After the third request the pope, speaking in Latin, declares this ancient charge: 'In honour of the holy and invisible Trinity, for the exaltation of the Catholic faith and the increase of the Christian religion, by the authority of our Lord Jesus Christ, of the holy apostles Peter and Paul, and by our own, after mature deliberation, ever imploring the divine assistance, by the advice of our venerable brethren the cardinals of the Holy Roman Church, the patriarchs, archbishops and bishops present in the Eternal City, we decree and define and inscribe in the calendar of saints the Blessed ——, ordaining that their memory be celebrated with devotion every year in the universal church.' It is a solemn pronouncement, generally followed by prolonged applause, for clapping in church is quite common in Italy. The *Te Deum* is sung, while the great bells of the basilica sound out the news, quickly taken up by the bells of every church in Rome.

The last canonization I attended was in 1970, when the cause of the forty English and Welsh martyrs, initiated by Cardinal Manning in the nineteenth century, finally came to fruition. Many pilgrims came from Britain to be present, and passed under a shield bearing the cross of St George and the English rose and Welsh daffodil in its quarters, hung high above the main portico of St Peter's. They were clearly moved as the long list of names was read out, and applauded fervently when the Pope declared them saints. It was the end of a long and disputatious road, in which the rules for canonization were bent to allow them all to be enrolled.

They were declared saints on the evidence of one miracle shared by the entire group. Their cause was considered controversial, especially in these ecumenical times, since the men and women who died for their faith were considered traitors by the supporters of Queen Elizabeth I. Many other brave Protestant men and women were likewise sent to their deaths on the scaffold during the short reign of Mary Tudor. In fact, more were executed at Smithfield than at Tyburn. However, the Anglican Church has no canonization process, and therefore the Roman Catholics hold an advantage in heavenly accolades. The causes of Pope John and Pope Pius will doubtless take a long time, for the Vatican thinks in terms of centuries. Canonizations do not take place all that often.

The official declaration of new saints can give great satisfaction to the faithful, however. I recall the canonization of the first coloured saint in South America, St Martin of Porres. He was a lay brother to whom miraculous cures are attributed, and is, incidentally, the patron saint of barbers, for among his other duties he cut his fellow monks' hair. My wife and I had gone across to the church of Santa Maria sopra Minerva to hear the first negro cardinal of modern times, Cardinal Laurean Rugambwa of Tanzania, celebrate Mass in honour of the new saint. During the service we ran across a cheery, tubby English priest, Fr Vincent Smith, who until shortly before his death was rector of the English church of San Sylvestro in the heart of Rome. In a strong Mancunian accent he asked, 'What are you doing here? You must be the most Catholic Protestants in Rome.' As I was explaining that the service was of considerable interest a Dominican glided by in his black and white robes. Fr Smith plucked the monk by the sleeve and said, 'Have you any secondary relics for me?' It was my turn to ask Fr Smith what secondary relics were.

'Well, if a saint dies, his robes, his rosary, any holy books, medallions or other possessions which have touched his body, are kept, apart from the body itself, from which you may take the hair. If you touch these possessions with something else, there you have your secondary relic, and the faithful believe that they can have miraculous powers.'

The traffic in such secondary relics is considerable. Even greater is the whole business of papal blessings. A special Vatican office deals with the thousands of applications which pour in from all over the world each year. Many shops in Rome sell beautifully illuminated scrolls for the purpose, surmounted by the pope's picture and coat of arms which, after approval, are sent to families, newly-married couples, individuals and groups of other deserving recipients. In certain cases, where good Roman Catholics are about to celebrate a golden wedding or perhaps a birthday in advanced years, arrangements can be made for the pope to send a special telegram of congratulatory benediction. One of our oldest friends, a devout peasant woman of unshakable faith, was about to have her seventy-fifth birthday. In her remote Alpine valley she had gone to Mass every day, winter and summer, and though of modest means had given much of what she had to people less fortunate than herself. I spoke to a Vatican official on her behalf, and no doubt inquiries were made through her parish priest, who delivered the pope's telegram personally on the appointed day. While I was arranging all this, the official asked me whether, in addition, I would like an *Agnus Dei*. He explained that this took the form of a wax disc imprinted with the ancient Christian symbol of the Lamb of God. They are made from the candle ends of the tapers which burn on the pope's private altar in his personal apartments. The pope blesses them, and they are sent, for a special fee, to certain selected people. The official (who I discovered subsequently was an authority on freemasonry) told me that the faithful often apply the *Agnus Dei* to the affected part of the body and sometimes achieve, if not a miraculous cure, at least some relief from suffering. I suppose it is all question of mind, or

at least faith, over matter. The whole question of sanctity
and relics is undoubtedly linked with man's atavistic belief
in the supernatural, if not a residual superstition from the
dawn of time, translated into a sometimes shame-faced
credulity in fetishism and other alleged forms of magic
which are supposed to help and protect him on the difficult
path through life.

CHAPTER TWO

Roofscape

While I was coming to grips with the political, economic and religious aspects of my assignment, returning each evening to the Hotel de la Ville at the top of the Spanish Steps, my wife had been equally active trying to find somewhere more permanent to live. This was no easy task, for we wanted to be in the heart of the city, not only because it would be near the office – and I like walking whenever I can – but because Rome, like all other great cities, has an osmotic effect on one's living and writing. After growing footsore and disheartened, we had a stroke of good fortune. Like so much in Italy it arose from a chance personal contact. An old Italian friend who was visiting us put us in touch with a distant relative of hers, Princess Orietta Doria Pamphilj. As a result, the Princess invited my wife to tea in her vast palazzo on the Corso. It marked the beginning of a lasting friendship with one of the most illustrious houses in Italy. More important at the time, the Princess offered us the choice of a small apartment in a tower on top of her palace or much larger accommodation in one of the villas in her great park behind the Janiculum on the outskirts of Rome. We chose the former, and spent thirteen happy years in it.

We never lost the sense of privileged wonder at the view from our home, up among the pigeons and swallows. Sitting at the breakfast table I would look out across the fascinating roofscape of Rome to see the great cupola of St Peter's gradually arise out of the morning haze. At lunchtime the sun's rays would slant through the windows of Michelangelo's lantern tower for a few minutes, almost setting it on fire. Churches, domes, towers, parapets and statues were all about us, soaring above the roofs, with their ancient heavy tiles of sun-baked ochre clay. There were breathtaking views at all points of the compass. To the east, the imposing pile of the Quirinal Palace, now the official residence of the President of the Italian Republic and once the home of kings and popes. To the south, the massive marble monument to Italian unity, and next to it the graceful Capitol with the equestrian statue of Marcus Aurelius in its oval piazza. To the west, innumerable churches, including St Ivo with its unmistakable corkscrew tower and, beyond, St Peter's on the skyline.

Throughout most of the day, life was accompanied by the sound of bells floating across the rooftops. There were the hasty tintinnabulation of our nearby little church, the urgent clanging of the bells of the Gesù where the Jesuits seemed incessantly at prayer, and booming occasionally across the Tiber, the deep-throated bells of St Peter's, the largest church in Christendom. Opposite our tiny balcony sat Garibaldi on his horse on the Janiculum Hill, and punctually at noon each day we would see a sudden puff of white smoke nearby, followed a few moments later by the thud of the noonday cannon. This in turn set the bells of all Rome ringing out the Angelus. The Angelus is normally rung in the early morning, at noon and again in the evening. It was Pope John, out of regard for people's habits, who decreed that the morning Angelus should be rung at seven o'clock instead of the customary six, so as to allow people more rest. In a noisy city like Rome this was a thoughtful gesture, typical of that great and good man.

An anti-Fascist journalist friend once told me that, when he was a schoolboy, hating with all his adolescent fervour the strutting Duce, he conceived the idea of getting the noonday gun loaded with live ammunition, since he calculated a shell fired from it would wreck the Palazzo Venezia, where Mussolini had his headquarters, and thus put an abrupt end to the Duce and all his evil works. Of course it never happened, though an Italian finally did put paid to the dictator, and I saw the petrol station near Milan shortly after the bodies of Mussolini and his faithful mistress Clara Petacci had been cut down, after hanging ignominiously by the heels, to be reviled by the mob. The slogan daubed above the corpses was still there: it read, *Fascisti prenotatevi* – Fascists reserve your seats. It was a grim and cruel ending, though politically it cleaned the air. The Italians, unlike the Germans, did their own dirty work.

The tower, which was our home, looked out across the Palazzo Venezia where the Duce used to harangue the multitudes. Towers have always been very popular in Italy, and in Rome, as elsewhere, families vied with one another in seeing who could build the highest. San Gimignano is a classic example of this. Most such towers have disappeared in Rome, with the exception of the Torre delle Milizie, which still looks massively over Trajan's Forum and leans considerably, though not as frighteningly as either the Tower of Pisa, or the tower in Bologna. Our tower – or *altana* – was rather like the one on top of St John Lateran. It was originally a belvedere, open on all four sides to enable the owners to have a 360° view of the capital. Once glassed in, it made a perfect nest from which to watch the rooftop life of Rome. Down below, in the Piazza del Collegio Romano, teenagers played in front of the Liceo Visconti, for the old Gregorian University building had been turned over to secular use after the unification of Italy had ended the temporal power of the pope. The observatory tower of this ancient building, which the Jesuits, who had founded the Collegio Romano, once used to scan the heavens, still served as an observation post, though for the Ministry of Forests and Agriculture, which posted one of its weathermen there. This tower was only about 60 yards as the pigeon flew from our tower. Every morning, at precisely eight o'clock, a grey-haired man would come out and inspect the rain-gauge, take the barometer reading, verify the temperature, the strength and direction of the wind, note everything down and then retire until the same time in the evening. He was our closest neighbour, a high-level acquaintance whom I never had the good fortune to meet personally, and whom, no doubt, I would anyway have failed to recognise at street level, though probably I passed him hundreds of times without knowing who he was.

There is a special quality about life on the Roman roof-tops, for the Romans excel in making roof-gardens, no matter how small the terraces. And many roofs, with the help of seed sown by the passing birds, had a glory all their own, the *flora tectorum* of willowherb and lichen, of ragwort and buttercups. To these wild flowers around us we added our own – azaleas, lavender, oleander, honeysuckle, roses and my wife's special pride – herbs for the kitchen. Verena not only believed in watering the plants, but in talking to them as well – encouraging some and chiding others. I once did a short broadcast on this odd facet of our domestic life, and had a letter from a listener in East Africa who complimented me on having the good fortune of living with a wife who talked to the flowers and herbs, rather than to her husband.

Some of the loveliest rooftops are part of monasteries and churches. It was a common sight to see monks and nuns pacing the galleries of an evening, reading their breviaries. And what magic there is in the evening light! For about an hour before sunset, the whole of Rome is bathed in that soft golden glow which has attracted painters down the ages and which Canaletto catches to perfection. In fact, life on the rooftops never failed to fascinate. For years every morning I saw a not so young man keeping fit and bronzed by skipping on his terrace before most of the city's inhabitants were astir. Was he an actor trying to maintain his figure and youthfulness? One day he was no longer there. Had he been taken ill? Had he fallen on bad times and been unable to pay the rent? Or had he had a great success and moved on to a far more splendid penthouse? It was just another Roman enigma.

Many is the time that I have seen Roman beauties washing

their hair on the terraces and drying their locks in the sun. Or the chatter of crowds at a rooftop cocktail party would come drifting across the roofscape, snatches of voices, the strumming of a guitar – sometimes the more insistent sound of a transistor radio at full blast. The rooftops were often festooned with washing – I have frequently thought that a string of washing is the unofficial national flag of Italy. 'The nuns are having a field day with their washing,' my wife would sometimes remark, pointing to a long line of ecclesiastical laundry fluttering in the breeze and adding its special splash of colour to the skyline.

Apart from people and flowers, no mention of a Roman roofscape is complete without a reference to the birds. Pigeons fly heavily between the campaniles where they roost, sometimes disturbing the owls, who hoot at night like fog-bound ships. Swifts dart from the eaves, wheeling and side-slipping in the warm air, catching insects on the wing and uttering their sharp little notes in a kind of crazy round-Italy cycle race, miraculously avoiding head-on collisions by a hair's breadth. Filled with incredible *joi de vivre*, we would watch them time and time again, as they soared and tumbled effortlessly in the heavens.

All these pleasures came as a result of that chance meeting with the Dorias. They were the kindest landlords we ever had. When we first met Orietta, her father, Prince Filippo, had just died, and she was managing her vast possessions and coping with the incredible legal tangles of inheritance as best she knew single-handed. Prince Filippo was a well-known anti-Fascist. He had suffered at the hands of Mussolini, who hated him so much that he ordered not only his deportation to a remote village in Southern Italy but even changed the name of the narrow road skirting the Prince's home from Vicolo Doria to Vicolo della Pace. During his studies in England the Prince had met and married a Scots girl, Gesine, and she was throughout her life a staunch supporter of her husband. She refused to cast her wedding ring into the urn in which Italian women were ordered to place them in order to help Mussolini finance his Abyssinian campaign, and when her husband was banished, to that harsh part of the country so tellingly evoked by Carlo Levi in his *Christ stopped at Eboli*, she went with him to share his exile. Her daughter Orietta, then in her teens, stayed with friends in Trastevere. They not only hid her but also her precious family jewels, which she kept concealed in a shabby shopping bag ready to grab should the police track her down and try to arrest her. In the end Prince Doria managed to escape and, though he lived again in his palace, the police never were able to track him down in its thousand rooms and corridors.

After the fall of Mussolini and, in 1943, the setting up of the Badoglio government, Orietta joined a women's organisation helping run canteens for the Allied troops advancing from the south. 'They called us the cakes and wads girls,' she said with a smile. During her duties she met a young lieutenant in the RNVR – the 'wavy navy' – and fell in love with him. The young man from Bristol, Frank Pogson, made a note of her address and promised to look her up when he had leave in Rome. He told me that he was staggered to find that his girl-friend lived in a palace the size of Selfridges. The romance blossomed. Prince Filippo was appointed first mayor of liberated Rome, but he was not up to all the party intrigues and subsequently retired to administer his estates. Before then, however, he had seen to it that the street near his palace had reverted to its old and rightful name. Once more there was a Vicolo Doria on the map of the capital.

Before the old prince died, he gave his blessing to the marriage of Orietta and Frank. He had one request, that the name Doria should not lapse. His great ancestor, Admiral Andrea Doria, had been faced with the same problem and had adopted children to keep the name alive. The couple were married quietly in London. The Italian press was initially hostile. It was said that this great Italian heiress should have married into the Italian nobility, or at least should have chosen a British peer as her partner. They were difficult early days, but the young pair bore them gracefully and showed what a happy marriage could be. The criticism has long since died away. It was, after all, by no means the first time that this great Italian family had been linked with Britain. Apart from her father's marriage to a Scot, in the nineteenth century Orietta's great-grandfather had married Lady Mary Talbot, a lady-in-waiting to Queen Victoria. To this day one of Orietta's favourite pieces of jewellery is a modest diamond and ruby ring containing a wisp of the Queen Empress's hair which she gave to Lady Talbot as a memento of her coronation.

The marriage of Orietta and Frank was not blessed by children, so they adopted two British youngsters; Jonathan, who also has the name of his illustrious adopted ancestor Andrew, and Gisene, who bears the name of the princess's Scottish mother. They are two lively children who will carry on the name of the Dorias.

A few ancient families still manage to live in the palaces which were built by their ancestors in more spacious days. The Dorias, the Colonnas, the Torlonias are among them. Very few, however, are now able occupy the entire space which was designed for the days when the great families held their own courts, had their own private bodyguards, their army of lawyers and musicians, artists and scholars, innumerable relatives and other hangers-on to accommodate. Today most such families content themselves with the *piano nobile* – the high-ceilinged first floor of the palace in which are the State apartments, the ballroom, the chapel and private rooms for the family. Taxes and death duties have forced them to let off the rest. Some are no longer occupied at all by the families which once owned them. The Palazzo Chigi, which was built by a prosperous banker who financed several popes, is now the Italian prime minister's office, after having been for years the Foreign Ministry. Some palaces are now put to far more mundane use as offices and workshops and warehouses. Quite often, as I walked round inner Rome, I would come across a carpenter's shop, or a picture frame maker's, a garage or a haberdasher's store, behind the great grilled windows of a once noble mansion.

Much of the Doria palace has thus been put to other use. The ground floor, once the stables, coach-houses and lumber rooms, has long since been converted into shops and offices. There is a printing works in the basement, there are bookshops, banks, a vast emporium selling household goods and toys, a perfumier, a clothing store, a shoeshop – and until recently even a circulating library, one of the very few in Rome. Even the *piano nobile* has been invaded. What was once the papal throne room was turned into a ballet school. The once world-famous dancers Alexandre and Clotilde Sakaroff used to put young dancers through their paces, as the piano tinkled beneath the not-altogether approving portrait of Pope Innocent X, perhaps the greatest ancestor of the Doria-Pamphilj family, the Pamphilj Pope who saw the completion of St Peter's, and whose coat of arms, the dove and the olive branch, adorn its pillars. After Alexandre died the ballet school lingered on – it was still there in our time – but finally it was disbanded. Its graceful, lofty rooms were avidly snapped up by a group of bankers, and Clotilde, who in her time had inspired Rilke to write ecstatic poems about her dancing, got on with her memoirs. She was an astounding woman who had walked with beauty all her life, who had known many of the great painters of her day – and who was convinced that she was the re-incarnation of a wayward aunt who lies buried in Cairo. To hear her talk in French, or English, or German (for she surprisingly came from an old Prussian officer's family who were appalled at her choice of the ballet as a career) was to catch the lilt of far-off, enchanted days. She died last year, at the age of eighty.

There are more offices on the upper floors of the palace, and a few apartments, culminating in our tower at the very top. When the lift failed to function – which was not all that infrequent – our home was reached by the ascent of 150-odd stairs. The tenants of this great honeycomb include a number of pensioned-off retainers. There are also several clergymen. One friend there is Mgr William Purdy, a stalwart Derbyshire man who works in the Vatican's Secretariat for Christian Unity and who, in spite of his 60 summers, is never happier than when on the cricket field. Another priest has the privilege of living next to the private chapel where Pope Pius IX celebrated his first Mass after ordination. There used also to be the friendly Ladies of Bethany – an order of Dutch nuns permitted to perform their ecumenical duties in ordinary clothes. Before the traffic of Rome was the *kamakaze* horror it is today I used to see them setting boldly forth on sturdy bicycles to guide people of all ages and religions round Rome. They are now housed in another Doria palace in the Piazza Navona, whose church of St Agnes, opposite Bernini's fountain of the four rivers which bears Pope Innocent X's coat of arms, is within the gift of the family. These Dutch nuns today run a simple *pensione*, and welcome hundreds of visitors each year in their Foyer Unitas, which has become a centre of practical Christian friendship. I have rarely seen a more happy group of women, who show that religion need not be a miserable kill-joy affair.

There were many other inhabitants – the Italians use that splendid word *inquilini*, which sounds somehow far more dignified and classical – in this great palace with its four courtyards, after the Quirinale possibly the largest in Rome. There were lawyers and journalists, party and government officials, one or two diplomats, a doctor, a brace of stock-brokers, a chemist, several teachers, as well as a florist, a policeman, a composer, a sculptor and an engineer. There were also several elderly ladies living on peppercorn rents who busied themselves with pious activities of one kind or another. Among other offices were those of an ex-service-men's organisation and one dealing with orphans, two news agencies, and, Rome being a sort of Hollywood on the Tiber, at least one film star at any given time. On a rooftop across the main courtyard from us was the Anglican Centre, set up by the Archbishop of Canterbury under the aegis of Canon John Findlow, a kindly priest well versed in the Greek and Slavonic languages, another happy Christian who went to his reward far too early in life. His successor was an Australian, Dr Harry Smyth, who presides with equal enthusiasm over the centre with its fine library, donated by Anglicans all over the world, where Roman Catholics and others may consult books on every aspect of reformed religion. Quite frequently lectures and ecumenical services are held in its spacious rooms. I once asked Princess Doria how many rooms there were in the palazzo. 'I have never really counted them,' she replied, 'but I think there are about a thousand or so.'

Some of the finest on the *piano nobile* are open to the public three times a week. Frank and Orietta have followed the tradition of the British stately homes, though they don't go as far as the Duke of Bedford in inviting unknown visitors to sumptuous dinners, at a price.

There is a steady stream of visitors to see the magnificent private collection of pictures and statuary, who wander round lofty frescoed galleries and through the lovely apartments, which are adorned by artists of the seventeenth and eighteenth century. Some of the gorgeous tapestries hanging on the walls had been in storerooms for decades, and now can be seen once more in all their glowing magnificence under gilt-coffered ceilings resplendent with coats of arms. One of the Gobelins was a gift from Louis XIV, and is emblazoned with the *fleur-de-lis* and the sun of *le roi soleil*. Another was woven by Flemish craftsmen in the fifteenth century, and was given by Charles V to the Admiral Andrea Doria – there is always at least one ship in the Italian navy which bears his name. Although the gold and silver threads of this great tapestry have been dulled by the centuries, the

39

colours are still warm and lovely. Legendary scenes in the life of Alexander the Great form the motif. You see him descending in the depths of the ocean in a great glass sphere, much as Professor Piccard was to do centuries later, or again, soaring into the heavens in a kind of floating sedan chair, borne aloft by four strong-pinioned cockatrices being urged ever higher by, of all things, succulent legs of mutton fixed to the ends of long poles. Visitors are also shown the gracefully proportioned ballroom, its ceiling painted like the sky, with doves with olive sprigs in their beaks flying against the pale blue – the crest of the Pamphilj Pope who lived here once artistically adapted to this delightful room.

The pride of the whole palace is undoubtedly the portrait of Pope Innocent X by Velasquez. It is one of the very few signed by the artist, and Ruskin held it to be one of the ten greatest portraits in existence. There Innocent sits, on a golden throne (still in use in the papal summer residence in Castel Gandolfo), holding a document and looking at you with piercing disillusioned eyes, which follow you wherever you stand. Next to it is a bust done by Bernini of the same pope in his last days. He is seen hollow cheeked and hagridden, the victim of his rapacious sister-in-law, Donna Olympia, who left him to a pauper's funeral, taking what was left of his personal fortune from under his bed before the corpse was cold.

The bust of this formidable lady stands nearby, done in exquisite alabaster and showing clearly the 'no-nonsense' character she possessed. When the Allied armies liberated Rome, some British troops were billeted in the galleries of the palace and referred to this termagant's bust as 'the matron'.

It would be idle to list the entire collection, for each visitor will have his own favourites among the Caravaggios and Poussins, the Piombinos and the del Sartos and the glowing primitive altar pieces. For British visitors there are, however, two pictures of especial interest which could easily be missed.

One is a portrait of the Old Pretender, the father of the tragic Bonny Prince Charlie, who lived in his own world of regal fantasy in the Palazzo Muti, only a stone's throw away across the Corso in the Piazza Santissimi Apostoli. The other is of Isaac Newton talking with the Earl of Gravesend, the unmistakable figure of Britannia, dressed as the helmeted goddess Minerva, standing between them.

Apart from the pictures and ancient statuary there are many other beautiful things to admire: decorated clocks of all kinds, collections of intricately carved amber, ivory and coral figures, mirrors and cabinets and inlaid tables, papal relics – including the case in which the ceremonial hammer was used to tap the dead pontiff's head thrice before pronouncing him dead and the Holy See vacant – an uncomfortable-looking carved cradle, embellished with the papal tiara and military and naval emblems to suggest the career its occupant might follow, a child's sledge, a sedan chair, suits of armour and pikes and lances and also, forgotten in a corner, an ancient Roman iron bucket. There is also a chapel unused for generations until the adopted Doria children made their first communions there in 1972. It contains many splendid pictures and carvings, relics by the dozen, including the bones of early Christian martyrs, one entire skeleton being attired in the uniform of a Roman soldier with a sword grasped in his bony hand and a martyr's crown of gilded laurel around the skull. There are also serene majolica stations of the cross round the walls, and the vaulted ceiling is painted with *trompe l'oeil* scenes which give a remarkable impression of looking upwards into the open sky.

Throughout the *piano nobile* the floors are a joy to behold, whether the inlaid marble floors of the State apartments, the encaustic tiles of the galleries or the highly polished parquets of the private rooms. Here is the house of a *grand seigneur*, still lived in and enjoyed.

When our daughter was married in Rome, the Dorias most kindly suggested that the reception should be held there. All the grandeur was displayed for the guests to admire, and my wife and I had hastily to inform some of them that we did not actually live in such state, but occupied a small home right on the roof. Princess Orietta, a tall and handsome woman of great dignity, enjoyed herself. It was the first wedding in her house for over 70 years, and she arranged all the flowers, while her husband proposed the toast of the bride and groom in his own bluff, naval way. There will no doubt be other weddings nearer home in this noble setting as the years pass and the young Dorias come into their own. We were often there at their hospitable table, and never tired of being shown round with other visitors after dinner – it is always wonderful to enjoy others seeing lovely things for the first time.

The custody of such treasures is a great responsibility. Some years back, on a Friday morning, as the gallery opened at ten a man dressed in holiday attire and wearing sandals on his bare feet came to look round. He did not stay very long. On the Sunday morning, when the gallery opened again at the same time, a monk, also in sandals, was one of the first to enter. He had a brief look round, and left within half an hour. Shortly after his departure an attendant noticed that a small picture by a Flemish artist, a charming portrait of a woman, was hanging slightly askew. He went to put it straight, and found that the original had been replaced by a passable imitation. The presumed monk had left with the masterpiece under his habit. Princess Doria was immediately informed and the police alerted. I sent a swift dispatch about the theft to the BBC, and soon other journalists were in hot pursuit.

In the face of such instant publicity it was obvious that the thief would find it hard to dispose of the picture by smuggling it out of the country. Within three days the Rome police had an anonymous call telling them to look out for a parcel placed behind the main door of the church of Santa Croce in Gerusalemme. A flying squad car rushed to the church

and there found the stolen picture, quite undamaged. Today
the placid face of the unknown Flemish woman still smiles
sweetly at her admirers, few of whom know her strange
adventure.

Since that time art thefts have reached gigantic dimen-
sions and, though there is a special branch of the police
which succeeds in recovering the more notable works stolen,
many disappear over the frontiers to add to private collections throughout the world. Today, however, the pictures in
the Doria collection are firmly screwed to the walls, and
other anti-theft devices have also been installed. In a country
such as Italy, so richly endowed with such treasures, it is
impossible to keep watch on everything. Churches in particular are often the targets of sacrilegious thieves, while the
tombaroli, the tomb robbers of ancient sites, also manage to
carry on a lucrative trade. Some pieces are smuggled across
the frontiers buried in sand or other building materials.
Not a few are discovered by the customs men, but they cannot
stop the traffic entirely.

The Dorias suffered considerable losses from their villa
and park on the outskirts of Rome. This 500-acre estate,
known as the Villa Pamphilj, has as its chief monument the
grand house designed by Algardi. The park is a peaceful
oasis on the fringe of Rome, with gentle pastures and pine
forests, trees of every variety, fountains and formal gardens,
waterfalls and great stone stairways leading to loggias and
marble balconies, all once adorned with busts, statues and
urns. But the art thieves had their eyes on what could be
taken away, and most of the statues of artistic merit have
either been removed or defaced.

Apart from the main villa, other smaller houses, cottages
and a few small holdings are dotted about the grounds. In
1972, the whole park was taken over by the municipality for
a much-needed open space for the crowded inhabitants of
Rome, who have less than a square yard of green per head.
Before this happened we were among those privileged to use

the park whenever we wished, for picnics and walks. Often one would encounter a cardinal reading his breviary wandering in the shade of the ilexes. There were sheep grazing on the slopes round the Arch of the Four Winds, the scene of the final battle between Garibaldi's troops and the French *Zouaves* of the pope. Prince Filippo, with consummate fairness, had memorials erected to the fallen of both sides within the grounds. Yet amid its frame of oaks and pines, cedars and palms and many other rich and rare trees, the villa stands out against the clear sky like a Piranesi etching, and the flora and fauna have changed little since the days when Caesar built a villa for Cleopatra on this very site.

Its broad acres are honeycombed with unmapped catacombs, on top of which, until recently, the flannelled fools of the English sports club used to play cricket at weekends. Behind one wicket the great dome of St Peter's loomed up, a kind of ecclesiastical sight screen, while behind the other a sturdy grove of stone pines formed the background. It was a delight to see the bowlers send down their googlies from the Vatican end, and to see a typical English village green, complete with the clatter of the teacups and the gurgling of bottled beer, as the metal figures clanged on the scoreboard.

Many happy hours were spent walking and talking about the two thousands years of history enshrined in its bounds, bordered on one side by the ancient Aurelian Way, whose aqueduct running along the top of the wall is still in use to this day. All popes tried to curry favour with the populace by bringing in water for the lovely fountains, and anyone who wants a complete picture of how this was done can read with pleasure H. V. Morton's fascinating book on the waters of Rome. In more recent times the Villa Pamphilj was used as a summer residence for popes and cardinals. Early in the last war it was occupied by the Germans, then requisitioned by the Allies, and subsequently used as the private residence of the Belgian ambassador. He almost succeeded in buying it for his country, but a piece of last-minute legislation prevented him from doing so. Today the villa stands neglected, for the Rome municipality has debts of millions of pounds unpaid, though the open spaces where once Cleopatra dallied are now pleasure grounds for thousands of Roman families.

Those fortunate enough to have lived in the grounds before they became public have long since left – not without regret. An Italian senator occupied one of the loveliest houses. The indefatigable English writer and historian Georgina Masson lived in a converted stable, a long, whitewashed room ideal for writing. She came to Italy during the Second World War and stayed on to earn her living, working hard at her writing and photography. She had a hard time at first, but this energetic woman, with her bright eyes and insatiable curiosity for the past, was not easily discouraged. She told me how she had plodded round Italy with her second-hand camera – when at work she always wore an apron, with kangaroo pockets for her lenses and filters – industriously photographing the villas, palaces and gardens of Italy which she published in memorable books. Her patience was incredible; once she waited for more than three hours to get a picture of peacocks strutting across the lawns on the fantastically beautiful Isole Borromee on Lake Maggiore. Her interests ran far and wide, from wild flowers to such enigmatic historical figures as Frederick II Hohenstaufen and Queen Christina of Sweden. But perhaps her lasting memorial is the compendious *Companion Guide to Rome*, a classic *sine qua non* for all who would know more about Rome and many aspects of its kaleidoscopic life. Whenever she is 'with book' Georgina Masson is a difficult woman to contact, for she cuts herself off from her friends and goes single-mindedly at her task. Between whiles she is a delightful companion and conversationalist, wears her great erudition lightly. She also has the remarkable quality of never having lost that first fresh enthusiasm for all things Italian, which she manages to communicate with zest to her readers. She now lives near

Florence, and no doubt will find much in that wonderful city and the surrounding Tuscan countryside to enchant her readers for many years to come.

CHAPTER THREE

The Italian Character

There are any number of odd angles to working as a journalist in Rome. One is the effect of the weather on its inhabitants. They are nervy and tend to explode when the sirocco blows, are cheery when the cold *tramontana* whistles down from the mountains – and above all they have a deep dislike of rain. When it rains in Rome, it pours – in fact, the annual rainfall of the city is as great if not greater than that of London. It tends to bucket down around Christmas and the New Year, and then the Romans, normally such a vivacious and merry lot, look suitably woebegone. They take the foul weather almost as a personal insult. On one occasion an old Italian friend, a naval officer whom I had known in Cape Town and who was quite at home in the roaring '40s, rang me to put off a meeting. 'It's raining,' he said. I replaced the receiver and thought what a strange excuse to give for not coming. Yet doctor and dentist friends confirmed that many of their patients cancel their appointments when the weather is bad. They feel affronted – and perhaps some, jealously guarding their *bella figura*, don't wish to risk spoiling their clothes in the bad weather.

Another strange thing is that, though the Italians are inveterate telephone users, a journalist cannot achieve much behind his desk on the telephone – at least, not at first. You have to be known personally to anyone you ring up before he will utter much, and even then he is often on his guard. Some say this is a throw-back to Fascist days, when telephone lines were tapped as a matter of routine – to judge by recent reports, these bad habits die hard – while others have told me that every Italian fears that the telephone caller may be the tax man in disguise, and no self-respecting Italian wants to deal with him unless he really has to. One of my dearest Italian friends, the soul of probity, once confided that if an Italian were to make an absolutely honest tax return he would be bankrupt; for by the same token no tax official ever expects anyone to tell the truth when giving details of his income and fortune, and adjusts the tax accordingly. There generally follows a long bartering session, and the final tax figure hovers either side of a half-way mark between what the taxpayer says he should pay and what the tax-gatherer demands. Consequently lawyers flourish in Italy, for a good lawyer can save you a lot of money.

To describe the legal situation in Italy would need a thick volume to itself. Everything is in arrears, and it is quite common for a civil process to take several years before it reaches the courts. In penal cases, the unfortunate accused may have to spend months in prison before his case is heard. If he is acquitted he has no redress for his incarceration, though if he is found guilty the time he has spent in gaol is subtracted from his sentence. It is an unfair world indeed. Some courts are overloaded with work, others have relatively little to do, yet it is rarely possible to transfer the backlog. In consequence most of Italy's prisons are very overcrowded. One way of controlling the situation is by the president's annual amnesty, which automatically wipes off certain cases unheard – I have even heard it said that, if you choose your time carefully for your crime in Italy, you can get off scot-free. Yet something generally sticks, for the laws of libel are far less rigid than in Britain. It is normal to read about 'hideous monsters' and 'ruthless murderers and heartless swindlers' long before the cases come up for a hearing. Only a wealthy and persistent character would dare to take issue with the newspaper concerned.

Though there are hundreds of newspapers in Italy, the Italian, on the whole, is not an avid newspaper reader. The largest newspaper, the *Corriere della Sera* of Milan, has a circulation of just over half a million. Most newspapers are supported financially by industrial or political groups, but the readership for such a large country – Italy has nearly 55 million inhabitants – is relatively small. The Italians prefer reading illustrated magazines or watching television. This is particularly true in the south, where illiteracy is still far higher than is often imagined. It is quite common to see adults reading *fumetti*, or books of comics, so-called since what dialogue there is is contained in little clouds of smoke.

Italian journalists are able to spread themselves far more than their Anglo-Saxon counterparts. It is not unusual for a correspondent to fill three full columns of closely-set italic type on the front page. There is not the same fashion of compressing the main facts of the story into the first paragraph to form what is known as a 'punchy' lead. The story unfolds at a far more leisurely pace, and every conceivable detail is drawn in. Sometimes the article will open with a historical introduction reaching far back; there will follow a description of the landscape and the climate; and only then will the writer feel obliged to get down to the facts, which sometimes are left right to the end of the piece. One or two papers have tried to be crisper, but it seems that the average Italian prefers the long-drawn-out account, laced with every detail possible. In spite of the fact that the Italians have some of the most persistent press photographers, there still is a demand for the artist on the spot, and the *Corriere* publishes a weekly with lurid pictures of terror-stricken people fleeing from earthquakes, gory representations of explosions, traffic accidents and murders. The artists have a free hand, and their work is extremely melodramatic.

Most of the daily newspapers have a special page devoted to more cultural topics. It is known simply as the *terza pagina* – for page three is always the one to which those who want to read about the arts turn first. Journalism in Italy is a highly protected calling, with its tightly organised associations into which no one is admitted unless he has passed a qualifying examination. Some years back people were astonished to learn that the well-known writer Alberto Moravia had decided to take this examination, which, needless to say, he passed. With his slight limp, Moravia is a shy man, quite unlike any of the characters he portrays. He speaks in a very soft voice, about his work, almost self-deprecatingly. Tall, with iron grey hair and deep-set eyes, he can often be seen walking near the Piazza di Spagna at the time most of Rome takes its *passeggiata* – a stroll in the cool of the evening. His glowering glance under bushy eyebrows gives him a Mephistophelian air, but he is, in conversation, the gentlest of men. Though in my view by no means the best of present-day Italian writers, popular English translations of his works make him perhaps the most widely known. His books reflect much of the boredom of our consumer society as they affect the decadent, pleasure-loving folk he revels in describing.

Moravia takes his journalism seriously, and is one of the highest paid in his field – and top-flight Italian journalists, unlike the bulk of their colleagues, are very well paid indeed, with fifteen months' salary a year, lavish holidays, and, most amazing of all, often a retirement pension higher even than the money they earned when fully employed. By the same token, foreign correspondents in Italy share a lot of the advantages enjoyed by the Italian press, though not such generous terms of employment. Still, they can apply for membership of the *Associazione della Stampa Estera*, and once admitted have the right to a number of useful aids in their work: free telephone calls within the Rome area, a desk, and even a typewriter in the spacious rooms of the Foreign Press Club, cheap tickets on railways, airlines and motorways where tolls are still paid, and any number of trips on which they may take their families, even free of charge. Every province and city of Italy, it seems, encourages these press trips – often they present handsome prizes to journalists who turn in an article which will help tourism in their particular part of the country.

As I was for several years president of the Foreign Press Club, I was able to see how many of my freelance colleagues looked to these free trips to help them make ends meet. Though I rarely had time to go on them myself, I did sit on a number of juries which had the task of selecting winning articles for a particular prize. That delightful publicist Professor Vinciguerra, who used to preside over the sessions for the Rome Prize, once turned to me and said, 'We have so many prizes in Italy, the difficulty is to find sufficient journalists to give them to.' Not only journalists, but film actors and writers, painters and poets, all have a chance of winning a million lire, or, in the case of the Premio Rusti-chello of Pisa, half a kilogram of golden sovereigns. Rusti-chello, as far as I could ascertain, was a kind of public relations officer to Marco Polo, and his name is recalled annually when the local tourist authorities award a prize for the best articles on their area. I served for several years on that committee, and saw how hard-fought the decisions were. Yet there is something delightful in these practices, for we are all at heart children and love to be told that we have merited some special prize for work already done – especially if it comes in the form of cash, an illuminated scroll, a medallion or, as in the case of Pisa, a clutch of golden coins in a supple leather bag. The city fathers of Pisa go out of their way to be hospitable, and hold the ceremony in the *aula* of the university with the seated statue of Galileo brooding over the proceedings. They often make the prize-giving coincide with the feast of the city's patron, St Ranieri, which turns the leaning tower and the banks of the winding Arno into a fairyland of flickering lights.

The Foreign Press Club was founded more than 60 years ago, and is probably the oldest in Europe. It was started during the first World War when the Italian authorities found that journalists were taking up a lot of time and space in the main post office in the Piazza San Sylvestro. They offered a few rooms of their own, with cable and telephone facilities. When Mussolini came to power in 1922 he, as an old journalist, saw the advantages of pampering the foreign press, and placed at their disposal more spacious premises and introduced many facilities, which Italian and foreign journalists still enjoy today, though naturally without strings attached. In the Fascist era the Foreign Press Club was a convenient centre for keeping an eye on journalists, and not a few were thrown out of Italy, among them Vernon Bartlett, who was helped to freedom through a back window by one of the post office staff before the police had time to arrest him.

The fortunes of the *Stampa Estera* waned in the second World War, when membership diminished considerably. However, when the Allies liberated Rome there was in the vanguard an American correspondent, Reynolds Packard, of the *New York Daily News*, a rumbustious character who boldly requisitioned the premises on behalf of the Allied correspondents. He had been a member before the war, and felt he had the right to act as he did. A hearty writer, with a Rabelaisian bearded countenance, he produced two books which achieved some notoriety. One was about Mussolini, *Balcony Empire*, and the other a novel about the life and hard times of a news agency man in Paris, which was called *The Kansas City Milkman*.

Since those early post-war days the Association has grown, and today boasts over 500 members. Its salon and bar have seen most of the newsworthy people of our time, and quite a number who hope to hit the headlines. The members, as anyone who has had a hand in helping manage the affairs of the *Stampa Estera* knows, are highly individual, not to say downright eccentric. I once had to use all my tact to prevent two irate colleagues from fighting a duel. Yet on the whole this corner of Rome serves an extremely useful function as a meeting place of the highly diverse points of view which go to make up the very essence of what journalism is about. Although the majority of members are non-Italian, there are some Italians working exclusively for foreign papers and agencies who are admitted as members and who play a useful part in the management of the association's activities. Whenever a news conference is held, the Italian press as a whole is invited, and many abiding contacts are formed. Italian journalists are among the most generously jolly if completely undisciplined colleagues in the business – especially the press photographers, to whose brave hearts nothing is sacred when it comes to getting that extra picture which may sell for hundreds of dollars. They certainly earn their money, carrying round with them everywhere the heavy accoutrements of their calling. They can never afford to be late for an event, yet, once the story has been covered, they ship off their film and are done with it all, unlike their writing colleagues, who have to sit and ponder their hastily written notes.

This is not true, however, of television cameramen, who have to fill in a 'dope sheet' giving precise details of every foot of film they have taken. The TV cameramen and recordists I worked with in my years with the BBC were among the hardest-working, most courageous and friendly men I have ever had the good fortune to meet. Their precise powers of observation are a godsend to the man who has to contrive his report or programme, and their buoyant behaviour in times of trouble is a great comfort, as I saw not not only in Italy, but in Cyprus, Algeria and Tunisia. One of those with whom I worked frequently was Bill Baglin, the ace BBC cameraman who has got out of more dangerous and difficult situations than anyone I know. He was rightly honoured by the Queen for his devotion to duty and his dash. There are many more with whom I have toiled in Africa and the Middle East as well as in Europe – men whose names are scarcely known outside their own intimate circle, but whose work is of vital importance to the electronic journalists of today.

In spite of what the pundits say, broadcasting, though more immediate in its impact, can never replace the newspaper and illustrated magazine. It is complementary to them, it provides healthy competition, but it can never meet the needs of someone who wishes to take his time over inquiring about any issue. In Italy television is followed by millions who shun the fatigue of reading, for, as already mentioned, the Italians are not avid readers and it is quite common to find no books at all in many an Italian household. Nevertheless, Italy can boast some of the most penetrating journalists of our time, several of whom it has been my good fortune to know well. One, whose name is known far beyond the frontiers of his own country, is Luigi Barzini. For many years he was a foreign correspondent of the *Corriere della Sera*, but he made his name when he published his views on his own countrymen, *The Italians*, which has run into many editions and been translated into a score of other languages. Barzini, who spent many years in the United States, wrote the original in English, very much with an American readership in mind. It became a best seller, though he told me that that was largely because millions of Americans of Italian origin bought it in the belief that they would read laudatory chapters on their famous forebears such as Christopher Columbus and Enrico Fermi. Instead, having bought it, they read about Cagliostro and Cola di Rienzo, Mussolini and the Mafia bosses; cynical portraits of popes and kings. Yet the affection was there all the time underlying the shrewd cynicism. It is required reading for anyone who attempts to understand the complex Italian mentality, and above all it is a book about real human beings who have sought in their various ways to come to grips with all the complexities and injustices of our imperfect world.

Barzini is a handsome man with the profile of a Roman Senator – in fact, for some years he was a Liberal member of parliament and one of the most trenchant critics of its decadence. He actually translated his own book from English into Italian, and expected a hail of abuse from his countrymen when it was published. But, after the furore of the American version, the Italian edition, though it sold well, did not stir up the same consternation, for the simple reason that the Italians knew at first hand that what he wrote was palpably true. I used to meet him often at official dinners in the Club dei Scacchi just off the Corso and at receptions in the presidential palace of the Quirinale, looking at the scene with a quizzical air. I would sometimes visit him at his well-appointed house out on the via Cassia. He loved all things English, smoked a pipe, drank tea, raced his yacht and even rode to hounds, for Rome still has its own pack, which hunts along the Appian Way. He told me how he had once been talking to a rather boring Italian when he suddenly felt himself gripped by a heart attack. He managed to get rid of his visitor before slumping to the floor. Yet Barzini bears no mark of the cardiac neurosis which afflicts so many who have suffered similarly, people who have made a perfect physical recovery, but who fear that they may blow up again at any time. He has a moving account of this happening in his equally successful book *From Caesar to the Mafia*, which, if anything, is even better than his first book.

Barzini puts his finger unerringly on human weaknesses and ambitions, as perhaps only a really successful man can afford to do. 'In the heart of every man,' he wrote in *The Italians*, 'wherever he is born, whatever his education and tastes, there is a small corner which is Italian; that part which finds regimentation irksome, the dangers of war frightening, strict morality stifling. That part which loves frivolous and entertaining art, admires larger than life solitary heroes, and dreams of an impossible liberation from the strictures of a tidy existence. The consolations which Italy afforded at all times have become more infinitely precious today than they ever were. . . The art of living, this disreputable art developed by the Italians to defeat regimentation, is now becoming an invaluable guide for survival for many people. More and more come to Italy, drawn to the place where the new perplexing problems of the world are familiar monsters, problems with which the natives have learned to live long ago. In a minor way, Italy has perhaps become once again a teacher of nations.'

Barzini told me that he believed this to be especially true of Britain, whose people, after generations of imperial glory, were having to learn to live with the harsh facts of reduced circumstances. I think he is right, though some of my countrymen living in Italy perhaps go a little too far in their efforts to be a law unto themselves. The old tag *Inglese italianizzato, diavolo incarnato* – an Italianised Englishman is the devil incarnate – is often true. Some of the worst road hogs on the *autostrade* are foreigners aping the Italians, whose reflexes are that much quicker. More than one modest English maiden lady trundling around in her Mini thinks nothing of keeping the British number plates on her car long beyond the permitted period, so as to avoid paying road tax, driving across the frontier occasionally to get vouchers for cheaper petrol and returning for a further six months as a 'tourist'. The Italian police generally get them in the end, but few would think that these gentle souls, who would be more at home crooking their little fingers winsomely over the teacups in Cheltenham, would stoop to such illegal practices. The Italians know and understand, and have a sneaking admiration for anyone who can get away with it. Many do, and not only English spinsters. There is a way round most things in Italy, with its interminable bureaucracy, and many short cuts as well, if you have the right contacts or are armed with the proper *raccomandazione*, that vital adjunct to any dealings with officialdom which oils the wheels and opens the required doors. One thing in Italy you learn is never to accept no for an answer.

Luigi Barzini, in one passage in his book on his countrymen, likens Italy to a *trompe l'œil*, a smooth coloured surface over a multi-coloured reality. He has no illusions about the merits and defects of his compatriots, and quotes Vittorio Alfieri in his support: 'the plant, man, grows in Italy second to none.'

'Single men, in the heart of their families, developed superior qualities. Added together, however, millions of them always amounted to no more than a weak, gullible and foolish mob,' adds Barzini for full measure, and goes on: 'The Italian nation never managed to solve its element-ary problems and the Italian army rarely succeeded in defeating their enemies. Italy has never been as good as the sum of all her people.'

Personally I find Barzini over-harsh on his own people, and I suspect, good journalist as he is, that he knows the attraction of overstating his case. Controversial opinions always sell well, even if they do not find agreement. Barzini also likens life in Italy to a slab of clear glass over a stormy sea. The non-Italian sees little of what goes on underneath, except for the frequent demonstration or strike which may disrupt his holiday for a while, but which, as often as not, provides a point of interest in an otherwise carefree stay. Even those who come to Italy on business see little of this underground turmoil. Italians overwhelm their guests with hospitality, and one soon becomes accustomed to the agree-able habit of the *pranzo di lavoro* – the working meal which can extend over several hours, especially a lunch which will last into the afternoon. This shocks the newcomer, until he realizes that the siesta habit dies hard and that most Italians will think nothing of working in the evening until eight o'clock if need be.

The tendency is to eat later than in Britain, though usually not so late as in Spain. I have seen latecomers order dinner in a small restaurant at midnight and the owners not turning a hair. Eating and drinking are serious matters in Italy. No one thinks of hurrying over a meal. There is something almost sacramental about it, and to this day people will make the sign of the cross before cutting a loaf of bread. I have learned a lot about the Italian way of life in innumerable *trattorie* up and down the country, for these are the obvious meeting places with acquaintances and friends, who tend not to invite one into their homes. One soon learns in Italy never to drop in on people. Adequate warning must always be given, except in cases of emergency or with Italians who have lived a long time in Britain or the United States, and have grown accustomed to the open house principle.

The open house goes for the Italian's immediate family, but not far beyond. The Italian has a strong clan feeling and will help those even remotely related to him, expecting, as a matter of course, help at some later date in return. Altruism is not widespread, and I recall my surprise when one lady, collecting for charity in the streets, insisted on showing me her accreditation before pinning a flag on my lapel. Such women are rare. Charity is left largely to the Church. There was one old monk who used to go round restaurants with his worn leather collecting-satchel at meal-times. Most succumbed to giving him a donation, though psychologically I always thought it akin to hitting below the belt.

Every now and then some scandal concerning the corrupt organisation of an orphanage or a hospital comes to light; it is a nine days' wonder, and then slips into oblivion. The Italian has an ambivalent attitude towards authority of any kind. He would like to be part of it, so that he can use its influence and patronage to his own advantage. At the same time he tries, and very often succeeds, in dodging his civic duties when it comes to paying tax or even military service. Fit young men in Italy have been known to get out of their eighteen months' conscription by knowing the right people, or by offering an appropriate inducement. Sometimes they simply absent themselves abroad at recruitment time and come back years later when their papers have become irretrievably buried in the archives.

It was often remarked to me that Italy is a wonderful country to live in if you are rich, or if you are a foreigner. This may be a cynical simplification, but there is some truth in it. Certainly the Italians are the least xenophobic nation I have met. They like foreigners. It enables them to get on another wavelength, to show themselves off to better advantage. Foreigners also bring in useful currency, but though tourism is the great invisible export of the country, which until recently more than balanced the annual trade deficit, it is not only that which makes the foreigner popular. They often give him a new lease of life; he becomes a Walter Mitty, achieving things he never would in the humdrum surroundings of his own tight family circle. They become attractively larger than life, as Barzini maintains, and are happy to instruct their newly-found foreign friends in the 'disreputable art of living'.

Yet the Italian, in spite of his surface gaiety, is at heart a pessimist when it comes to civic and national affairs. Parliament, the one body which should in theory be able to put things right, is admitted to be relatively powerless. There are too many cross-currents of interest to make it effective, and these cross-currents are most strongly felt in the government of the day, which, since the war, has always been an uneasy coalition led by the hopelessly divided Christian Democrat party, which enjoys Vatican support, its most stabilising factor. The Italians revel in elections, when the piazzas are loud with election propaganda and the streets awash with leaflets, but the results are nearly always the same, despite the immense expenditure of time and money lavished by the dozen or so parties. The Palazzo Montecitorio, which houses the Chamber of Deputies, has been likened to a Grand Hotel without bedrooms, where the members may eat and drink and talk, take a bath and even have their hair cut while waiting their turn in the debating chamber.

To be an Italian deputy is to have a reasonably well-paid existence, with many fringe benefits. As a matter of course the members pay a certain percentage of their salary to the party funds – the Communists taking the largest slice. The legislative process is slow, and so hedged about with provisos and safeguards and the general rigmarole of bureaucracy that little is achieved. A recent example is the vast sum of money voted to the victims of the earthquake in Western Sicily in 1968. Apart from a few barracks, nothing has been done to construct permanent houses for the homeless of Gibellina, Salaparuta, Santa Ninfa and other towns in the Belice valley. In one case attempts to set up a new market were blocked for six months because the relevant documents were held to be incomplete: they were tied together with ordinary string and not with a tricolor tape as the regulations prescribed. Fatalism is a common trait among the Southern Italians, especially the Sicilians, and goes some way to explaining the existence of the Mafia and its rule of *omertà*, or honourable silence. The Italian electorate does not expect all that much from its legislators anyway, unless they happen to be related to one of them. The *raccomandazione*, as I have noted, plays a significant part in everyday life, for without the signature of a politician or party official even those of outstanding merit often fail to progress. It is accepted as one of the facts of Italian life, deplorable yet seemingly inescapable.

This is why some believe that for centuries the Italians have sought a release from this underworld of intrigue and graft by turning to the arts, in which they have so often excelled – perhaps most of all in the art of living itself, as Barzini maintains. Certainly the Italian has a flair for living for the moment and enjoying life as it comes, rarely planning far ahead, since that would mean looking for disasters on every level. The visitor sees little of this side of Italian life, and the very fact that he probably does not speak more than a few words of the language endears him to many Italians. There are, in fact, times when even the Italian-speaker does well to conceal his knowledge. In hotels very often it is more advisable to speak English if you want good service; it puts the Italian staff on their mettle, switches them over to another wave-length and helps them to forget their immediate troubles and pressures, transporting them into a different and, as they imagine, fairer world. They are not hampered by any exaggerated chauvinism, as the French tend to be, but are individualists who get on easily enough with those around them; perhaps this is why they make such good international officials. Their background is not that of a closely-knit nation; their loyalty is to far smaller groups, the province, the city, the village even and above all the family. With such a personal tradition behind them they can work easily in international institutions where survival depends not only on nationality but on the ability to look after your own personal interests.

Having said this, I would by no means wish to leave the impression that the average Italian is a self-seeking egoist, to the exclusion of everything and everyone else. Many former Allied prisoners of war could testify to the contrary. There were many simple and unassuming countrymen who concealed and fed them at the risk of their own lives and who still keep in touch with those friends who were on the run during the latter stages of the war after Mussolini's downfall, when the Nazis moved in *en masse*. Several gripping stories have been written about these experiences. Writers such as Eric Newby, Stuart Hood and others who owe their lives to the kindness of Italians have narrated their tales convincingly.

These Italian countrymen, shrewd and cautious, are perhaps not completely typical of their compatriots, in that they acted without expecting many plaudits. The Italian is certainly seen to fullest advantage when in the limelight, not least by himself. His is the cult of the *bella figura* – he loves cutting a dash. He will run into debt to have a car which he may not really need and but rarely uses. He will spend more than he can afford so that he can say that his wife and family are having their annual *villegiatura* – the tradition whereby they move to the mountains or to the seaside, leaving the husband to toil away in the summer heat of the city. They will see to it that their children are sumptuously dressed for carnival time and for their first communions. And when it comes to weddings they are inclined to throw all caution to the winds to ensure a really magnificent *festa*.

I find this love of showing-off very pleasing. It had something of an effect on me, for I was never more careful about my dress than when I was doing the rounds of Rome. The Italians judge a great deal by outward appearance, which is why you see relatively few Italian blue-jeaned hippies. It cuts across all that they believe to be right. Psychologists try to explain this devotion to the *bella figura* as an expression of insecurity. I am not so sure; from what I have observed the Italian likes to please himself and give pleasure to others by arousing admiration for his turn-out. The Italian male has something of a peacock quality, and likes to strut about in his finery. This is another reason why he will stay at home when it rains – his feathers won't get bedraggled. In such a mild Mediterranean climate he is not confined for very long. The very weather makes it easy to live far more in public, and full advantage is taken of this agreeable fact. It also explains, to me at least, why the standard of public building is so much higher than that of domestic architecture. The home is largely a *machine à vivre*. The bulk of real life is led in the full public gaze, which the Italian enjoys uninhibitedly, whether in church, in the theatre or opera house, or just sauntering along the fashionable streets looking at the shop windows or chatting in the Piazzo Navona or by the Trevi fountain.

I had a friend who for many years had been a municipal official of Rome, and who, though long since retired, helped the mayor in some of his more formal duties, which included marrying couples who did not wish to have a church ceremony. (In Rome, to be married in Michelangelo's palace on the Capitol is as impressive a ceremony as anyone might wish for.) He loved Rome, and every morning of his life was up early, wandering round the streets of the old city taking measurements of some of the ancient buildings. He showed me many corners I would otherwise have missed, and was proud to have disovered that quite a few of the buildings so much admired had been built by eye, so that not all corners were true angles of 90° as one would have thought. He was a bald and tubby little man, who would always be impeccably dressed even in those early hours when we would sometimes meet, he with a carpenter's rule in his hand, carrying it like a wand of office, and I, called out early on some story which would not wait.

It was on such stories that I got to know some of my Italian journalist colleagues. Nothing helps so much as the early assignment, whether it be at the airport waiting for an important visitor to land, a sky-jacker to bring in his plane, or some matutinal Vatican occasion – for the Church normally pursues its labours shortly after cock-crow. I grew to learn that early morning was in fact the only time when you could really appreciate the beauties of Rome and many another Italian city, before the lovely squares and fountains became cluttered with parked cars and the whole place turned into one stinking, honking open-air garage. Siena, Bologna and one or two other enlightened places have banned the motor-car from their centres, but in most of Rome and, alas, in many other lovely cities, this has not yet come about, partly because the public transport system is so inadequate.

Only now are they building an underground railway in Rome, though plans for it have been prepared for half a century at least. I once spoke about the project with a civil engineer who lived on the Aventine. He had long since retired, and was living a withdrawn life in his book-lined flat. He showed me plans he had drawn up more than 50 years earlier for an underground railway – plans which had been shelved again and again, in spite of warnings that the traffic situation, with the rapid spread of motor transport and the impossibly narrow streets intersecting the centre of Rome, would steadily grow worse. One valid objection was naturally raised by the Fine Arts department – that many valuable finds would be destroyed as excavation and tunnelling proceeded. And all along, Rome's financial situation remained very much in the red, so that today it runs a deficit of well over a thousand million pounds, and is barely able to meet the interest due on the loans it has taken down the years.

However, work is now finally under way. An answer has been found to the objections of the archaeologists by sinking shafts far more deeply, so that the tunnels will not disturb the layers of ancient civilizations above. Rome is so rich in archaeological finds that virtually any building operation is likely to be held up for months because the contractors have unearthed something of interest. Very often they hush the whole matter up, so as to be able to get on with their work. I recall once being invited by a professor of antiquities at the Vatican to inspect catacombs under the via Latina. They had come to light by chance, simply because a block of flats erected above them had developed an alarming tilt. Upon investigation it was found that, while digging the foundations, the builders had found catacombs, with lovely frescoed walls, had shored the foundations up with columns of ferro-concrete, and had gone on with their construction. Only years after was the discovery made, and by then the frescoes had faded and were in any case disfigured by the emergency operations of the builders.

One Italian journalist who throughout his life campaigned vigorously for the preservation of ancient Rome from the builders was the late Silvio Negro. He was a remarkably energetic man, whose profound knowledge I came to respect as I grew to know him better. We used to lunch together with another distinguished Italian editor, Domenico Bartoli, at the agreeable restaurant of Ranieri's just off the via Condotti. Ranieri had at one time been a chef to Queen Victoria, and had gone to Mexico with the ill-fated Emperor Maximilian, who ended in front of a firing squad. The Emperor's demented wife, Carlotta, returned to Italy in a vain attempt to persuade the pope to save her husband's life. As she lived in mortal fear of being poisoned, her cook came with her, and stayed on in Rome to found the restaurant which still bears his name. Silvio Negro was a splendid table companion, a hearty eater, though this never seemed to interrupt the flow of his conversation which ranged over all periods of history of his beloved Rome, about which he wrote several books, including one with the memorable title *Roma non basta una vita* – One Life is not enough for Rome. In this he was absolutely right, for one life is by no means sufficient to get to know all that Rome has to offer.

Domenico Bartoli was often with Negro on these occasions. He was a spare man with a mischievous smile, perfect English and an understanding of Britain enjoyed by few foreign correspondents. He was for six years the London correspondent of the *Corriere della Sera*, a man with a talent for writing, a witty conversationalist, and a good listener (the last being by no means common in Italians). He still writes regular articles on topics of importance for the *Nazione* of Florence, which he edits. Sometimes we were joined by a fourth journalist, the diminutive Vittorio Gorresio of *La Stampa*, with his grey hair *en brosse* and his Dantesque profile, one of the shrewdest and best informed of all Italian political commentators. The company of such journalists was valuable and stimulating, and went far beyond mere professional comradeship, as did that with another outstanding connoisseur of things British, Sergio Telmon, who for many years was the London correspondent of the Italian Television and whose face is now well known all over Italy, since he is one of the RAI's main news commentators. A man of stout Republican leanings, he was someone I regarded not only as a good friend but as a wise counsellor on all things Italian. His views on Britain, too, were balanced and full of understanding. His commentary from London when Churchill died moved many to tears. It was of the highest standard, informative, sympathetic, and not obtrusive. The danger of so many television performers is that they do not know how to let the pictures speak for themselves, and overlay everything with an endless babble. It was my friend Richard Dimbleby, a master of the television and radio technique, who once said wisely that the art of the radio man was to commentate, that of the television man to annotate. It is a lesson which few have learned in any country.

CHAPTER FOUR

Literary Visitors

Everyone turns up in Rome sooner or later. If you sat outside a café in the via Veneto or near St Peter's you would in time see everyone you had ever known. Rome is a magnet for artists of every kind, especially actors and writers. I made it a practice always to leave my office door open and allow anyone to come in, no matter what I was doing. I could learn from them, and it was always fascinating to find out what people were interested and engaged in. Of course I was sometimes had, like the time when an elderly Rumanian sea-captain came and told me a heartbreaking tale about having no money to catch his ship which was leaving from Genoa the next day. I gave him his fare, which he promised to return, but that was the last I heard of him. Itinerant nuns and monks – mostly nuns – came begging alms – one Order lived off what it managed to beg, and its members were among the most cheerful women I ever met. So many Italian nuns look sour, perhaps because some are forced to enter a convent at a young age, and find out too late that the life is not for them. The same occurs, especially in Southern Italy, with orphan boys who are dressed like mini-priests from a tender age. Some stay on to become priests, though whether they have a vocation remains debatable.

The usual number of young English girls used to come looking for work. Most, I suspected, had an Italian boy-friend and wanted to change from their *au pair* jobs to something which would give them more free time. Hardly any of them spoke Italian. I talked to them all, for I could not banish from my mind my own daughter, an art student in London, who often looked for holiday work. Some I was able to help in a practical way, others had to be content with a drink and a chat.

One summer morning a young, snub-nosed, red-headed girl came to my office. She had an introduction from another wartime colleague and friend, Wynford Vaughan Thomas, himself a commentator of the Dimbleby school. She introduced herself as Aeron Thomas, but added that she was no relation of Wynford's, merely that he had suggested she should see me. I love the chance visitor, much to the despair of a succession of secretaries. There is always something you can learn from them. I asked Aeron Thomas about her past education, for want of something better with which to start the conversation. She gave a rather startling answer – she had been to a progressive school in the West of England – 'with mixed nude bathing before breakfast and all that' – and then had switched to a Sicilian convent, where, she assured me, the girls draped mantles over the bath so that they should not look at their own nakedness. After that had come a stint as a nurse in a large Paris hospital, and now she had landed in Rome. All the time she related this, she looked at me with wide blue eyes. She was completely at her ease – a young woman who had clear ideas of what she wanted and could express them forcefully.

She quickly came to the point, and asked me what were the prospects of getting into journalism in Rome. I must have been asked the same question hundreds of times, not merely in Rome, but everywhere else I have worked. Rome was a particularly difficult place, since so many chose to live there, eking out an existence with freelance activities of one kind or another. I had seen from experience with the *Stampa Estera* just how sought after these 'stringer' posts were, and how tough the competition for them was. So I was rather off-putting in my reply. She insisted that there must be some opening for her, and so I suggested that she got in touch with the one English language newspaper in Rome, the *Daily American* – the successor of the wartime armed forces newspaper *Stars and Stripes* which, with its narrow budget, often took on promising youngsters. She succeeded in convincing them of her merit, wrote several well-observed and succinctly expressed pieces, and became a staff journalist within a short space of time.

I asked her about her parents, for every time a young woman comes for help I inevitably think of my daughter, and try to be helpful. 'What does your father do?' I said. 'He was a poet, but he's now dead,' came the totally unexpected reply. Then in a flash I saw the resemblance. She was undoubtedly the daughter of Dylan Thomas, though she had been careful not to mention it. 'And your mother, where is she?' 'She lives in Rome, though I don't live with her. We're on good terms, and if you like I'll invite you to meet her.'

A few days after this chance encounter, my wife and I went to see this remarkable woman, Caitlin Thomas, of whom we had heard and read so much. It took us some time to find her flat, on top of a new block overlooking the Tiber, passing along bumpy, unmade roads in an unbeautiful speculators' suburb opposite St Paul's beyond the Walls. The flats were new and mostly still unoccupied, and the lifts were not yet functioning. We climbed to the top floor and found the right door, outside which were a lot of empty bottles. A stocky, jovial, middle-aged Sicilian, an ex-carabiniere, opened the door and bade us welcome. His two-year-old boy Francesco was playing on the rug in the living-room, completely engrossed in his toys. Aeron greeted us warmly, and laid the table for supper. There was no sign of her mother. We chatted desultorily for about half an hour, Francesco showing me how his model crane worked. The atmosphere was a relaxed family one.

After half an hour Caitlin Thomas entered the room, glass in hand, and the whole atmosphere suddenly changed. She was a striking, spare figure of medium height with burning dark eyes which flashed a certain bitterness at the world in general, though this dark look quickly dissolved when a smile spread over her features. It was not long before she talked of Dylan, who, she averred, had used her as a pacemaker for his writing and drinking. Her conversation was very much along the lines of her book *Left-over Life to Kill*, intransigently honest about her husband's failings and laced with the same resentment about his ultimate success in New York, which led to his early death. She described how many of his 'boozing friends' came to see her off on the liner which brought Dylan back in his coffin to his native Wales. Before we left she gave me a copy of another book I did not know she had written. It was entitled *Not quite Posthumous Letter to my Daughter*, a strangely frightening book, with its almost savage account of her own deep and dark despair.

In it she had many harsh things to say about journalists – one of her less offensive descriptions of them was 'the scavengers of society', so I was perhaps honoured to be given a copy of her book. On the fly-leaf she wrote, simply, 'To Patrick Smith, to a friend in a future, I hope.' Throughout the evening she had drunk beer laced with Italian brandy, which seemed to help her through the conversation. She was clearly annoyed that her daughter had decided to become a journalist, and in a way envious that Aeron should have received a welcome because of her father, which she felt was her due, after all that she had been through with Dylan. Caitlin Thomas was a strange, disturbing creature, obviously of unusual talent, an uncompromising genius almost, though of a tortured kind, shot through with a combination of warm humanity and mysticism. 'I'm imprisoned here,' she said, 'and I can't get out.' Whether she meant in Rome or in the world, I have never been able to decide.

Our meeting went on till well after midnight. 'Come again,' she said, as we negotiated our way past the empty bottles. I often intended to do so, but never got round to going again. In fact I only saw her daughter a couple of times after that. She was happy at her success with the *Daily American*, and proudly showed me the articles she had written. Then she disappeared as suddenly as she came. The last I heard of her was giving an interview, a child's view of her poet father, which was freshly uncompromising about his virtues and his faults. Looking through the book her mother had given me, I read: 'Try to suppress this mania for putting down everything which is in your head: which is a special weakness of the print-mad English who feel positively undressed without a bit of print to bury their noses in. Just leave these effervescent bubbles in your head; and, with luck, they will evaporate in superficialities. If they don't, they may be dubiously worth conserving. Look outward, not inward. You may not be wise by so doing, but you will be happier.' Caitlin Thomas has an unexpected style, peppered with unorthodox punctuation. From her writings she emerges as a considerable poetic force. She ends her book thus: 'As a last purge to swallow is: the more you do, the more you can do. As inversely, the less you do, the less you can do. So keep going: even if you have got no lighted indication of where to go. To be asleep: or to be awake; that is the question. Best of all Aeron: to be awake. Even though you look: my angel sleeping. Your almost sleeping: but not angelically; Mother.'

Some time after this strangely moving encounter Wynford Vaughan Thomas dropped in to see me after re-visiting the battlefields of Anzio, about which he had written. Wynford was a trustee of the Dylan Thomas Foundation, and had many reminiscences about his old friend and compatriot. He recalled that when Caitlin saw her husband's corpse in its coffin, made up and elegantly clothed in the American manner, she said, 'What a terrible tie Dylan's got on. He wouldn't be seen dead in it. . . Oh, what am I saying?' When the liner reached Southampton, Evans the Death was waiting with his hearse to take the coffin on its last journey to Wales, but lost his way getting home. However, the funeral was finally held, where, apart from the more intimate mourners, a number of literary agents were gathered at the graveside in the hope of doing business with the widow concerning her late husband's writings. The imposing American style casket would not go down into the grave prepared. Back went the mourners to the church, while adjustments were made. Wynford stayed at the graveside to talk with the sexton, who said, 'Mr Dylan always loved bananas, and I thought he would like it if I dug his grave in the shape of a banana. But now I shall have to straighten it out to get that big coffin in.' This he proceeded to do, and the funeral, with its macabre touches of unintentional humour, was completed. Dylan would have chuckled. Caitlin was alone, with her left-over life to kill. I have often thought of this gauntly handsome, outspoken woman, with her fierce criticism of much that has been written about her husband's work since he died, and her burning resentment of the fact that few have paid tribute to her part in creating his unforgettable poetry.

Rome has always been a magnet for English writers. Perhaps, as Dr Johnson once observed, they felt an inferiority complex unless they had absorbed something of its atmosphere. Because of its many pleasant distractions, Rome is not as stimulating a place for a writer to work steadily in as for a painter. Yet its influence is profound. E. M. Forster confirmed this when I once met him in a quiet hotel near the Pantheon. He had been lecturing in Italy about the countries which had influenced his work. He impressed me as extremely modest, almost shy. He was fairly tall, and wore an old tweed suit and a cloth cap: he reminded me of a kind uncle who had spent most of his life secluded in some esoteric branch of the Civil Service. Forster reluctantly acknowledged, with some surprise, that he had turned out to be a well-known writer. We sat in the faded glories of the Hotel Minerva lounge over tea, discussing literature and the craft of writing. My questions were rather naïve, now I come to think of it, but from my notes at the time I recall his tolerant amusement as he answered them.

He was a thoughtful, slow speaker. 'England,' he said, 'built me up and stimulated my writing more than any other country. Most of my inspiration came from Hertfordshire where I was born and where the house still stands – which was the original of *Howards End*. But it was from Wiltshire that I derived most,' he went on after a pause, 'for there I got the idea of my favourite novel, *The Longest Journey*. Curiously enough, however, it was a visit to Italy which started me off writing. I can remember the exact spot – it's a little valley not far from Ravello and there I had, almost instantaneously, the idea for a short story, *The story of a Panic*. . . Italy is a country I so much love. After that short story I went on.'

Naturally I asked him about his most widely-read novel, *A Passage to India*. He thought for a moment, then said, 'Well, that is a particular experience and a personal one. I'm very fortunate about India because I really went out there since I had an Indian friend. I didn't go to govern the place, or to make money out of it, or to improve people. I just went out there to see a friend; through him I made other friends, and that's why, in a way, *A Passage to India* is the best documented of my work, because I did get to know a little about the country from the inside. I felt I was very much connected with the Indians with whom I was living, and I also, of course, had many British friends too. On that first visit the tension between Great Britain and India was already working up, and I had the interesting but rather painful experience of, as it were, moving from one camp to another. I think my first visit to India was full of discomfort, as well as of pleasure and of fun, and I think that discomfort itself may have helped me to write my book about the country.'

Forster spoke slowly and carefully, weighing every thought that he wanted to express. At one point in the conversation he took out a handkerchief and carefully wiped his grey moustache before continuing. I asked him what advice he would give to a young writer in the light of his long experience. I half expected a pundit's reply, but was utterly mistaken.

'My goodness, I've no advice to give at all. You see, when I was young, no writer was ever able to help me, so why should I be able to help young writers in my turn? I'd like to help them, but they must do the job themselves; there's nothing I was told, and nothing I can tell them.' He looked at me rather regretfully, perhaps seeing the look of disappointment on my face. Later, however, I reflected that his remarks were in essence the same as the advice Caitlin Thomas had written to her daughter: the more you do, the more you can do, so keep going. E. M. Forster made a profound impression on his Italian lecture tour. He told me that, though his love for Italy was deep, he had hitherto always regarded himself as a tourist. This was the first time that he felt himself to be 'half an Italian'. It is only a pity that he did not write more of the country he loved so well.

Few writers indeed can become assimilated completely by Italy. Whether Goethe or Stendhal, D. H. Lawrence or Munthe, they are essentially outsiders looking in. Only the Italians can get the real feel of their country. You have to read Machiavelli and Manzoni in the original to get close to Italian life, unless, of course you can live out your days in Italy, and even then not in Rome or any other great city, where you are bound to be thrown among a host of non-Italians. Yet many foreigners have written enchantingly of this many-faceted country. Cecil Roberts, for instance, as elegant in his appearance as in his writing, bestrides the Italian scene like some dignified senator. His book *And So To Rome* is deservedly a classic of its kind, sweeping across history in a fluent and eminently readable style. I used to go especially to the vast, Edwardian Grand Hotel in Rome, where he usually wintered, just to hear him talk. He chooses his words with meticulous care and pronounces them precisely, placing each one deliberately in the ear of his listener, pausing for a moment to ensure that the right effect has been achieved, before proceeding serenely. I could listen to him holding forth for hours; he is very much a *grand seigneur* of Rome, and a welcome guest wherever he goes. With him the art of conversation is still very much alive. I know of only one other writer living in Rome who approaches Roberts in his spoken style. He is the Yorkshire-born historian, Glorney Bolton, whose book on the centenary of Rome was not appreciated as much as it should have been. Except in speech Bolton is the complete antithesis of Cecil Roberts. Modest to the point of being unbearably shy, he has written well on such diverse topics as Czechoslovakia and India, and still turns in a very readable column for the *Yorkshire Post*, though already in his seventies. Writing keeps a man young; so long as a natural curiosity persists, the twinges of rheumatism pass largely unnoticed.

At the present time, perhaps the most popular and widely known writer on Italy is H. V. Morton, that *maestro* of the travel book to whom nothing, even the most unpleasant discomfort, seems to come amiss. He was a regular visitor – a quietly-spoken author of innumerable books, now in his eighties but nonetheless active and alert – who has written compendiously about Italy in three books which are a sheer delight to read or just to dip into. Curiously enough, I first met him while I was in the Cape shortly before I was transferred to Rome. He waxed enthusiastic when he heard of this and invited me to his lovely villa at Somerset West, which he had built on the crest of a hill, for all the world like a villa in Tuscany. Modestly he did not mention his own writings, but suggested that I should read Roger Peyrefitte's *Keys of St Peter* as an introduction to my future posting.

We talked for hours in his book-lined study, surrounded by model ships which he builds in his spare time. He told me how, as a young journalist in Fleet Street, he began to interest himself in stories with a historical background. He produced a series of articles on the ghosts of London, and quickly realised that he had found his *métier*, delving into the past for his stories. After some years he took the plunge and abandoned journalism to write a series of books, *In Search of Britain*, which laid the foundations of his subsequent success. It is rare to meet a writer who can make a steady living from his talents, yet this lovely home was the result of his labours.

Well liked for his entertaining style, Morton went further afield – to the Holy Land – and became world-famous with his *In the Steps of the Master*, and *In the Steps of St Paul*. Throughout his writing there breathes a lively awareness of history, intermingled with his own sensible opinions on the events and places he is describing. His travel books on Spain, Italy, Britain and South Africa, as well as his writings on the Holy Land, are all deservedly popular, for he has the great gift of lending the reader his perceptive eyes when viewing the passing scene, but lets him form his own judgement on what he learns. Though he is not afraid of giving his own views on occasion, he does so discreetly and unobtrusively. Above all there is a serenity about his writing – none of the breathless enthusiasm and hurry which mar so many other excellent guidebooks of our time. For H. V. Morton writes more than a guide; his books can be read with pleasure by those who have never been, nor even intend, to visit the countries he describes so well.

I had many happy times with him when he was busy preparing his book *The Waters of Rome*, tracing the sources of every one of the city's lovely fountains. He is a man of precise routine, getting up at dawn and surveying the scene before most of the world is astir. Some of his most felicitous passages, to my mind, are his accounts of seeing the church doors open in some little town perched on a hill in Umbria or Calabria, describing the half-awake faithful drifting almost in a dream to church before getting on with the daily task. He often used to come to lunch, and loved to admire the roofscapes of Rome from our tower. He never accepted any evening social engagements, for then he was busy writing and revising his notes before retiring early, so as to be ready for the following morning's search. All is set down in smoothly flowing prose – curious encounters and revealing information often of the most unexpected kind – which leads the reader on. Old-fashioned novelists used often to address the 'gentle reader'. H. V. Morton is the gentle writer *par excellence*.

One writer whom I met on my rounds in Rome was of an entirely different stamp. Vladimir Nabokov came to Italy shortly after the uproar caused by the publication in Britain of his *Lolita*, which added the word 'nymphet' to the English language. He seemed mildly to enjoy all the fuss. Throughout our talk, his wife sat by his side with a small box open on her lap containing a card index of questions that her husband had been asked and the answers he had given. I was impressed by this debonair man's desire for consistency – or perhaps it was a means of saving time – anyway, as he answered my questions, his wife riffled through her cards checking his replies against what was written down. She did not have to remind or correct him once. I asked him whether he was worried about the censorship difficulties first encountered by his novel. He was more amused than bothered about it, he replied. 'I had the feeling that my censors had either not read the book at all, or had perhaps read some other book entitled *Lolita*. Banning a book because of its subject is a highly ridiculous act, since with the matter you ban the manner, and I question if the person or persons who call it obscene are sufficiently well informed to pronounce judgement on its style. I do not expect any rumpus in England [this was in 1959], but I imagine that the more literate of her Philistines may try to suppress the book by denouncing the style – and make fools of themselves, of course.'

Nabokov seemed utterly sure of himself and of his creative genius, and well aware also of the publicity-value of the controversy he had aroused. I asked him whether he thought in English or Russian as he wrote. 'I'm not so sure I think in words at all,' was his answer. 'Or, if I do, rather infrequently. I seem to think in images, and these begin to speak only when I start composing the actual phrase that I need. On the other hand, I notice that some certain, simple thoughts – primitive thoughts – may come in English, in Russian or in French, depending on chance associations and surroundings.' He then went on to tell me that he was engaged on a tremendous publication running into four or five volumes about Pushkin, whose *Eugene Onegin* he had just completed translating into English, adding an appropriate commentary. 'Once I have completed that, I shall settle down to the composing of a new novel, which exists in my mind in a folded state, with all its colours in miniature, and which will appear when it is ready to emerge.'*

His white-haired wife nodded approval at the replies he had given, and even noted down one of my questions to add to her card index – I think it was the one asking in which language he thought. Nabokov was a pleasant showman, and, like all showmen, on his guard. He reminded me of Salvador Dali, and I left wondering what he was really like underneath. Perhaps, like so many others used to the glare of publicity, he had assumed the personality outlined in the many articles written about him.

I confess I find neither Nabokov nor Forster easy reading. They are too cool and cerebral – Nabokov far more so than Forster, who, as we now know after his death, was tormented by his special affections which he kept secret for most of his life. His early novel on the love of two young men for each

---

* Both projects were completed. The Pushkin translation, together with an introduction and commentary by Nabokov, was published in four volumes by the Bollingen Foundation, New York, 1964, and by Routledge and Kegan Paul, London, in the same year. Princeton University Press are soon to publish a revised version. The novel is *Ada*, published by McGraw-Hill, New York, and Weidenfeld and Nicolson, London, in 1969, and by Penguin in 1970.

other was not, in fact, published until after his death, and caused hardly a ripple.

This whole problem of homosexuality arouses emotions of widely differing kinds. One afternoon I was sitting at my desk watching the swallows performing their acrobatics above the rooftops when the admirable Laurence Gilliam, who was one of the real pioneers in the art of broadcasting and of writing features for the medium of radio, rang me from London, asking me to go to Tuscany to interview a former colleague, Lionel Fielden. Fielden had recently published a disarmingly frank autobiography called *The Natural Bent*. This was an unusual request, not routed through the proper channels. My first task was to gather news, and anything as literary as this would mean spending several days away from Rome. Hard news is what counts, even though most of such stories are soon forgotten. An earthquake, a riot, a plane crash: Why did they happen? How many victims? What did the survivors say? Can such events be prevented in future? The news-hungry public has a right to know, and it is the correspondent's job to help satisfy their hunger. I mention this in passing, since the Lionel Fielden interview meant being away from Rome for three days and laying complicated plans for instant recall should anything 'blow up'.

As luck would have it, permission was given for me to leave Rome. Lionel Fielden had a talent for living in lovely houses – lovely, that is, after he had put a lot of hard work converting them from crumbling villas into desirable residences. He received me in one such lovely home, rescued from decay in Tuscany. The spacious house was surrounded by extensive grounds planted with cypresses and vines and with a broad terrace overlooking the valley to the mountains beyond. When I went, in October 1960, it was at its autumnal best. Fielden had carefully prepared his thoughts for my visit, and spoke frankly and easily about his 'natural bent', adding: 'Perhaps we should not mention it on the BBC, you know what people are.' There was a twinkle in his eye as he said this. He was a striking man to meet, tall, with a sun-burned, lean face and clipped grey guards-officer moustache. His hair was grey, shading to white at the temples. In some lights you could almost have taken him for an Anglo-Indian, he was so tanned. He had, in fact, worked in India for several years, re-organizing the radio in the subcontinent before the war.

I listened to his reminiscences of a BBC I had hardly known. He was a fascinating raconteur. He told me over dinner that he had found it extremely difficult to write about the BBC, so much so that he had cut out most of what he had put down about his years with the Corporation. Fielden had many memories. I asked him who was the outstanding broadcaster of his day – man or woman. 'I think the best I ever knew was Walford Davies, because he was entirely natural, he didn't care whether the microphone was on or off, he simply was himself and conveyed an extraordinary enthusiasm for music which I've never heard done so well again. And then there were others: Vernon Bartlett, Stephen King-Hall, and in another sense there was Winston Churchill, perhaps the best broadcaster we had in many ways. It's extraordinary that women have not made a great mark, not in talks, that's to say. In other things of course, but not as straightforward talkers. I don't think there has ever been a good woman broadcaster that I can remember – not really naturally outstanding and memorable. I haven't the vaguest idea why this is. I never could make it out. I worked very hard with a lot of them to try and make them good, but somehow they never quite hit the jackpot.'

Lionel Fielden had been a talks producer in the early BBC days, and besides his work in India was also a capable musician, had worked with the League of Nations, and had served as a soldier in the second World War. At its conclusion he had driven out to Italy in an ancient Rolls-Royce inherited from his family with enough money to set up house in the Tuscan hills. In his autobiography he describes his search for the right house.

We drove to a part of the country, north of Florence, which I had not seen before. When we came to a huge bare-looking house, with an unkempt lawn and great doors from which all paint had peeled, I said at once that it was no good at all, and I did not even want to go inside. While I was turning away, the great doors were slowly opened by a tiny woman who seemed to have stepped straight from the Middle Ages. Beyond them the sunshine fell on a vast court-yard, surrounded by a shady cloister of delicate soaring arches. It had a stunning quality of peace and beauty, and was entirely unexpected. I stepped in, and saw beyond the cloister a small but exquisitely made doorway. Beyond it was a formal rose garden, some 35 yards square, bounded by ancient box hedges and grey walls: and this garden seemed to hang suspended above a view of Tuscany, stretching away to the Chianti hills, so romantic, so perfectly arranged, so peaceful, that it seemed unreal. Inside the house, bare as a barracks, were great rooms whose vaulting floated up like clouds, or drifting white smoke, so light it was. Eight huge sitting-rooms, twelve bedrooms, a colossal granary, and one extremely ancient and probably unworkable bathroom. This house I had to have. I asked the middleman the price. 'Twelve millions.' Too much for me: far, far too much. I said I would offer the owners five (at that time about four thousand pounds) if I had the reply by the next morning, because (as was true enough) I was already more than half committed to another villa. The reply next morning was in the affirmative. Thus, in a freakish moment, I acquired the idiotically large house, with some fifty acres and three farms known as 'Le Tavernule'. Oddly enough, my snap decision was right not only aesthetically but also financially. I lived in it and loved it for six years, and I still think it one of the most beautiful houses in the world. When I had to sell it, which was inevitable with my comparatively slender means, it fell, luckily, into good hands, and is beautifully tended today.

The rescue and redesigning of old houses is a game which attracts some people and frightens others. I have always found it one of the most entrancing, and in every way rewarding occupations imaginable. Some eight transactions of this kind have fallen to my lot, and each one has not only been a delight, but also a successful financial gamble.

I imagine Lionel Fielden must by now be living in at least his tenth house since settling in his beloved Tuscany. One of his most engaging qualities as emerged from our long talk was his absolute frankness about himself.

I don't like work. I never did like work. I hate being in offices, I hate all kinds of administrative jobs. I like to sit in the sun and look at the view, and paint a bit and play the piano and be thoroughly lazy. I am a dilettante, and I shall remain so until I fall into the grave. The only thing I would like is to be young again. At the moment I'm trying hard to write a book about a bulldog, because all my life I've had bulldogs and I'm extremely fond of them. I fear they are a race which is dying out in England, and that's a great pity. I go less and less to England now. You know, one gets older, one's friends die off and one's interests in England get less. I miss the theatre, but I don't like the climate of England. I find that most of my friends turn up here sooner or later, and I like seeing them here very much better.

I was only to see Lionel Fielden once after that, when I visited him again for his views on Lord Reith which the BBC wanted for a programme on the great man to go out on television after his death. Fielden was obviously not nearly so much at home in front of the unwinking eye of the camera as he had been before the microphone. He told me afterwards it was an excruciatingly painful experience through which he would much rather not have gone. He was about to move house once again, but still lives happily on in his Tuscan hills, cultivating his garden and enjoying being a fascinating host.

He has communicated his enthusiasm for living in Italy to a number of friends, among them Vernon Bartlett, who, after a distinguished career as a journalist, broadcaster, independent MP and writer of books, had come back from his new career, undertaken in his sixties in Singapore, where he was chief commentator on the *Straits Times*, to seek a home in Italy. By chance he ran into Fielden, who took him and his wife Nelly round the countryside. Vernon Bartlett told me that he had dreamed of a small house by the sea. However, it was not a dream he fulfilled. He and his wife were involved in a road accident. Vernon escaped relatively unhurt, but his Belgian wife Nelly did not get off so lightly and had to spend several weeks in Lucca hospital. Between visits to her Vernon continued his search for a home, and finally found what he wanted. It was a small villa on a hill, with its own chapel, a barn and another farmhouse next door, surrounded by some fourteen acres, mainly of vineyards. It was quite unlike what he had had in mind, yet it appealed to him and he settled in as soon as Nelly was well enough to leave hospital. He has written affectionately about it and of his efforts to adapt himself to rural life in Italy in two enchanting books called appropriately *Tuscan Retreat* and *Tuscan Harvest*.

I have always admired the sheer professionalism of Vernon Bartlett. For me he was the ideal foreign correspondent, always seeing just that bit farther than the average observer of the international scene, never losing sight of the human factors involved in the making of great political decisions, in action rather retiring and unobtrusive, never letting his own personality stand in the way of his readers and listeners. And what a natural genius he had for radio, exuding a strong and almost affectionate understanding for all the wayward-ness of human nature, yet inflexibly devoted to the demo-cratic way of life. Over the years our paths have crossed frequently, and a steady friendship sprang up in spite of our different generations, for we were both in the same game, and age counts for little in journalism.

I have had many hilarious visits to his home in the Apuan Alps, where he pours out his own wine with pride and talks of times present and past with equal shrewdness. He is a stockily built man, now pushing 80, though he remains young at heart in all he does and says. His face has a habitual expression of puzzlement, registering the innate curiosity of the active writer. He can look sad and then suddenly explode into a great gust of laughter, throwing his head back as he roars at a good story. He is one of my favourite companions, whose humanity I admire as much as his great ability as a writer. Apart from all his journalism – and he was already an outstanding commentator on international affairs in the thirties, both for the BBC and also for that once great newspaper, the *News Chronicle*, which died such an ignominious and unnecessary death – he has written well over twenty books, ranging from early autobiography, which was turned into a highly successful play on television, to works on Africa and Malaya as well as on his beloved Europe. He has an inventive mind, and has many more books in him. He not only wrote his own obituary, but broadcast it, proving remarkably detached and critical about himself. He talks as well as he writes, which is not all that common, and his company is precious to all who enjoy his friendship. For many years helped by the faithful Giuseppe and Annunziata, whom he immortalised in his Tuscan writings and who now have earned an honourable retirement, he goes on peering quizzically into the future – an unrepentant optimist and artist, both in his life and his books.

On my first visit, shortly after he had set up house near Lucca, he proudly showed off his cows, one of which had just won a prize at the local show. The last time I called he was actively planning the conversion of the neighbouring farmhouse, into which he has since moved. His enthusiasm never wanes and, as a result of his writing, several of his friends have come to live out their days in Tuscany. He perhaps unwittingly described the key to his humanity in one of his books in which he wrote: 'Even after the experiences of a lifetime, I cannot find it in myself to distrust more than 1% of my fellow men.' This happy confidence shines through his writings. He is critical yet never sardonic; he holds strong views yet is never bigoted; and above all he has the art of choosing the right words and putting them in the right order.

Vernon Bartlett has written so much about his own life and times that it is not easy to sum up his many-sided character in a few words. I see him as a very humane person, who has seen suffering and disappointment, as well as happiness and success in abundant measure, writing on in his Tuscan study, surrounded by his books and papers and occasionally glancing out of his window at the Tuscan landscape which frames his life. The cypresses stand, stirred by the wind, dark sentinels across the valley, and little is heard except the steady tapping of his ancient typewriter as yet more of his thoughts on the strange, passing scene of life are committed to paper.

CHAPTER FIVE

Of Keats and Danilo Dolci

A writer cannot spend all his time at his desk. In Rome, I frequently would walk out on to the terrace, look at the roof garden which I had planted, and then peer over the parapet at the Piazza di Spagna below. It is not the peaceful place it was when John Keats came to spend the last few months of his life in the house just to the right of the famous steps. Alas, it is often crammed with coaches, and on hot summer days scores of holiday-makers sit round the ancient fountain designed by Bernini's father, dangling their toes into its cool waters. This lovely fountain, *La Barcaccia*, or the sinking galley, is the focal point of this famous place, and its water splashing at night was probably the last sound the poet heard before he died.

For all the many thousands who wander up and down the Spanish Steps when they come to Rome, only a small percentage, I imagine, bother to go into the house where Keats died. It is a peaceful place, with touching relics of the great poet and of his contemporary, Shelley, who was drowned off La Spezia over a century and a half ago. Within its lofty, cool rooms are housed one of the finest existing collections of books on the English Romantic Movement. Many students from all over the world come to study there in the course of the year. They always look reverently at the narrow room, with its high, coffered ceiling, where Keats breathed his last. In a showcase are set out mementoes of those tragic few months when Keats sought in vain to regain his health: a lock of the poet's hair and some handwritten manuscripts, the ink a faded brown, and touching drawings of the poet on his deathbed done by his faithful friend, the artist Joseph

Severn, who now lies buried beside him in a corner of the English cemetery by the Pyramid of Cestius at St Paul's Gate.

The Keats-Shelley Memorial house is lived in and looked after by one of the kindest people in Rome, the gentle Signora Vera Cacciatore. She first came after finishing her studies years back to assist for one summer, and has remained there ever since. A novelist in her own right, she is, appropriately enough, married to a Sicilian poet. She has devoted much of her love and her life to these three poets, the one living, the others immortal. Her quiet manner conceals a determination to safeguard this hallowed corner of Rome, so precious to lovers of poetry. She has herself given a moving account of the vicissitudes of the collection during the war, how they were moved to the Benedictine abbey of Monte-cassino and how the precious books and manuscripts were ferried back to Rome in German army lorries disguised as the personal baggage of the archivist Don Mauro Iguanez, a Maltese monk, before the entire abbey was bombed into rubble by the Allied air force. Once back in Rome, the collection was kept in cupboards until the liberation in 1944. Vera Cacciatore tells how she saw the sprawling bodies of Allied soldiers recumbent on the Spanish steps, drunk not only with victory but with the local Castelli wine, whose potency they had underestimated. For her Keats is still alive, and she keeps his memory fresh by going often to lay violets on his grave and see that souvenir hunters have not torn up the flowers planted there.

Some years back this corner of the English cemetery was restored to something of its former beauty. The then British ambassador, Sir Evelyn Shuckburgh, who was at that time chairman of the body administering the 'non-Catholic cemetery', to translate its official name, told me that during his years accredited to Italy it was this work that gave him the most pride. The pine trees overshadowing Keats's grave had long since been smitten with blight, and were in a dangerous condition, so they were dug out. In the process, Sir Evelyn told me, he saw that one of the tree's roots had become firmly entwined round the bones of the poet, having grown right through the rotted wooden coffin. The remains of the poet were transferred to another coffin, new trees were planted, the whole graveyard returfed and set with flowers. It was a great moment when the tombs were reconstructed. The poet and his friend sleep on under the watchful guard of the Pyramid of Cestius which marks the corner of this 'foreign field which is forever England'. The sadness of the epitaph, 'here lies one whose name was writ in water,' never fails to move me when I pass it, nor the simpler tomb in which Shelley's heart lies buried, plucked from the funeral pyre on the beach of La Spezia by his friend Trelawney. The stone bears the simple inscription, *Cor cordium*.

Vera Cacciatore knows most of Keats's poems by heart, and it was a great moment in her life when the late poet laureate, Cecil Day Lewis, came to Rome with his beautiful actress wife Jill Balcon and visited the house. There in its peaceful rooms she read some of the famous odes with exquisite tenderness. However, Vera Cacciatore is by no means a sad person at heart, for the memory and poetry of Keats give her an inner serenity. She can be gay in company, and she and her husband Eduardo can be seen most evenings taking their *passeggiata* in the narrow streets leading from the Piazza di Spagna, greeting many friends as they pass, and sometimes asking them back for a glass of wine on their terrace. I have often sat with them there in the cool of the evening, watching the shaggy-haired young in their ragged blue jeans meander on the steps, perhaps some new Keats among them. The Cacciatores inhabit a world of beauty and goodness and truth indeed. The house has its special serenity – not the calm of a monastery or convent with their overtones of religious strictures. It is a light and airy peacefulness, difficult to describe, which lifts the soul of all who enter. Outside, the roar of Rome's traffic blares on. Inside, all is tranquil and inspiring. Vera Cacciatore is its presiding spirit. 'Dear John Keats,' she often says in conversation, as though she would not be at all surprised to see him come in from his room. And he is, in truth, never far from her thoughts. The world of poetry and kind-hearted people everywhere owe this gentle person an unpayable debt for preserving the records of this young Romantic and keeping his memory alive. It is strange that an Italian should have devoted her entire life to his greatness.

Some writers who live in Rome do not find it conducive to creative work. They tell me it is too overloaded with tradition to favour original writing. Certainly I know of few capitals where one can pass the time more agreeably and at relatively little cost. If you are hard up, you can manage better in Rome than in many other places, for the Romans are generous when it comes to credit. One woman I know who lost her job told the restaurant keeper where she habitually ate of her plight. 'Don't worry, signorina,' he said, 'you can keep on having your lunch here until you get a new job.' She accepted gratefully and, when she had found new employment, told the *padrone* the good news and offered to pay him back for the lunches she had eaten. He would not hear of it. Then there are always *vernissages*, or previews, at the scores of art galleries, where, in addition to admiring the pictures, you can generally pick up a drink and a canapé or two. And if you have a few hundred lire to spend, you can always sit at a street café, not necessarily on the via Veneto, where the price of the view is added to that of your coffee, but in a quiet backwater where the passing world is less stereotyped and far more colourful and genuine.

A favourite Roman habit, sometimes copied by foreigners who settle there, is to live in a seemingly shabby street and then to furnish your home luxuriously. Much of Trastevere, for example, is little more than a picturesque slum. Guests ring at a nondescript door, and are taken aback with wonder when they enter the unexpectedly beautiful rooms beyond. Cynical Romans say that this habit keeps the tax inspectors at bay, though I doubt it. In fact, when one came to visit me, I asked him whether he had much difficulty in assessing the riches of the Romans. He had come to assess me, and had looked round the flat in the Palazzo Doria, asked me what belonged to me and what to the Princess, whether the car he saw parked under the portico was my own, how much I paid in rent and what were my earnings. I dealt straightforwardly with him, though I winced a bit at telling him my salary. It is an odd quirk that, though people will reveal almost anything about their private life, they hedge at laying bare their financial position. Either they want to appear richer than they are, or the reverse – according to the company. My particular tax inspector was something of a psychologist, for after our amicable chat over a glass of wine he left with the splendid pay-off line, 'One thing I learned very early on in my job is that it only takes the first few minutes to ascertain whether people are telling the truth or not.' And with a smile he was gone.

His was a particularly difficult area of action, for he would have to try to value the canvases of struggling artists in their studios, or writers in their attic flats – though to live in an *attico* was a sure sign that the occupant was reasonably well-off, for the rents rise with the storey in Rome, as in most other places.

In a narrow, cobbled alley running at right angles to that pleasurable street, the via del Babuino, I once made my way to a small flat up among the rooftops where the successful novelist Richard Mason used to live. 'Baboon Street' takes its name from the battered fountain of a much disfigured, recumbent, stone male figure, now almost entirely commandeered by the neighbouring flower stall. The disrespectful Romans, who regard statues not just as carved lumps of stone but as having a life of their own, quickly dubbed this one 'the baboon', and the street took on the name. Via Babuino has several bookshops, apart from its antique galleries and boutiques. One, the Lion bookshop, used to be run by two formidable maiden ladies, locally known as the Lionesses, though their growl was far worse than their bite. In fact, once you had got to know them, they were extremely kind and helpful. The other was opened some years back by Feltrinelli, the rich, ill-fated eccentric who dreamed of turning Italy into some kind of Cuba in the Mediterranean, and who once staged a clandestine performance of Hochhuth's *The Representative* in the warehouse at the back of the shop, at which I was present. This controversial work, it may be recalled, had been banned from the Rome theatres at the insistence of the Vatican for its highly critical portrayal of Pope Pius XII.

I had to climb several flights of stairs before I reached Richard Mason's door – the lift had a scrawled notice, *guasto* – 'out of order' – on it. Mason was basking in the success of *Suzy Wong*, which had recently been made into a film after running as a play on Broadway for some months. He had a friendly, easy-going manner – a slight figure with something of the eternal undergraduate about him. He told me how by chance he had become involved in the Far East. He was serving in the RAF during the war, when he saw a notice requesting volunteers to learn Japanese. 'So I volunteered, since I thought this would mean all sorts of wonderful things. I took a course in Japanese at the University of London, then I went out East and have never stopped being interested in the East since.' As he sat in his old armchair, with his glass at his elbow, he seemed somehow amazed at his own success. He had scripted the film of his book himself and did not seem at all to mind that the directors wanted the story changed to fit their box-office tastes. Mason had been living in Rome for about two years when I first met him. I asked him whether he planned to draw on the Italian background for future novels, and he replied, 'That will probably happen, though one has to let it creep up on one and take its time.'

Another successful writer, unlike Mason, was furious at changes made in his books by Hollywood. This was the Australian, Morris West. I had met him soon after my arrival in Rome in 1958, when he had been given an assignment by the *Daily Mail* to write a series on how the Vatican worked. He came up against all kinds of obstacles, as most inquirers do when they attempt to probe into the lesser-known activities of the Holy See. He was infuriated by this obstructionism, as only a loyal Roman Catholic can be, yet managed to produce his highly informative series as scheduled. In the preparation of these articles he collected much material which proved a fertile seed-bed for his popular *Shoes of the Fisherman*. It was a resounding success from the date of its publication, for by one of those flukes it began with the words 'The Pope was dead . . .' and came out the day that Pope John died – as nice a bit of fortuitous timing as could be wished. The book was immediately a best seller, though the film was not an outstanding success. Morris West told me how upset he was by all the changes in the script, so much so that he wished for no acknowledgement of his work when the film was finally shown. However, in spite of its longueurs, it does at least capture the right atmosphere of the conclave, with all the jockeying for votes before the Holy Spirit finally guides the cardinals to their choice.

West registered his first notable success with a book on the slums of Naples and the valiant efforts of Father Borelli to combat the teeming poverty and vice of the city with his Casa dei Scugnizzi, his house of the street urchins. When I talked with Father Borelli on one of his fund-raising visits to Rome he told me how, after living amidst the squalor and crime with the boys he hoped to help, he had come up against every kind of obstacle before he was able to set up house. Since then he has helped hundreds of boys to get a reasonable start in life. He is a short, unassuming man, and, because of the inevitable publicity he attracted to himself, made many adversaries – human jealousy never being far below the surface. At one stage he fell out with his superiors, but his good work goes on.

This question of personal publicity is an inescapable one – and journalists, though they help, are also partly to blame for its adverse effects. There was a similar case which came my way when I was in South Africa and got to know another uncompromising priest, Father Trevor Huddleston of the Mirfield Mission. He had spent many years of his life in the Johannesburg slums – now ironically cleared to make way for the white population – fighting the battles of the under-privileged Africans, and he too had attracted much personal publicity.

He frankly admitted that, though he disliked it, it was the only effective weapon in his armoury. Now Bishop of Stepney, though his heart remains in Africa, he champions the cause of the East End children who have little space in which to play and develop. He and Father Borelli have much in common. Their attempts to stir the authorities into action by their sometimes unorthodox methods are, however, seldom forgotten or forgiven.

Social reformers are awkward customers, and I know of none more so than Danilo Dolci, whom I met a number of times in various parts of Italy, sometimes leading a demonstration in Rome, sometimes in a depressed corner of Sicily. Dolci was described by Aldous Huxley as a twentieth-century saint. His detractors – and there are not a few – brand him a political agitator. He is a quixotic character, often the despair of those who try to collaborate with him. He has an inbred hatred of all authoritarianism, whether of the Vatican, the Italian government or the Mafia. He is a thorn in the side of them all. In his 40-odd years of life this architect from Trieste has been jailed, had his passport withdrawn, gone several times on hunger strike and engaged in endless litigation. Somehow, however, he survives to fight on, appealing for social and educational reform in the western corner of Sicily where life is at its most primitive and ruthless. Those who have worked with Dolci all grant that he is a great-hearted, if not well-organized idealist. One Roman Catholic priest I know described him as a humanitarian who puts all Christians to shame.

In his bug-ridden life in the hovels of the poor, Dolci also knows the power of publicity, and gets his money wherever he can. 'I'll take funds from the devil or the Pope,' he once told me. 'I'm not fussy where it comes from.' In spite of the Mafia and other forms of obstruction he has succeeded in building three dams and setting up education centres. He continues his uphill task undeterred by apathy or opposition. Above all, he is up against the fatalist mentality of the Sicilians whom he is trying to help, who for generations have regarded all authority, whether temporal or spiritual, as necessary burdens, to be borne with a resigned shrug of the shoulders. Dolci, with his open-necked shirt and beret, his quick speech and engaging friendliness, will remain a prophet, one possibly without much honour in his own country but one who at least has done something to stir the conscience of the world. He is lionized when he lectures outside his own country – a Lenin Peace Prize winner who is not a Communist. Some think he should be a candidate for the Nobel Peace Prize. In the final analysis he has given hope to a forsaken and largely forgotten corner of his country, and helped some Sicilians towards a more bearable existence. Whatever view of him one may take, he deserves his place among the awkward squad of social pioneers. He follows the non-violent teachings of Gandhi, has been much influenced by Thoreau and remains an eccentric with a heart of gold.

The last time I encountered Danilo Dolci was in Sicily, just after the terrible earthquake in 1968. He told me that no one wanted to take on the responsibility of succouring the victims – fear of being blamed for taking any initiative is a deep-set trait of the Italian official's character. As I have already mentioned, five years after millions had been voted for their relief the unfortunate homeless are still housed for the most part in makeshift Nissen huts, waiting for their villages to be rebuilt. I flew to these shattered hamlets within a few hours of the catastrophe. The airfield at Trapani was crowded with inhabitants who had left the town and were camping out as best they could. I managed to persuade a young lawyer with a car to drive me into the town. It was an eerie experience – the street lights were still on, the petrol stations illuminated but deserted, and the whole town almost completely devoid of life, except for a few forlorn groups squatting round bonfires in the parks, enveloped in blankets against the chill evening air. Yet, amazingly enough, there were one or two taxis waiting at the station for the arrival of the last train of the day from Palermo, and I was able to induce the young driver of one of them to take me to the stricken area.

The moon was full, but at first there was little unusual to see as we drove inland. As we climbed higher, sagging cracked houses, all abandoned hastily, showed the first effects of the earth tremors. I walked across the little piazza in one such village. It was deathly still – so quiet in fact that I could quite easily hear the measured ticking of the town hall clock, sounding like a death-watch beetle. We drove on to the outskirts of the smashed town of Gibellina, which lay in a hollow in the hills. The army, complete with bulldozers, searchlights and other rescue equipment, were posted at the fringe of the area, but were doing nothing and would not, at first, allow anyone to go down to the village. However, at my own risk, I was finally allowed to go into the ruined village accompanied by a young soldier – a country boy with a rifle. As we walked carefully down the middle of what had been the main street dogs began barking at us. Donkeys and cows were ambling aimlessly, looking for their stalls in the mass of rubble of the collapsed houses. I thought, as I spoke to my companion, that there must be some survivors who could hear our steps and who were now filled with hope that rescue was at hand. As we walked on, the earth trembled and a great fissure yawned suddenly a few yards ahead of us. The country lad saw me freeze in terror and placed a kindly hand on my shoulder warning me to stand quite still. A nearby house quietly slid into a pile of rubble, then all once more was still – even the dogs had ceased to bay. After a further look round, I scrambled back to the top of the hill with a feeling of cowardly relief. I asked the young officer in charge why they had not begun rescue operations. He said that, though they had been there some hours, no orders had as yet been given to move in. In fact, the authorities in Trapani and Palermo debated for several days before deciding on a chain of responsibility, and by that time, those who might have heard us talk in that ghostly moonlight were long since beyond all help. I saw vividly the point of Dolci's remarks, and realized what he was up against.

He has written several graphic books about conditions in Sicily and what he is trying to do. The Mafia leave him alone. Perhaps they do not take him seriously, or are too conscious of their own power to worry overmuch. A parliamentary commission sat for over a decade trying to get to the bottom of this secret 'honourable society', but achieved little. Mussolini almost succeeded in rooting it out, but history overtook him. After his fall and before the Allies could land in Sicily, many of the imprisoned Mafia agents claimed, with some truth, that they were anti-Fascist. They were let out as soon as the British and American forces disembarked from North Africa and without doubt helped the Allies overrun Sicily with the minimum of resistance. Since then they have grown in strength and influence. In spite of all, Danilo Dolci continues to labour on the stony ground of Sicily, determined that his unpopular campaign shall not be forgotten – a campaign against fear, oppression and fatalism which brought the Mafia into existence in the days of the

great absentee landlords over a century ago. It is a cancer in
the body politic of the entire country, and is at its most
malignant in Sicily, where it was born.

CHAPTER SIX

City of Make Believe

Cliché writers have dubbed Rome 'the Hollywood on the Tiber'. Indeed, today more full-length films are made in Rome than in Hollywood, which has largely been converted to making shorter films for the insatiable television market. Scores of writers and journalists make their livelihood writing for films, and many more scratch a reasonable existence playing small parts as extras. Rome, of course, is ideally situated for film-making because of its excellent light and good climate. In any case its inhabitants are natural actors, so competition for the extra parts is tough. The Fascists built up a grandiose film city called Cinecittà to the south-east of the capital, and many films are still produced in its rather dilapidated studios and in the surrounding vast spaces. These spaces can be turned into lakes or prairies as required, and Italy now produces a fair share of the ever-popular cowboy films, known in the business as spaghetti westerns. There are also more modern studios built by the dynamic Neapolitan, Dino de Laurentis, on the via Latina well beyond Rome, containing one of the largest studios in the world: it was large enough to house a replica of the Sistine Chapel, to size.

I had occasion to visit Richard Burton once for a special broadcast appeal on behalf of the British Haemophiliac Society, in which he is deeply interested, partly, no doubt, because he has a brother suffering from this strange disease. At that particular time he was taking time off between two major films to act and direct a film version of *Dr Faustus* with a cast of young players from Oxford. Among the cast, which of course included his wife, Elizabeth Taylor, was the jovial professor who had taught Burton English at Oxford – Neville Coghill, authority on Chaucer and the English stage.

It was a harassing moment for Richard Burton when I arrived. Time was running out, and, with the film in its vital closing stages, the studio staff were threatening to strike. All film directors and actors of eminence have something akin to a court around them. It certainly was the case in this instance. I had to pass through the hands of several elegantly dressed individuals before I was shown into Burton's private dressing-room, where a coloured aide offered me a large gin and tonic. I was more than half-way through it by the time the great actor arrived, dressed in medieval film costume and perspiring slightly under his heavy make-up. He gave an impression of great strength, for he is ruggedly built with broad shoulders and moves purposefully, yet he is a gentle giant. I saw that he obviously had everything on his mind but the short appeal he was to record. However, he glanced through the script, and began. He made many slips, and repeated the passages correctly. It took me well over an hour to edit these 'fluffs' out, but at least I had the pleasure of learning that his appeal brought in a great deal of money, and many wrote to compliment him on the smooth flow of his delivery.

His voice is a wonderful instrument, which he controls perfectly in the highest tradition of the English acting profession. He could play on his words as Menuhin on his Stradivarius, and he created sound images which were sublime – all the result of long and arduous training, the art that conceals art and makes everything seem effortless and natural. Once this recording was over, he relaxed for a short while and told me about his wife, Elizabeth Taylor, obviously a favourite topic of conversation with him. 'She knows more about film making than anyone else on earth, and is even more talented behind the camera than in front. She has taught me more than I can tell.'

The film world, like that of television, is a realm of

fantasy mingled with hard-headed business. Only the really strong survive for long, for the technicalities overwhelm everything, and you have to be a dedicated actor to overcome them. Either the light is not right, or, when it is, an aeroplane passes just as you have begun shooting and you have to begin all over again. Then perhaps the camera will seize up, or the light fuses will blow, or, as the wretched Richard Burton found on the day of my visit, the studio staff would growl mutiny and threaten to knock off altogether. It is something of a miracle that films ever get completed. I once saw Charlton Heston on the set in *Ben Hur* repeating a sequence over and over again until the director had it exactly the way he wanted. Outside the studio, in a great arena, Texan horsemen were racing around, rehearsing for the chariot-racing scene, while a little farther on technicians were putting the finishing touches to part of a Roman galley. It was always interesting just to drive past the studios. Sometimes you would see a complete medieval town on the set, at others a large model of Noah's Ark, with all kinds of animals in cages, waiting for their cue.

Yet in the main I prefer to see the finished product, and not have my world of make-believe shattered, fascinating though the occasional insight into this larger-than-life operation may be. Most actors, by their very calling, are like flaccid containers, waiting to take on the shape of what is poured into them. Some never seem to stop acting, whether on stage or off. There are exceptions, and Richard Burton is certainly one. When you talk with him, you feel that his native Wales and all the privations and suffering he has seen are never far from his mind, in spite of his enormous wealth and success. He told me that, eventually, he plans to give up acting so that he can devote himself to teaching at Oxford. I wonder whether this will ever come about. If it does, his lectures on Shakespeare will prove a great magnet for the lucky undergraduates of the English faculty.

The Vatican occasionally holds a special service for those

connected with the world of entertainment, and invites journalists to share in the occasion – knowing wisely that much of journalism is a branch of the entertainment business anyway. I remember being asked to one such ceremony in St Peter's, where Pope Paul received all the great stars of the day – all except one, it seemed, for, as a cynical monsignore informed me, St Peter's was not big enough to hold both Sophia Loren and Gina Lollobrigida. I did see the young Claudia Cardinale, who at the time was much in the news because of her private life, and she created quite a stir by wearing a mini-skirt. Many thought the Pope would not receive her, but he greeted her warmly as she made her curtsey. Afterwards, when I chatted to her outside the basilica, she lifted her shapely leg to a horizontal position, displaying lots of thigh, and said to me, 'But this isn't a real mini-skirt, you know.'

I was sitting during the service behind one of Italy's greatest actors and playwrights, the Neapolitan Chekhov, Eduardo de Filippo. He is a wisp of a man, with sad eyes and sunken cheeks, a bent back and yet with a stage presence which is quite remarkable. He is in the tradition of the great actor-managers, and writes most of his own plays. His gestures, the flicker of his eyelids, the shrug of the shoulder, the tremendous range of his voice and his superb timing all proclaim the superb actor he is. He was very modest in front of the Pope, and said that it was the greatest day in his life to have been able to pay his respects in such a setting. He has brought his company more than once to London for the World Theatre season for so long brilliantly organized by Peter Daubeny. Though the audience may not follow the broad Neapolitan dialect which he speaks, the action and gestures are almost sufficient in themselves to make everything clear. One play he put on dealt with the fortunes of a third-rate travelling troupe, forced to cook their meals in the rooms of their mean lodgings, since they had not sufficient money to pay even for a simple meal in a restaurant. The plot is slight, yet you feel that the play could go on and on, the actors and actresses are so real. Eduardo de Filippo, though he orchestrates the entire production and is, as it were, soloist and conductor in one, does not hog the stage – every person in the cast has his or her clearly defined part to play, even though they be but foils to the great man of the theatre, who lives the role of the seedy strolling player wondering how to make ends meet. Living in the heart of Rome, I found it easy to slip out for an evening's play-going, and the Quirino Theatre, where Eduardo de Filippo used to perform, was always a favourite.

I also saw there one of the rare stage appearances of Anna Magnani, in the powerful, earthy Sicilian drama *La Lupa*, or the she-wolf, written by Verga, who also wrote the libretto for *Cavalleria Rusticana*. Anna Magnani was a great tragédienne, and seemed to consume herself with the fiery passion of her peasant role. She was the embodiment of that smouldering passion which the character demands. There was something terrible about the volcanic furnace of her acting which defies description. She was the tigress of the Italian theatre; beside her most of the rest appeared mere lay figures. Her tired, ravaged countenance was symbolic of much that lies behind the character of the average Italian woman, only now beginning to realize the joys and terrors of emancipation in a world hitherto almost completely dominated by the male. Right up to her death at the age of 65 she was a formidable star, and few will forget her last brief appearance in Fellini's film *Roma*, in which she dealt him a brief comic rebuke. She had finally overcome her mistrust of television as a medium, and was planning a drama series at the time of her sudden death following a gall bladder operation in September 1973.

Even with such consummate players as de Filippo and Magnani, however, the Roman audiences are relatively sparing in their applause. They do not show the same *tifoso* or fanatic spirit which they demonstrate over their football stars. They tend to arrive shockingly late – it is quite normal for the curtain to go up half an hour after the advertised time. Not for them prolonged applause and innumerable curtain calls; once the play is ended, there are only a few bows before the mass of the public rushes to the cloakrooms and makes its way home. Yet their theatre is nonetheless unforgettable, and the players real professionals who accept this brief appreciation of their talents as the most natural thing in the world.

I have often asked myself why this is. Perhaps because the Italian is a natural actor himself, and has an unconscious resentment at seeing others on the centre of the stage. Few countries outside Italy, I imagine, can draw on so many talented characters as the poet-film director, Pier Paolo Pasolini, and that grand old man of the Italian films, Vittorio de Sica, found many years ago. For one thing, the Italian is used to dressing up, and feels quite at ease in any kind of costume – or none at all. Zeffirelli has found that out too, in both his film making and in his great opera productions. It is no accident that opera is a very Italian art form – it suits their temperament entirely, and has its origin in the elaborate ecclesiastical ceremonies of the early Christian Church in the Mediterranean area, if not in the pagan rituals which preceded them.

Before leaving this digression on some fleeting aspects of the Italian world of entertainment, mention must be made of the charming Sophia Loren, whom we once invited to dinner with her director husband, Carlo Ponti, on a summer's evening at Romolo's, a restaurant in Trastevere. It was indeed a fitting setting for such an occasion, since it was in this house that Raphael had met his great love, the baker's daughter, *La Fornarina*, Margareta Luti – a beauty he immortalized in dozens of Madonnas which inspire the faithful in churches all over the world. It was touching to see a really happy couple, who have at last been blessed by two children whom they so ardently desired for many years.

Sophia Loren was a poor Neapolitan who could not even afford enough for a meal, let alone the ferry across to Capri, when she was a girl living in the slums. She became a small-part actress, and used to make extra money posing for photographs in illustrated magazines devoted to the simple kind of love story – the *fumetti*. She was then taken in hand, first by Vittorio de Sica and then by Carlo Ponti, who made her into a great star. Off stage she does not act, but is the most natural of company – generous about her colleagues, and as appealing to women as to men. Though she has the glamorous trappings of the great film actress, she is essentially simple, and is at her best in the role of a peasant woman dealing energetically with a rumbustious husband rather than in the elegant parts she is often called upon to play.

Despite her fame and wealth, her lovely flat overlooking the Capitol, her luxurious villa near Marino, in the Alban Hills near Rome, which was once the summer retreat of a hedonistic cardinal of the eighteenth century, and as well as further homes in Switzerland and France, she remains at heart a straightforward Neapolitan lass, slightly surprised at her good fortune, which she knows will not last for ever. Nevertheless, she enjoys it while it does, as a real artist in life should. It was a memorable meal, of which I recall the friendly atmosphere she generated around her. As she sat by my side, fussed over by the owner of the restaurant, who was bursting with pride at having such an illustrious guest, I thought of that other beauty, the love of Raphael's life. She would have rejoiced to know that, for one evening in her old home, her place had been taken by another beloved beauty, as famous throughout the world on the screen as *La Fornarina* is on canvas.

This handful of players have given unalloyed pleasure to millions who have never known them in the flesh. They provide entertainment as I understand it – but then my tastes are relatively simple. Though there is much to be admired in the avant-garde playwrights and their obsession with representing the problems of life in their depressingly sordid particulars, they are not for me. Life is too often an ugly business. When I pay at the box office I confess I hope to be whisked into a land bordering on the mysterious fairy-tales of my childhood, or shaken by some tremendous tragedy which I imagine could not possibly happen in real life. A certain amount of escapism is necessary from time to time. We need more beauty in this polluted world, not less. I salute those in Italy and elsewhere who succeed in giving real entertainment, lifting nations out of the muckheaps which so often surround them.

The cinema, of course, has to meet the challenge of television. One way in which it strives to keep up box-office receipts is to make films more shocking and perverse than television is allowed to show even in the more permissive countries. As a result, there is more frontal nudity, more violence and more general nastiness. I wonder why the public pays to see much of this? Are we becoming more hardened to such depressing themes, or is this the only way to appeal to jaded appetites? Financial successes some may be, but artistically many of them are disasters, and indeed can hardly be called 'art' in any shape or form.

I had many friends who made a reasonable living out of the film industry in Rome, among them actors who were experts in dubbing films – a lucrative industry which has sprung up as films received a wider international distribution. Some of them, also, eke out their retirement playing as extras. The dignified looks and bearing of one former British consul are much in demand when directors are casting for cardinals and judges and other dignitaries. The old chap quite enjoys his work on the set, though he told me, in a moment of confidence, that he had stipulated that he would neither accept parts in westerns which involved violence nor take part in love scenes of a suggestive nature – which is reasonable, I suppose, when you consider that he is now over 70.

People of all social strata get into films sooner or later: aristocrats, students with handsome faces and figures, workmen with every kind of feature, dwarfs, those monstrously fat women so beloved by Fellini, and pretty well every other type that can be imagined. Quite apart from the extras, a whole host of experts flock to the studios to advise on anything from ancient Roman gladiatorial combats to the intricacies of ecclesiastical ritual. One good friend of mine, Fr Prospero Grech, a jolly Maltese Augustinian monk, who is a great scholar of the Bible, and almost as much at home in Hebrew or Greek as he is in his own Maltese language, once told me how he was pushed on to the set by a harassed producer anxious to start filming in the mistaken belief that he was an extra costumed as a monk. It is one of his treasured memories, for his life is normally cloistered and academic.

The Rome Olympic Games of 1960 are a fading memory for most now that Tokyo, Mexico and Munich have come and gone between. Yet the run-up to the Rome Olympiad is something which haunts me still. The Japanese were particularly quick off the mark, and sent over hordes of journalists and technicians well in advance. So too did the Germans. Accommodation was being snapped up and it was one of the rare occasions when my wife, during my absence in North Africa, took the law into her own hands and rang the BBC to say that she had discovered an unfinished hotel within walking distance of the Olympic stadium, and proposed reserving it in its entirety for the 80-man BBC team. The administrators came rushing out clutching cheque-books and signed up the entire place. We found an Italian duchess, Nelly Lante della Rovere, who was prepared to act as house-mother to the BBC team, and well she served them, bullying the management into providing meals at all hours of the day and night to fit in with the broadcasts, and making sure everyone was as comfortable as could be in the pressing circumstances.

RAI regretted that they had no special studio accommodation exclusively for the BBC, but we got round that problem by hiring several large caravans which we parked outside their offices in Mussolini's grandiose Foro Italico and recorded and edited our material from there. The largest caravan had been used just previously by Elizabeth Taylor on set for some spectacular film. To the horror of one strait-laced colleague from London it was found to contain, among its other accoutrements, a bidet. It was used, as I recall, to keep the wine and beer bottles cool until a fridge was installed, and then cushions were placed on it to make an extra seat.

It is amazing how much is spent on such sporting encounters without apparently the turning of a hair. The public demands a ringside seat for everything, and the host country sees that all the radio and TV networks throughout the world pay their proper share. An Olympiad gives that country the chance of doing many public works on which otherwise they would have dragged their feet for years. The Italians had already built a magnificent Olympic stadium out of the proceeds of the football pools; new roads were cut to make the distance between the various venues shorter; Professor Nervi erected a daring, covered stadium to the South of Rome, and the authorities drained some swampy land, cleared away slums and built the Olympic village in record time.

There was a moment of comedy when they discovered that at the entrance to the Old Foro Italico, earmarked as the training stadium, there was a great marble golden-tipped obelisk inscribed with 'Mussolini Dux'. There were angry debates in Parliament. The Socialists wanted it removed, as they considered it would be an affront to the progressive nations of the world. The Christian Democrat-led Government hit on a compromise. They pointed out that they were just as anti-Fascist as the opposition, but that the cost of uprooting such a huge mass of marble was not worth the effort. Everyone knew what they thought of the *Duce*. He had vanished into the limbo of history. So it was left there, though as a gesture some of the smaller Fascist bas-reliefs nearby were hastily chipped away. It showed a certain maturity on the part of the Italians, in my view, to leave the obelisk where it had been placed. It had slipped into history and would gradually become just another sight in the city of a million such memorials to men whose past deeds and misdeeds were largely forgotten.

Before every Olympiad there are always political problems. Those out for publicity know that the journalists of the world are conveniently concentrated in one place, and therefore offer a ready-made opportunity for the airing of views. Similarly, such an occasion offers a field day for the sociologist. The competitors at the 1960 Olympiad were all asked to answer a questionnaire. What was their race; were they one of twins; were they left-handed, single or married; were they smokers; were they drinkers, and if so did they drink beer, wine or the hard stuff? There was a group of questions on their athletic prowess, but the questioners then returned to their preferred hobby-horses. What were they studying or working at; what languages did they speak; what did they read – newspapers, scientific works, travel books, novels or detective stories or the lot; what was their favourite colour; did they collect stamps or coins; what were their favourite foods; had they made a success of their careers to date; how did they rate their own temperament; and had they made a success of their marriage? I suppose all the answers were computerized and served some useful purpose, though I never came across the results of the probe into this specialized branch of Olympic market research.

There was one practical exemption. They were all asked well in advance what kind of bed they preferred. Asian competitors asked for beds made of plaited rope; French competitors plumped for horse-hair mattresses; the Irish settled for foam rubber; while the Indonesians wanted their mattresses filled with kapok. The Australians wanted interior sprung mattresses, whilst the United States team diplomatically requested that half their beds should be soft and the other half hard. An official I spoke to at the time, who had the job of meeting all these diverse requests, wiped the sweat from his brow and said: 'I haven't had a request for a bed of nails yet, but no doubt we could oblige if desired.'

The Rome Olympics, were the first ever to be televised, and were seen simultaneously in both Western and Eastern Europe. This was before the days of satellites, and some American TV networks chartered planes specially equipped with developing and printing rooms to hurry their film across the Atlantic to the insatiable public in the United States. All sorts of strange little items of news came to light as we toiled to serve up interesting Olympic fare for our audiences. One such item was that the famous opera composer, Mascagni, had composed both the Olympic fanfare and the Olympic hymn. Another was that the Rome municipality had issued a special blue parking ticket printed in four languages telling the owner of the foreign car when he had transgressed the parking regulations. The ticket did not, however, threaten him with a fine, but wished him a pleasant stay in Rome. This gallant courtesy has persisted ever since.

Pope John came down from his summer residence in Castel Gandolfo to greet thousands of athletes in St Peter's piazza. I don't know what they made of his Latin address, but the athletes cheered and waved their panama hats in the air when he had finished. And when the Games were officially declared open by President Gronchi, the bells of every church in Rome pealed out a welcome.

There was a touch of comedy about a controversy which blew up over the waters of the lake near Rome where the rowing events were held. It is normally called Lago Albano, and is a volcanic lake just below the Pope's summer residence.

The people of the village would dearly have liked it to be known as Lago Castel Gandolfo, though somehow the name never caught on. The official signposts put up for the Games tactfully pointed to 'Lago Olimpico', whilst the Italian Ministry of Works signs read simply '*Al Lago*'. However, it is still known as 'Lago Albano', even though valiant attempts have been made to call it 'Lago Olympico' and even 'Lago Romano'. Fringed with forests and vineyards and not far from the clangour of Rome, it remains a pleasant, relaxing place, whatever the thousands of Romans may call it who come down at weekends to bathe, row, canoe or simply picnic or take their ease in the dozens of *trattorie* along the waterfront.

By the time the Games were at an end I think we all had the Olympic rings permanently before our eyes. Yet I also have memories of one of the most graceful athletes I have ever seen, the twenty-year-old American negress, Wilma Rudolph. She was about six feet tall, had short curly hair, an easy-going kind-hearted smile and moved with the natural unthinking grace of a gazelle. She won three gold medals, and when I saw her win the 100 metres in record time under the blazing sun on the Olympic track her action was a poem to watch. Even as she breasted the finishing tape there was a dreamlike smile on her face. This coloured grace from Tennessee was the embodiment of all that is finest in the now sadly tarnished Olympic world. She was always the first to turn and congratulate her rivals, and would saunter across to the prize-giving podium – clutching a straw hat, from which she never wished to be parted, even when the medal was hung round her neck – then meander off the track for all the world like a teenager out for a stroll. She remained unspoiled by the ballyhoo of success, and was the darling of the Rome Olympiad. Her victories were all the more remarkable, since she had suffered from polio as a child and for four years her legs were in irons. She came from a poor family with 18 brothers and sisters, and said: 'If you have as many in the family as I have, you learn to run when it comes to mealtimes.' Known as 'Skeeter' to her friends, she said: 'I just run, I don't know why I run so fast, I just run.'

CHAPTER SEVEN

Men of the Cloth

Rome always springs surprises, and many a cheery character lurks beneath a clerical robe. If you see a priest eating in a trattoria you can be sure that such a place will be well worth visiting for the amplitude of its dishes and for the reasonableness of the bill. One of the social conveniences in Rome, as my wife soon found, is that you never need be short of a man at table. There are always clerics happy to get away occasionally from their refectories, and they are in the main very good company. They abound with the latest quips about the pope and the Vatican. Even so, I was taken aback when a saintly Irish abbot, now dead, told me that Pope Pius XII's alleged vision of the Virgin Mary was due not to the Pontiff's devotion to the Mother of God but to an inefficient oculist, who prescribed the wrong spectacles. Another, admittedly younger, priest told me, after Pope Paul had issued his controversial encyclical *Humanae Vitae*, condemning artificial forms of birth control, that it had quickly become known as the epistle of St Paul to the Fallopians. Like Scotsmen and Jews, the Rome clergy seemed to take a special delight in spreading stories about themselves.

Although I cannot recall Father Grech's particular stories —and he had as large a fund as any – I came to appreciate his solid friendship. He is a jovial-faced monk in his forties, and one of the happiest men I have met. Though a profound scholar, and today Rector of one of the theological seminaries – the Augustinianum, situated in the shadow of St Peter's – he wears his great erudition lightly. Part of his happiness is no doubt due to the fact that he has no money problems. He is housed, fed and clothed by his order of Augustinians –

the Austin friars, as they were called in England, and the order incidentally to which Martin Luther once belonged before he married a nun – and is quite happy with the minimum of pocket money which he is allowed. When I first knew him he invariably wore a cassock, which is a cheap form of apparel and suitable for every occasion. After the Second Vatican Council he started to wear what the Italians delightfully call *il clergyman*, in other words an ordinary dark suit, so I imagine he is costing his order a little more these days.

The Augustinians have by tradition always been the sacristans of St Peter's, and through Father Grech's kindness I was able to see most of those treasures of the Vatican not usually on display to the general public. Many of these wonderfully rich vestments and other accoutrements are stored in rooms behind the Sistine Chapel. They fill a series of carefully guarded strong-rooms, lined from floor to ceiling with cupboards and drawers. The first sight of such splendour takes one's breath away. Here are papal tiaras, great brooches and clasps, diamond-studded chalices, flaring mitres in cloth of gold, rings set with huge jewels, altar plate of solid gold, crucifixes, reliquaries and croziers of the richest workmanship. One outstanding triple crown is set with so many diamonds and other precious stones that it is too heavy to be worn. It was given by a penitent Napoleon when he sought pardon for ordering his troops to loot the Vatican. As is recorded, they did a thorough job, stripping it of its finest statuary, pictures, vestments, plate and jewellery, though much of it was later returned. Near this splendid tiara is another of no intrinsic value. It was made in one night by skilled craftsmen working round the clock for the coronation of Pius VII after his return from imprisonment in France in 1814. There was no tiara left for the ceremony, so this one was made from silver foil, metal and paste. At least it had the merit of being the lightest of the papal crowns.

Originally the pope wore a single crown, as did other

temporal monarchs. Boniface upstaged his fellow kings by adding a second circlet in the thirteenth century and Benedict XII went one better by adding a third in the fourteenth century. The papal tiara was worn for probably the last time by Pope Paul VI, in 1963. When he was crowned he wore a new triple crown donated by the faithful of Milan. Artistically it was a disaster, looking for all the world like the nose of a shell. He found a way out of the difficulty by handing it over to the then Archbishop of New York, Cardinal Spellman, to sell for charitable purposes. Since then Pope Paul has never worn any tiara, even for the most magnificent of ceremonies. Father Grech, pointing to the cupboards crammed with all this bejewelled ecclesiastical haberdashery, turned to me and said with a ring of regret in his voice, 'You know, the Pope won't wear any of these any more. He likes the simpler vestments.' Opening a small cupboard, he produced a linen mitre embroidered austerely with the symbols of the four evangelists. 'This is the only headress he allows himself these days, though we occasionally persuade him to wear a more gorgeous one.' Then, shutting the door on the cupboard which contained the mitres and heavily ornamented chasubles and copes, Father Grech added, rather wistfully, 'Perhaps the fashion will change again. He might even wear a chasuble that I once designed [it was fittingly ornate], but for the present triumphalism is definitely out. The Pope feels it's not in keeping with the times.'

It is sometimes suggested that many of these treasures should be sold and the proceeds devoted to charitable works. The hard fact is, however, that most of these precious objects are gifts from devout Roman Catholics down the ages, and cannot thus lightly be disposed of. Peruvians, for example, gave Pope Leo XII an enormous golden clasp set with precious stones, representing the earth supported by angels. Queen Isabel of Spain donated to Leo XIII another clasp, made entirely of the finest diamonds. The Italian House of Savoy presented a delicately wrought golden chalice. Nor did the gifts come only from the Christians. A sultan once gave Pius IX a black charger complete with a saddle worked in gold and a caparison studded with diamonds, which were then wrought into one of the most opulent chalices I have ever seen. It now stands unused in one of the strongroom cupboards together with thuribles, incense boats, candle-sticks and monstrances. Occasionally papal diplomats come to see that the former gifts given by their countrymen are still there.

Father Grech pulled out wide drawers to show me albs and surplices of the finest gossamer-like lace, once worn by armies of clerics at the great services in St Peter's, and went on to exhibit the bejewelled gloves and embroidered slippers of successive popes and a whole array of croziers which the present Pontiff has abandoned for a modern tortured crucifix on a simple staff. Gone are the *flabella*, the high Persian fans, which used to flank the pope as he made his triumphal entrance into the great basilica on his portable throne, the *sedia gestatoria*. Gone too are the silver trumpets which, until recently, sounded their fanfare under the great dome as the choir intoned the *Tu es Petrus*. Pope John hated being carried on this throne; he said it made him feel seasick. Yet every pope submits to the ordeal so that thousands may catch an unimpeded glimpse of the man whom tradition claims is Christ's vicar on earth.

An American archbishop, Paul Marcinkus, who heads the financial operations of the Vatican – an office known as the Institute of Religious Works – once told me the wry story of two American priests who watched such a papal entry. When the service had ended one found to his dismay that his wallet had been stolen. The other grinned and quipped, 'Now you know why the Pope is carried high above the crowd on his portable throne.' Church services have always given the unscrupulous thief his opportunity. Pickpockets abound in crowds. The Vatican police once ran to earth a man dressed in monk's habit whom they noticed frequently kneeling, his hands joined in reverent prayer. They found, on closer inspection, that these hands were made of plaster and allowed the thief ingeniously to pick the pockets of his unsuspecting neighbours. It is an offence under Italian law to wear clerical habit if one is not entitled to do so, for obviously it forms a splendid disguise for criminals of every kind. Apart from pickpockets, the churches up and down Italy are sitting targets for the hardened thief who often gets himself locked in at night so that he can detach the works of art undisturbed and make off with his booty at first light. Antique shops and even flea markets have no shortage of such objects, and many is the lampshade I have seen made from the parchment of old psalters.

Perhaps those in the Vatican should let loose the thieves in the *floreria* – a storehouse where most unwanted items are stacked away, along with crimson and gilt furniture, dinner services once used for cardinalatial banquets, statues and pictures of doubtful taste, busts of forgotten dignitaries – the accretion of centuries – some frankly hideous. It is often said that the cellars of Windsor Castle and other British royal households are similarly crammed with gifts offered to monarchs, particularly to Queen Victoria. They are difficult to dispose of, for, who knows, someone somewhere may take it into his head to ask to see them. Yet the best of the Vatican treasures are on view, even though extra security precautions have now to be taken against insane attacks, such as that in which a crazy Hungarian smashed Michelangelo's priceless *Pietà* in 1972. By painstaking labour it has been restored perfectly. In fact, in the process of restoration the experts found that it had suffered damage long ago and had been repaired wrongly, so now the hand supporting the dead Christ is back in its rightful posture. The whole, however, can only be seen behind shatter-proof glass in the dark side chapel to the right of the main entrance of St Peter's.

I got to know one monsignore who worked in the Vatican, called Father Charles Burns, a chubby-faced Scot, brisk in

manner and humorous of speech. I met him first sitting in the
next barber's chair in a small hairdresser's shop in the centre
of Rome. We fell into conversation, and I discovered that he
was employed in the secret archives of the Vatican and was in
charge of the many priceless documents which that fabulous
library contains. It was not long before Charlie Burns became
a firm friend, and, when he offered to show me round some
of the more interesting parts of the library, I naturally
jumped at the invitation. He showed me an ancient decree
allowing smoking in churches in Bulgaria; a surprising collection of documents supporting the canonization of Don Juan
– believed in real life to have been a seventeenth-century
nobleman from Seville who repented of his profligacy in
later life; a papal decree permitting an order of nuns to wear
ordinary civilian clothes; and a special dispensation for one
nun, who ran a girls' village on the outskirts of Rome, to
wear a fur coat, have her hair permanently waved and use
cosmetics, apparently so as to set an elegant example to the
young ladies committed to her charge. Father Burns opened
drawer after drawer of papal bulls, heavy with their great
seals, conducted me along miles of shelves containing reports
dating back centuries from papal legates in distant lands. He
showed me too the Tower of the Four Winds, where the
details of the Gregorian calendar were finally calculated.
And, of especial interest to anyone connected with England,
there were love letters written by Henry VIII to the ill-
starred Ann Boleyn, acquired, no one knows quite how, at
the time when Catherine of Aragon was doing her best to
keep the Pope from declaring her marriage to the king
invalid.

For those who have the time and energy, the Vatican
library holds an inexhaustible store of information on almost
every aspect of human activity. Until his death in 1972 the
Vatican library was directed by the redoubtable French
cardinal, Eugène Tisserant (whose family originally came
from the Alsace and were called Weber until the annexation

of Alsace Lorraine by France, when many changed their German names into the French equivalent). This venerable grey-beard was one of the best-known figures in Roman society. He was invited everywhere, and often was among the last to leave. He was one of the last of the princes of the Church of the ancient regime, and lived his life to the full. He once told me, sipping his whisky with obvious enjoyment, that he had taken a liking to the drink when he was a young liaison officer serving in Syria during the first World War. He was Dean of the Sacred College of Cardinals for years, accompanied successive popes on their travels, and was clearly incensed when, with the passing of the years, his powers in the Vatican were reduced. He left behind him some highly controversial memoirs, which are probably locked up in the secret Vatican archives, where even Father Burns is not able to go.

In their scarlet robes, cardinals tend to stand out at any reception, and so experienced hostesses prudently wear dark and simple dress when they invite such eminent guests. They also wear the minimum of jewellery, at most a pearl necklace, for they cannot begin to compete with the sparkling pectoral crosses and rings of these top dignitaries. In the old days cardinals would be received with flaming torches, and even today the State of Italy generally mounts a guard of honour of two carabinieri in front of the house where the cardinal is visiting. Yet, taking a leaf out of Pope Paul's book, today even cardinals tend to dress with less outward show. Gone are the silver buckled shoes and the long trains. Many a cardinal feels happier in a simple black cassock, and one Italian archbishop I know, Cardinal Michele Pellegrino of Turin, discourages his flock from calling him *Eminenza*, preferring them to address him as 'Father', as they did when he was newly ordained. I had many talks with him during the Second Vatican Council, and found him to be a man of liberal views which clashed strongly with those of his more traditionalist colleagues.

Until last year, for the first time in its history Scotland could boast two cardinals. One was the veteran William Heard, who for many years was Head of the Sacred Rota, the Vatican's court of justice. He died in September 1973, aged almost 90 – a spare, bent figure who lived in retirement in the English College and whom I often saw walking in the Villa Pamphilj, accompanied by a young seminarist, or by the vice-rector, Mgr John Brewer, himself now a bishop. Heard was a testy character, not very approachable – at least as far as journalists were concerned. Perhaps he knew too much of the press criticism of the Vatican's methods of annulling marriages. Right up to the time of his death he loved the sensation of speed, and could not be driven fast enough in his ancient car with its Vatican numberplates. Perhaps his joy at moving fast dated back to the days when he was an Oxford rowing blue.

A more outgoing type was the other Scottish cardinal, Gordon Gray, who is Archbishop of St Andrews and Edinburgh. He too is happiest out of his ecclesiastical vestments and in his spare time likes to walk in the gardens of his rather austere residence in Edinburgh accompanied by his two Scots terriers. Gordon Gray is a patriotic Scot with a fine sense of humour of the old-fashioned kind. He recounted to me once in the new Scots College on the via Cassia over a delectable whisky that he had once been invited to take part in an ecumenical service. He drove slowly behind a large group of people making their way towards St Giles. He was in his cardinalatial robes, and only when his driver overtook the procession did he see that it was headed by banners inscribed with the slogan, 'Down with Popery'.

Cardinal Gray is an inveterate pipe-smoker, and it is rather incongruous to see him in his robes, smoking his pipe at receptions in Rome. At one, I recall how the British ambassador to Italy, Sir Patrick Hancock, a tall and imposing diplomat also blessed with a good sense of humour, offered the cardinal a fill of his own favourite brand, 'Parson's Pleasure'. 'No thanks,' said Cardinal Gray, 'I'd rather stick to my own Presbyterian Mixture.'

The Cardinal Archbishop of Westminster, John Carmel Heenan, is certainly by far the best known of the British princes of the Roman Church. He has always been a controversial figure, and he certainly does not shun publicity, which he knows how to handle. A notable preacher and pastor, he is one of those few who has a complete mastery of the treacherous medium of television. Created a cardinal in 1965, he was among the last batch ever to receive the *galera*, the wide-brimmed flat-crowned red hat. The presentation of this betasselled headgear, which hangs over the cardinal's tomb, has since been abolished, and now only the scarlet biretta and ring are given as a token of the high rank of the recipient.

Heenan is an imposing figure, and beams at you searchingly through his trifocal spectacles. He marshals his thoughts carefully before expressing them, which he then does with a deceptively simple clarity, and is a joy to work with both on television and on radio. He is a professional who knows exactly what is required of him, and also the value of letting the interviewer have his head. I had occasion to cross swords with him during the Vatican Council, yet he remained kindly and considerate in his relations with me throughout and is a man whose faith I admire. In November 1963 I was having dinner with him in the frescoed refectory of the English College. Before dinner we drank one of the college's famous and strong aperitifs, and finally made our way into the dining hall. All those from Britain taking part in that second session of the Vatican Council were ranged on either side of the long table in the centre of the hall and were in relaxed mood, for agreement had just been reached on liturgical reforms, and the Council fathers no doubt felt that they had earned their dinner. When the dessert was about to be served, however, the college porter came in to summon me to the telephone. When I got to his lodge, there was my wife on the other end, almost frantic. 'Thank God I've finally got through,' she said, 'I've been trying for such a time. The porter said that the bishops were not to be disturbed at dinner, but I finally persuaded him that it was urgent.'

'What's happened?' I asked.

'President Kennedy has just been shot and is believed dead.'

I said that I would leave immediately, but before doing so went back to the dining hall. I slipped into my place beside Heenan and told him the tragic news. He tapped on his glass for silence and announced what I had just told him. I shall never forget the incredulity on the faces of those round the long table. Some jaws dropped in disbelief, and everyone had a look of horrified shock as if suddenly frozen by the tragedy. Heenan asked all to stand, while he said a prayer for the repose of John Kennedy's soul, and I hastily took my leave to gather reactions for an emergency broadcast. All, from the Pope to the Communist leader Palmiro Togliatti, who always impressed me as being a kind of Kremlin cardinal, were at one in expressing their grief at the violent end of a young president who only four months earlier had been given a warm welcome with his wife when they paid an official visit to Rome.

I saw much of Cardinal Heenan, both during and after the Vatican Council, and in spite of our religious differences we became good friends. He has a phenomenal memory for people and places, a gifted pen and fluency of speech. He always has something apposite to say; one may or may not agree with what he says, but he is never pompous or dull. Despite a façade of moving with the times he is at heart a traditionalist. He rose from humble beginnings to one of the highest posts in his Church, and is determined to keep the faith of his fathers – and if possible to bring back Anglican Britain to the 'light and learning' which Henry VIII is said to have shown when he wrote his disquisition against the heresy of Luther, before himself breaking with Rome. The students of the English College, as they gather on the staircase for prayers each evening before retiring, still pray for the re-conversion of their countrymen to the 'one, true faith'. It is an open secret that Cardinal Heenan has often been in religious conflict with Dr Michael Ramsay, the Archbishop of Canterbury. Ramsay said to a friend on one occasion, 'I am all for a bridge between Lambeth and Westminster, but I don't want it to be one-way traffic.' The Archbishop of Canterbury, I may add, though not the extrovert that Heenan is, is nevertheless no mean performer on television, as I had reason to know on his visits to Rome. He has not written as much about himself as Heenan, nor, so far as I know, did he rebel when young against episcopal authority, as Heenan did. Cardinal Heenan, now at the apex of Roman Catholic authority in England and Wales, has to deal with a new generation of turbulent priests as well as with the growing phenomenon of the laity demanding a greater say in the affairs of the Church.

Some disillusioned Roman Catholics obviously feel that the high promise engendered by the Second Vatican Council and by Pope John's whirlwind reign has become smothered under the more cautious leadership of Pope Paul. Perhaps the Roman Church should become more Anglican rather than the other way about, and there are signs that in some ways it is moving in this direction. The laity are being given a greater say – it is no longer a question of 'pray, pay and obey'. There is greater insistence on the Bible, and services are at last held in the vernacular instead of Latin, much to the chagrin of some of the die-hards. Yet, with all this, one should always remember the prayers being said, not only in the Venerable English College in Rome, but in many other places, for England to return to Roman Catholicism. It is a sobering thought amidst the loose euphoria of ecumenism which so often confuses unity with union. And today much of the steam seems to have gone out of the ecumenical movement. Perhaps people realise to a greater degree that there is a usefulness in diversity, and that such divisions as exist, and which have seemingly almost always existed in the ranks of Christianity, are man-made and therefore not of fundamental significance. Uniformity can be the death of everything. Diversity is no bad thing whether in religion or anything else.

CHAPTER EIGHT

Roman Easter

Rome exerts a great fascination on those who see it for the first time, but never more so than at Easter. There is elation in the air. The first tourists are at the street corners with their guide books in hand and cameras at the ready, anxious not to miss a thing. In earlier days they were known as pilgrims, today most are just tourists. The general principle of the journey, however, is the same. Not only do they mean good business: the Romans are very proud of their capital, and they like others to admire it too.

Rome is beautiful for a thousand different reasons. In spring-time, with the trees in bloom and sprays of blossom adorning houses and shop-fronts, the city puts on its best Easter bonnet for the first visitors. In the confectioners' shops there are enormous Easter eggs, some at least 5 feet high and weighing 150 pounds. No one in his right senses buys an egg of this size, most of which are melted down afterwards into more mundane bars of chocolate.

Then there are the bakers. The Via Panisperna, which meanders up and down from the centre of the city out to the great basilica of Santa Maria Maggiore, is full of such shops, each with an intriguing variety of loaves, rolls and Easter cakes, catering for the most fastidious tastes. Some of the shapes go back to pagan times, including one large biscuit baked in the form of a woman who startlingly boasts three breasts – no doubt a pagan symbol of fertility.

Holy Week sees some of the richest and most moving ceremonies the Catholic Church has to offer the faithful. People throng the churches, each of which has its special relics on show. Many of the ancient churches have more than one relic. I once made a point of following some of the pilgrims on their rounds. In St John Lateran, for example, there is the Maundy Thursday ceremony of 'Mandatum', where the Pope washes the feet of twelve old men or twelve young boys, some of them cripples, recalling how Christ washed the feet of his disciples. On Good Friday there is the service of Tenebrae celebrated in all churches, commemorating the three hours' darkness over the earth following the crucifixion. One by one the candles are put out, until only a single flame is left, symbolising Christ as the Light of the World. Devout Roman Catholics visit several shrines, doing penance at each. Near the great basilica of St John Lateran there is the Holy Staircase, brought back to Rome by St Helena, the mother of St Constantine, the first Christian Roman Emperor. This staircase is believed to be the one down which Christ walked after he had been scourged and sentenced by Pilate. All day long the faithful wait their turn to go up the 28 steps on their knees. I saw creaky-limbed old and nimble young praying as they did so; they would then pause solemnly at the top for a final prayer at the old chapel altar, which existed long before the great church of St John Lateran was built.

St John Lateran houses the skulls of St Peter and St Paul. They are in finely wrought silver monstrances in a kind of cage over the altar. In St Peter's and other churches there are fragments of the 'true cross' brought back to Rome, the spear with which Longinus pierced Christ's side, thorns from the crown of thorns and various other relics.

The smaller churches of Rome – many of which are passed over by the tourists, who are pushed relentlessly through the pipeline by the travel agencies – have some of the most touching relics. In Santa Prassede, for example, with its uneven marble floor and glowing mosaics, there are the bones of thousands of early Christian martyrs; there are three thorns from Christ's crown and a fragment of his garment; and in a side chapel there is a portion of the marble pillar believed to be the one at which Christ was scourged, a relic of particular veneration.

This whole controversial question of relics comes up time and again in discussions on religion. Many tend to think cynically of the Canterbury Tales and the pardoner with his bogus relics. St Helena was one of the first to start the cult by bringing back many early Christian relics from the Holy Land to Rome. As well as being Constantine's mother, she is believed to have come from Yorkshire, and to have been the daughter of Old King Cole. The Holy Staircase was one of the most imposing of the relics she brought to Rome. Just how authentic such things are is a question which can never be fully answered. I once asked an English monsignor I knew, now a bishop in the Midlands, what he thought of relics, since some enlightened Roman Catholics were, I found, rather embarrassed by the devotion shown these generally rather grisly remains.

His reply surprised me. 'Even if they are not demonstrably genuine, it's a wonderful thing that people believe in their miraculous powers and, if they work, well, it should be left at that.' His answer did nothing to set my mind at rest, but smacked rather of the confidence trick played on the gullible.

Good Friday is the day when the pope goes to the Colosseum (the place where so many early Christians went singing to their deaths and won their martyr's crown) to recite the stations of the cross in flickering torchlight.

On Easter Sunday, the piazza in front of St Peter's fills up. About a quarter of a million people can find room in the great space, embraced by the massive colonnades of Bernini, and said to have been built to show how the Church embraces the whole world.

People come from all parts of Italy, some with banners and flags; there are tourists from foreign countries in their coaches, and many others on foot. They all converge on St Peter's. The yellow and white papal flags fly from the

Vatican palaces. On the stroke of noon the pope, robed in white and escorted by two of his most senior cardinals robed in crimson, appears on the balcony high above the main door of the basilica. Many of the faithful kneel on the hard flagstones as he comes forward, blessing the crowd with out-stretched arms. The pope's Easter message is a lengthy affair. It generally touches on a number of spiritual and temporal matters. At the end, the pope gives his traditional blessing, *Urbi et Orbi*, to the city and to the world. The bells of Rome peal out. Nowadays the ceremony has become far more familiar, since it is seen by millions throughout the world on television. The pope generally has a few words of greeting in English, German, Spanish, Portuguese, French and, of course, in Italian and Latin for the faithful. In recent years the languages used have included Russian, Arabic, and Chinese. Long after he goes to his private apartments, great crowds stay on, slowly filtering away to begin the secular part of their Easter holiday.

It is an Italian custom for the Church to come into the homes of the people at Easter – it is one of the few times clergy do so. You see priests in their robes, accompanied by young acolytes bearing holy water, in every quarter of the city, visiting houses, apartments and offices to bless and to receive alms, or sometimes the traditional Easter food – boiled eggs, salami and a special pie made from cheese. Generally there is something new in the home to bless, a baby's cot, some china or maybe a coffee mill. They all receive a special benediction.

On Monday of the Angel, or 'Pasquetta', as the Romans call the traditional Easter Monday, most inhabitants leave Rome to take their first picnics by the seaside or in the gently rolling countryside of the Castelli. On that day the tourists, perhaps a little foot-sore, but still clutching their guide books and their cameras, have Rome almost entirely to themselves.

Easter is a time when Rome is at its best. It is an unforget-table experience to assist at some of the ceremonies or merely to live in Rome, even if one isn't particularly religious. There is this lightness in the air, a certain hope of Spring, which seems to transmit itself and communicate itself to the hearts of all those, young and old alike, who feel that life is worth living and that Rome is one of the best places in the world in which to live it.

Paradoxically, one of the reasons why it is so pleasant living in Rome is that one can swiftly get out of it, by car, tram or train, or in one of the roaring buses which career along the country roads, honking as they go.

In the years that I lived in Rome, I've certainly not seen everything. You can go on discovering new things every day: a water clock in a tucked away courtyard, a statue on the sky-line one has never noticed before, a charming balcony or decorated window frame. The variety of man-made beauty is endless. Outside Rome the natural beauty continues.

The Victorians rather pooh-poohed Lazio, the province round Rome, or 'Latium', as it was known in ancient times. Yet it is pleasant to go up into the Castelli – the Alban Hills – to wander through the narrow streets of Castel Gandolfo, where the pope has his summer villa, where busy and friendly Australian Jesuits look at the stars every night through their telescopes. It is pleasant, too, to seek out a little trattoria overlooking the shimmering waters of Lake Albano, far enough away for the buzz of the outboard motor-boats to be hardly more disturbing than the humming of a bee.

The Castelli Romani are the favourite excursion spots for the Romans: Rocca Priora, Frascati, Marino, Castel Gandolfo. My own particular favourite is the village of Nemi, above Lake Nemi, a small volcanic lake, sometimes known as 'Diana's Mirror'. According to one legend the lake was formed by tears of the goddess Diana. Another claims she used it as her mirror. It is a charming, lonely lake, in a rather remote part of the Castelli; one can easily drive past without ever seeing it. You have to go right into the little village of Nemi, with its old Ruspoli castle, before you can actually see its limpid waters, surrounded by flower gardens, strawberry beds and vineyards.

In ancient times the lake was a pleasure resort. Nero ordered two great galleys to be built on this lake, floating palaces of amusement. In time they rotted away and sank to the bottom. One of the things which Mussolini did, to his credit, was to have the lake drained, so that the hulks of these two great galleys could be recovered. It took years to do this; the hulks were hauled up, restored, and two large museum halls were built to house them. There they remained throughout the war until the very end, when a German NCO blew up the museum as a final act of vengeful vandalism before withdrawing to the north.

The museum is still worth a visit; there are anchors, helmets and brass and bronze rings in lions' heads which once formed part of the rail round the galley. It is also one of the saddest museums in which I have ever been – for what is so obviously missing. You can see where there was once a splendid poop and prow; now just a few charred remains of timber lie here and there, and the rest sketched in light metal tubing to show what was once the grandeur floating on Lake Nemi.

Everybody has their favourite part of Italy. There is the sophisticated beauty of the Tuscan towns and the wild beauty of the south. There are the lovely cities of Padua, Verona, Venice and many more. It's not sensible to attempt to choose which one prefers; all have their particular attractions. To the south, within a few hours of Rome, you can still see old women sitting at their doors and in the piazzas wearing the full skirts and large-sleeved blouses, the costume which their ancestors have worn for centuries. They wear it unaffectedly; the young, however, prefer mini-skirts and blue jeans to the pleated full-skirted costumes of their grandmothers.

There is always the risk, when talking of Rome and its surroundings and indeed of Italy in general, of thinking in terms of churches, paintings, monuments, ruins and landscapes. Most vitally interesting of all are the people. For anyone coming to Italy, quite apart from ticking off sights which are on the list, it is well to sit at one's ease in a piazza, drink an *aperitivo* or coffee and just watch the world go by. One of the best places to do this in Rome is the Piazza Navona, once an ancient Roman circus. Apart from its churches, palaces and magnificent fountains, it is also teeming with life. The profiles on many a Roman coin spring to life. Young children take their first steps in the piazza, or hazard their first wobbly yards on a bicycle; old people sit on the stone benches; soldiers chat to young girls; students and artisans rub shoulders with each other; occasionally priests go by, looking humble or haughty as they glide along in their cassocks to say their offices in some pillared church or chapel. That is the way to enjoy Italy. Not just to go, guide book in hand, but to watch the people.

Italians are quick to laugh, and also quick to anger. Psychologists don't make much of a living in Italy, because emotions are very near the surface. Italians either blow up with fury or explode with happiness or sorrow. You don't find many glum Italians, or at least they don't stay glum for long. They are friendly and flattering. If you say just a few words in Italian they immediately raise their hands and tell you encouragingly that you speak the language fluently. Conversely, the average Italian speaks very little of any language but his own. They experience a euphoric feeling – a sensual pleasure, almost, merely from talking; they love the sound of their own voices; they love the sensation of language as it issues from their lips; and they tend not to engage in conversation, waiting for their friends to answer, but to talk simultaneously past each other, yet somehow miraculously catching from the edge of the sound track, as it were, the gist of what their companions are telling them. That is why, even if only two or three Italians are talking together, they sound like a quarrelsome crowd. They are seemingly impervious to noise, and certainly don't mind the sound of their own often strident voices. It is a curious paradox that an extremely musical nation, one which produces some of the loveliest music from instruments and voice in the world, has harsh and penetrating voices, such as will cut through any background of motor cycle engines and traffic. And if all else fails, they fall back on the rich language of gesture.

The Italians are a gregarious race, perhaps frightened of being alone too long. They enjoy their pleasures cheek by jowl – you only have to look at the beaches to see that – and they like congregating in piazzas to talk. They like to surround themselves with their family and their clan. One of the most dangerous Italians is the lone driver of a car; if he has no one to talk to he drives like Jehu and hoots every now and then, just to keep himself company. Conversely, when the driver has a companion, he is likely to take both hands off the wheel to gesticulate. The Italians rarely if ever give hand signals – if you see a hand out of the window it is merely that the occupant of the car is emphasising a point in his conversation.

It takes a long time to know the Italians well, their way of life is so different. Superficially they are extremely easy to know, but deep down you find they have their own, special attitude to life. This is summed up well, as I have related, in the controversial book called *The Italians* by Luigi Barzini. Barzini told me, when his book first came out, that the Italians were far more realistic in their approach to life than most other nations. They didn't waste time on hypocritical courtesies; they just went straight for what they wanted. He gives many examples of this Italian singleness of purpose, some rather terrifying. His book has come in for much criticism from his own countrymen. From my own observations it is basically true, and not as uncharitable as some people, who have only glanced at it, would have one believe.

The Italian does not have a gentle sense of humour, but

rather a biting form of satire. He is extremely cynical of the powers that be, which makes him debunk everybody, from the pope and the president downwards. Nothing is sacred to an Italian, or at least nothing about those in authority is sacred. The Italian tradition has always been to shoot cynical darts at those who set themselves up above their fellows. The Roman 'dialect' poets Belli and Trilussa are loved for this. You can hear and read many cynical things about the government of the day which would be considered libellous in Great Britain, and you would hear more anti-clerical jokes in the Vatican than anywhere in the world. A typical Vatican joke or *barzaletto* is the following:

Question: What is the difference between Pope Pius XII, Pope John XXIII and Pope Paul VI? Answer: Pius believed in the Church but not in God, John believed in God, but not in the Church; poor Pope Paul just can't make up his mind.

Basically the Italian is rather uncertain of his place. He is never sure whether the system under which he works is going to last or not. That is hardly surprising. Italian national unity only celebrated its first centenary in 1970, and the country is not deeply united even now. One of the first pieces of information any Italian tells you is where he comes from – he wants you to be quite certain that, if he is a Venetian, you don't mix him up with one of those arrogant Romans; and, of course, if he is a Roman, he wants you to know how proud he is to be a citizen of the capital of Italy. Very few will admit to being just Italian. The northerners on the whole still have a great disdain for those from the south. Provincialism dies hard.

A common remark to be heard in Milan or Genoa or Turin is: 'Italy would be one of the richest countries in Europe if it only stopped at Bologna.' It is an ironic fact of the industrial expansion of the north in the past decades that much of it has been due to the influx of workers from the south who, nevertheless, still find it hard to integrate their lives with those of their countrymen in Upper Italy. To many of their northern countrymen they are virtually foreigners.

There is an abundance of labour in Italy, though much of it has emigrated from the south to the north and beyond to Switzerland, France, Germany and Belgium. In Southern Italy there are many almost deserted villages where the fields are tilled by old men and by women. The emigrant workmen send money home; houses are built, shops are restored and opened and there's a general air of thriving absentee land-lordism of a modest, working-class kind.

The south and the north are being linked more closely as the great arterial roads, the motorways, are opening up, and travel becomes swifter. One of the greatest links in pulling Italy together is television – a wonderful medium for a country where standards of education vary so much, from the well-educated northerner to the more primitive southerner, who is not necessarily less intelligent, but who, because of backward and inefficient local government, has not had the chance of schooling. They can all see the same television programmes. Sometimes it is difficult for the producers and planners to know just how to pitch the level of such pro-grammes; yet the southerner today can see what's going on in Milan and the people in Venice can see what's going on in Calabria, and perhaps they see many points of similarity as well as of difference.

Two characteristics unite most Italians. One is their innate sense of religion, even if they are over-familiar with church services and dealings with the clergy. Another, probably linked with this, is a deep feeling of superstition. There is a surprisingly widespread belief in the powers of the evil eye, and many other strange superstitions which we do not meet with in Britain: beliefs and practices concerned with such important matters as birth and death, marriage, love, spells, amulets, charms, as well as patron saints to turn to in time of specific trouble. Marital troubles, hopeless causes, lost treasures: there is a saint for every case. It is quite common to see lorries careering about Italy with a large notice on the cab saying: 'St Joseph have mercy on us,' or, 'May the Madonna bless us,' and dangling from the radiator a large bull's horn to ward off the evil eye. This strange combination runs through both the pattern of Italian life and the personality of the Italians themselves. It makes the Easter pilgrimage a continuation of something which has been going on long before Christianity came to the West. Before there was a pope there was a Caesar, and before there were nuns there were vestal virgins, and so on. The parallel is very close. Those who have studied the Mithraic religion can see why it was that the Christians put it down so fiercely, for this was the one religion which threatened to oust their own as the pagan world collapsed.

The early Christians were not nice people. They suffered, but they were tough, and in turn they were great iconoclasts and arrogant, exclusive authoritarians when their time of power came. Their great coup was to convert Constantine the Great to Christianity, and their greatest worry in the early world was when Julian the Apostate tried to put the clock back.

Rome is a layer cake of religions. You only have to look at some of the excavations, such as those in San Clemente, to realise how one civilization has superimposed itself on another, and how the Christian civilization at the top is crumbling noticeably today, through indifference born of affluence and corruption of ideals – partly due, no doubt, to the wider education of the masses. That is why the Christian Church, with the Roman Catholics in the vanguard, are trying to bring their religion, as practised and organized, in line with the twentieth century, knowing that the old authoritarian days when people did as they were bid are over.

There are two inescapable landmarks in Rome. One is the dome of St Peter's, the other the great white marble monument to King Victor Emanuel – the first king of united

Italy. Wherever you go in the city, you are bound to catch sight of one or other of them before you get very far. The one is the symbol of the Roman Catholic Church, the other a reminder of how comparatively recently Italy overthrew the temporal power of the papal states and became a unified country. It would be patently unfair to dwell on their respective aesthetic appeals. Michelangelo's dome is a master-piece, and to see it dominating the Roman skyline is always an inspiration. The same can hardly be said of the marble mausoleum which dwarfs the Capitol Hill. It is one of the ugliest things in Rome, its unrelenting white marble columns and gilt statues evocative more than anything else of a rather unsuccessful wedding cake. Some irreverent Italians refer to it as the typewriter which has been left out in the snow. Yet this mass of Brescia marble is a shrine, not only to Italy's unknown soldier and the dead of two world wars, but also to the victory over the papal states and their absorption into a united Italy. It is the altar of the country, and as such it is an historic symbol of significance.

After 1870 and the unification of Italy, the pope, as is well known, called himself 'the prisoner of the Vatican'. Few would deny, even today, that apart from his religious authority he wields political influence far beyond the confines of his small kingdom. Many Italians still like to regard him as the indirect monarch of their country. In some ways he is. Certainly the influence of the Roman Catholic Church makes itself felt in many fields – in finance and politics, in educa-tion and in all forms of entertainment, to mention but a few.

The sheer weight of the Church on daily life has brought into being the strong counterweight of anti-clericalism. Over the whole issue Italians show something of a split mind. They are naturally at home in their churches to an extent few of us are in ours. Yet many of them resent what they consider to be the interference of the clergy, not only in political matters but in affairs of everyday life. The unbending attitude of the Church towards divorce, for example, is one source of perpetual controversy; another is the Vatican's negative attitude towards birth control, in a country where the rapid growth of the population and the accompanying upward curve of unemployment are constant problems. So far as divorce is concerned, the Italian parliament, largely through the unceasing efforts of the Socialist deputy Loris Fortuna (himself a happily married man, incidentally), finally got the ban on divorce lifted in 1970. It is estimated that some five million men, women and children, almost one in ten of the Italian population, were, until the divorce laws, leading an illegitimate existence. The Lateran Pacts signed by Mussolini and Pius XI in 1929 are incorporated in the Italian constitution and uphold the Church's traditional ban on divorce. The new law permits divorce when a spouse has been abandoned for a long term, and for other reasons. The neo-Fascists and some of the Roman Catholic Christian Democrat party were almost alone in opposing this innovation. Their plan now is to allow a referendum, in the hope that it will be reversed. Such a move would revive a *Kulturkampf* atmosphere which most would like to see remain dormant.

I often used to discuss this controversial matter with Italian friends. One reaction I did not expect was from a cynical man of the world, who said: 'I am against the introduction of divorce, because there are many unhappily married men like myself who find it very convenient to tell our mistresses that we would love to marry them, but that it is legally impossible. Once divorce is permitted, a great army of mistresses will arise and demand that their lovers should marry them.'

Pope Paul's upholding of the ban on birth control in his *Humanae Vitae* encyclical has also proved extremely unpopular. It is illegal for any publicity to be given to the sale of contraceptives, though every device can be had at most chemist shops, either over or under the counter. Foreign women have no difficulty in buying the pill without a prescription. Italian women find it harder, unless they know their chemist well, since the pharmacists are always worried about possible police intervention and subsequent prosecution. One friend of mine, an Italian working man, contrasted rather bitterly the wealth of the Church and the apparent comfort in which many clergy live with the poverty and overcrowded conditions in which so many lay Italians still find themselves. 'Just think,' he told me, 'only the other day a priest came to visit my sister and her three children. She lives with them and her husband in one room, without windows. And do you know what the priest said to her? "You should thank God," he said, "there are many others far worse off than you are." Well,' asked my friend, 'what sort of comfort is that? Why doesn't the Church help?'

Another Italian friend, a devout middle-aged Catholic woman, held the opposite view. She said to me: 'It doesn't matter about all this poverty; there will always be the poor. However much money you spend on them, you have nothing to show for it in the end, for the people die anyway. Now our Church has created most of the beauty you see in Italy today. Isn't it worth it?' My second friend, I may add, is not well off either; she is a working woman who is inordinately proud of her country and her Church, though I am not quite sure in which order she would put them.

A cardinal friend, when I taxed him with these views, said in reply: 'You know, you really have to be a Roman Catholic priest to understand anti-clericism. It is an old problem, which we know all too well. But the Church goes on in spite of it all, which is another reason why we believe it must be divinely protected.'

Yet most Italians agree that the hold of the Roman Catholic Church is not as strong, especially on the younger generation as it was before the war. Growing opportunities for education provide one reason for this. Some of my Italian friends tell me that they think the hierarchy is against too widespread schooling facilities. They would prefer to have the masses relatively ignorant and unquestioning, looking to the clergy for a lead. These days are passing, if not already past. They add that the Roman Catholic Church also is not against poverty, for it gives scope for the exercise of charity. One man of left wing views said to me: 'I admit these priests, monks and nuns do good work, some of them, but they mean nothing in terms of economic production, and they have got to be supported to live.'

Yet even the staunchest Communists – and they form the second largest political party in Italy, and the largest Communist party in Western Europe – still fall back at certain times on the Roman Catholic Church and its traditions. They are quick to protest if the priests fail to come to their homes to impart the Easter blessing. They will go to Mass, and then at election time go to the polling booths and vote for the Church's greatest single enemy – Communism. The Roman Catholic hierarchy is too wise to threaten them with excommunication for doing this. Often a Communist and a Roman Catholic are one and the same person in Italy. The red in their national flag suggests to some Italians the colour of a cardinal's hat, to others the red flag of international Communism. For a great many, however, it is an inextricable mixture of both.

Newton's law, that action and reaction are equal and opposite, applies to Italian politics just as much as to physics. Perhaps one of the main reasons why the Communists poll so many votes in Italy is that the Vatican interferes in everyday life and politics. The Christian Democrat party is its main instrument for this – a large amorphous political group which has led the government since the end of the war, though it rarely, if ever, has a parliamentary majority to carry through its programme. It has always had to form a coalition with the left or the right, and for the past few years has been in a not-too-happy coalition with the Socialists. In fact, were it not for the cement of the Roman Catholic religion, or more precisely of the Vatican, the Christian Democrats would long since have fallen apart as a party, containing as it does members of almost the whole range of political spectrum, from neo-Fascist members on the extreme right to advanced trade unionists on the left.

How, then, does the Vatican exert its influence on them all? And on others besides? The answer is partly historical and partly geographical. Italians tend to 'own the pope'. It is well-nigh inconceivable to them that he should not be an Italian. It would indeed be difficult for a non-Italian to understand all the ramifications which exist between the Vatican and Italy, a kind of ecclesiastical 'old boy network'. Throughout the country, cardinals and archbishops have great influence well beyond the religious sphere. To obtain a job in Italy, a recommendation from a prelate will often clinch the deal; conversely, opposition from the Church will make the candidate's chances slim indeed. The *raccomandazione* is still all-powerful in Italy, whose citizens are realists enough to grasp the fact.

The fact that the tiny Vatican State is in Italy is not without significance. It is a postage stamp State whose sovereign has wide sway far beyond its narrow territorial borders. With the help of the House of Savoy, Pius XII in his day made all his nephews princes. They became influential directors of banks and other enterprises in Italy. Pope John, to his everlasting credit, resisted promoting his farmer brothers. There is the story that, shortly after he was elected pope, one of the senior Vatican officials inquired of Pope John what titles he would like to confer on his brothers who led, and still lead, the lives of simple farmers in Bergamo in northern Italy, tending their vines and looking after their modest livestock. Pope John replied '*Non sono conti, ma contadini*' (they are not counts, they are countrymen). Nor has there been any suggestion that Pope Paul has any ambitions in this direction. His brother was, until his death, a senator (of the Christian Democrat party, as might be expected), and the Pope has to tread warily in the Italian political arena, though he does not hesitate to uphold the Lateran Treaties with Italy and speak out against divorce and abortion when he sees that the Italian coalition government shows increasing tolerance in such matters. It does not add to the Pope's popularity.

Apart from the strong moral, historical and geographical influence the Vatican has on Italian affairs, there is another, the financial, which is not perhaps as widely known, even to many Italians.

However much one tries to probe into the financial operations of the Vatican one comes up against a wall of secrecy – and this gives rise to extraordinary rumours. The cardinals in their black limousines look affluent, though often they are not. The grandeur of Vatican ceremonies, the expensive diplomatic missions in many lands, the financing of the Vatican Ecumenical Council and of synods, charitable institutions, schools and universities, all make heavy demands.

Yet the Vatican is one of the great financial powers in Italy and, indeed, far beyond. An informed estimate of the value of Vatican shares held in Italy is in the order of one thousand million pounds sterling – a considerable slice of all the shares issued in the country. The Vatican has large holdings in several banks, one of them, appropriately enough, called 'the Bank of the Holy Ghost'. It controls a chain of hotels and cinemas, and owns much real estate. It helps such concerns as insurance companies, gas and water-supply undertakings, the production of ceramics, building materials and even spaghetti. Its financial ramifications are almost endless. The Vatican therefore has every reason to exert its considerable influence to keep an Italian government in power which will safeguard this important financial stake in the country's economy. When the government of the day veers too far to the left, the Vatican sells some of its Italian shares and invests the money elsewhere.

Under the Lateran Treaties of 1929 the Vatican was exempted from all Italian taxes. In 1962, however, a law was passed putting a tax on stock market properties. There was no mention of any exceptions being made. The Vatican claims that it is still exempt. The opposition Communists and Socialists argue, however, that it is not, and that it has a large unpaid tax bill since the new law was passed amounting to well over 30 million pounds. This the Vatican describes as absurd. Nevertheless, in 1969 the Vatican withdrew a considerable share of its holdings in Italian industry and reinvested the money in Paris. This was presumably done for two reasons: one, to cut down on its capital in Italy in case the tax was enforced; two, to bring pressure to bear on the Italian politicians, particularly the Christian Democrats. It was in other words a warning, to put it in its politest terms, to go slow on such controversial issues as divorce. However, the concordat signed in 1929 between Mussolini and Pius XI regulating relations between the Vatican and Italy will obviously have to undergo bilateral revision before long.

Where does the Vatican get its money? Its basic wealth comes from money paid by Italy at the time the Lateran Treaties were signed; this has been shrewdly invested over the years not only in Italy but in many other countries, including Switzerland, France, Britain and the United States. Financial experts, by no means all of them Roman Catholic, handle these portfolios, and secrecy surrounds the exact nature and extent of the investments.

The Vatican also has its own bank, called 'the Institute of Religious Works'. At its head is a US prelate, Archbishop Marcinkus. Its clients are carefully selected. Apart from the religious, only a few laymen, such as diplomats and others who have special relations with the Holy See, hold accounts in it. Its transactions are as secret as those of any numbered account in Switzerland. No doubt it would surprise many in the Vatican itself if a roll-call of its clients were ever to be published. It would probably include some of the bitterest political opponents of the Roman Catholic Church who, nevertheless, through third parties, use the Vatican banking facilities for their international dealings. Discretion is the heart of sound finance. The Vatican exemplifies this to a most refined degree. *Pecunia non olet.*

The cynical and disillusioned Romans maintain that the registration letters on the Vatican limousines, SCV – *Stato Citta' Vaticano* (The Vatican City State) really stand for *Se Christo Vedesse* (if only Christ might see). However, it is fair to say that, though the Vatican receives much revenue from the faithful, it dispenses most of these funds with careful charity.

Pope John tried to lift the Vatican above Italian politics. The Council put a great strain on Vatican finances. He was obviously out to share the wealth of the Church – raising the pay of Vatican officials, and generously distributing funds for every kind of project. He was a man who cared little for worldly possessions.

His successor is a more careful administrator, but he too knows that the demands for help (if the Roman Catholic Church is to develop further in the world) will continue to increase.

The Vatican has many priceless treasures, most of which will never be sold. Apart from its investments, the Vatican can count on bequests and 'Peter's pence', contributions from all over the world which are made on St Peter's day each year. American Catholics account for almost half of this. They are generous, and well organised by their efficient and enthusiastic clergy, and on the whole much richer than their fellow-believers in other countries.

However, so long as the cardinals are sworn to secrecy, so long as no balance sheet is ever published, and so long as the financial operations of the Vatican remain in the hands of an expert few there is bound to be disquiet, suspicion and even fear in the minds of many, whether they profess the Roman Catholic faith or not.

To help him administer this vast wealth for the good of the Church, the Pope has round him experts both clerical and lay – cardinals, stockmarket experts and papal aristocrats who keep an eye on Vatican affairs and work closely with the Apostolic diplomats accredited to many governments throughout the world. In all fairness, it must be said that the Vatican provides colour, dignity and solace to countless millions who pass through Rome each year – possibly for the one and only time in their lives – with its magnificent ceremonial and courtly proceedings; and it seeks to maintain a standard of simple dignity and continuity of services in even the humblest of churches. There is a sense of belonging to a great and powerful organisation, which uplifts and sustains many of the faithful; a sense of being on the right side, supported by some of the ablest intellects in the world. This is a cause of envy to many outside its fold. It is the reason why, every year, there are conversions to the Roman faith, often of people of highly discriminating mental fibre, who feel, especially as they approach the end of their lives, that they need the moral support of a well-grounded religion which has thought up, from the wisdom of the early Church fathers onwards, the answers to many of the questions which bedevil life in our modern, unquiet times.

The Vatican Ecumenical Council and the subsequent meetings of three synods have made it abundantly plain that the Roman Catholic Church is going through a crisis of faith and authority. Quite a number, who in the past would have easily been converted simply because Roman Catholicism seemed to have the definite answer to all problems, are now holding back, because the once monolithic Church is no longer so sure of herself. In some parts of the world, such as Holland, she is in obvious ferment, bordering on disarray. This could be the start of a belated reformation inside the Roman Church. As such it is to be welcomed, though the present is perhaps one of the most turbulent periods in its recent history, with vocations decreasing, with many openly questioning the authority of bishops and even of the pope himself, and casting doubt on many of the old church traditions, such as clerical celibacy. At the head of it all an anguished Pope Paul is striving desperately to keep the barque of St Peter from capsizing in the stormy waters of the late twentieth century.

The pope is a mixture of absolute monarch and democratically elected head of the Church. Anyone may become pope, providing he is male and a Roman Catholic. In theory he need not even be ordained, though I cannot recall that a layman has ever been elected to this supreme office. In a century or two this just possibly could happen. The Pope is far easier of access for ordinary people than the Queen of England or the President of the United States. People can be received in audience every week *en masse*, they can call on the pope privately if they are suitably sponsored, and they can receive his blessing every Sunday in St Peter's piazza or in the summer at Castel Gandolfo.

How then is such a man, the Vicar of Christ on earth, the successor of St Peter, the Patriarch of the West, the Bishop of Rome, the Sovereign of the Vatican City State – to give him a few of his age-old titles – elected in the first place? Why is one man preferred to another? What outside influences, if any, come into action at the time of a papal conclave, when the cardinals of the Sacred College are walled up until they have elected a new pope? Who wants to be pope anyway, one of the loneliest and most awe-inspiring tasks in the world? Is there much difference in the way successive popes act? Can anyone imagine what it is like to be pope?

Two writers in English have tried to imagine themselves as pope of Rome. There was the strange ex-student of the Scots College in Rome, Frederick Rolfe, later known as Baron Corvo, who wrote the remarkable fantasy, *Hadrian VII*, which has proved a great theatrical success on both sides of the Atlantic. More recently, as I mentioned earlier, the Australian writer Morris West made a valiant effort in his fascinating novel *The Shoes of the Fisherman*. Perhaps it stretched the readers' imagination and credulity just a bit too far, but some of its pages catch the aching loneliness and ultimate responsibility which a supreme pontiff must undoubtedly experience – a man who believes himself answerable directly to God.

CHAPTER NINE

The Successor of Peter

One of the daunting impressions anyone has coming to
Rome for the first time is of the overwhelming mass of books
which have already been written about it. One feels that
everyone is far more knowledgeable than oneself, and must
already have written and covered every possible angle of the
scene. Nevertheless, one has the advantage of coming into a
place with a fresh eye. When I first came to Rome early in
1945, having been wrenched from a war job which I rather
smugly had considered very important, I thought that I
would soon be going on to Vienna. I soon discovered that I
was stuck. The Vienna trip was off for a long time to come,
because the Russians, although they had captured Vienna,
weren't allowing the Western Allies in. One morning I was
sitting glumly at the breakfast table in the Hotel de la Ville
at the top of the Spanish Steps. Opposite me was Eric Linklater, whom I had known in the Savile Club, an erudite
writer with a superb sense of the comic, as shown particularly
in his *Juan in America* and *Juan in China*, and, in what I
consider his masterpiece, *Private Angelo*. He said to me,
'You're looking very down.'

'Well, I *am* feeling disheartened,' I replied. 'I was expecting to go to Vienna and here I am stuck fast in Rome.'

'There are many worse places you could be stuck in. Do
you know Rome very well?'

'I don't know it all that well yet. I've been round a bit and
I've looked at one or two things.'

'You must go on seeing more. Have you seen the Pope?'

'No, I haven't seen the Pope.' (That was, of course, Pope

146

Pius XII.) 'But I thought of going along to one of his general audiences.'

'You don't want to go to a general audience. You must go to a private audience.'

'Have you been to a private audience?'

'Oh yes,' he said.

'What's the difference between a private audience and a public audience?' I asked.

'There is not all that difference really, except the numbers are far smaller and the Pope has more time to talk to individual people.'

'What does the Pope say?'

'Oh, well,' he said, with a rather wry smile, 'he always says roughly the same thing, "Welcome to sunny Italy".'

The pope is a great attraction for pilgrims and tourists. The Venerable English College, for example, started out in the thirteenth century as a hospice for English pilgrims, who made the adventurous journey across Europe to Rome. It was set up to protect the English pilgrims from the rapacious Romans. Times don't change all that much. There are still rapacious Romans and there are still, of course, gullible pilgrims and tourists.

Talking to my colleagues who had been in Rome for some considerable time, I received rather cynical advice. First, that people generally were not all that interested in the ramifications and complications of the Italian political scene, at times too complicated even for the Italians to understand. All people outside Italy wanted to know, they informed me, was whether the Communist party, the strongest in the West, would ever seize power from the Roman Catholic-controlled Christian Democrat government. The same cynics added: 'If you fall on thin news days, you can always write about the Leaning Tower of Pisa, leaning another millimetre a year, or, at the right season of the year, about snow on the gondolas or the Piazza of St Mark's in Venice being flooded, and people taking boats into church.'

Years later, in 1958, I recalled Eric Linklater's advice about seeing the pope. Thanks to a colleague in Vatican Radio, it was not difficult to obtain a ticket for a general audience.

I went on a March morning. It was snowing, a rare thing in Rome and a story in itself. I made my way across St Peter's square. I had a large and impressive ticket from the pope's major domo, and a Jesuit father conducted me to my place on a tribune in St Peter's near to the papal throne which was set up in front of the place where the faithful believe St Peter to be buried. It was a long and cold wait, but there were thousands whom I could watch whilst I was waiting, of every colour and from almost every country in the world. I noticed a priest at a side altar nearby, assisted by a young server, and with only a handful of women present, achieving his lifetime's ambition by saying Mass in St Peter's basilica. Every altar in St Peter's, and there are dozens of them, and those in the crypt with its many side chapels, is booked for months in advance.

It happened to be the nineteenth anniversary of the coronation of Pope Pius XII. The Vatican police, resplendent in their dark blue Napoleonic uniforms, cockaded hats, capes and swords, were strutting about importantly, hardly deigning to control the crowds who were held back behind strong timber barriers. Adding more colour to the scene were ushers in plum-coloured damask livery and knee breeches – the *bussolanti*. They are the people who have the privilege of waiting on the pope, and also carrying him on the *sedia gestatoria*, the portable throne. They also have the final duty of carrying him in his triple coffin when he dies. They scrutinised all admission cards. The snow was fluttering down past the sixteen windows which fret Michelangelo's great dome. After a long pause the Swiss guards marched in, erect and unhurried in their orange and blue uniforms slashed with scarlet, carrying their seven-foot-long halberds and cutlasses, standing round the throne in their ruffs and breastplates, as they have done ever since the sack of Rome more than 400 years ago, when their staunch defence of Pope Clement VII gave them this special privilege to be next to the pontiff wherever he goes.

The congregation pressed closer. Around me men and women started singing in many languages. Soon all languages suddenly became a great unison as they intoned the Creed in Latin. Then, with great theatrical effect, hundreds of chandeliers blazed into light, illuminating in all their splendour the mosaics of the dome and the cream and gilt roof of the apse, making the bronze barley-sugar pillars of Bernini's *baldacchino* look more improbable than ever. At the same time, groups of the faithful in the congregation raised flags and shouted, '*Viva il Papa.*' Their cries echoed through the great basilica, as the Pope, a frail figure in white, was borne by ten men through the main door on the *sedia gestatoria*, his gilt throne set on a crimson velvet litter. Before him marched a detachment of the Swiss Guard, in their helmets with scarlet ostrich plumes, led by an officer in plum-coloured velvet. Then followed the Noble Guard, dressed in black and gold helmets with long horse-hair tails reaching down to their belts.

Pope Pius XII, with both hands outstretched in typical Italian fashion, showered his blessings on the throngs who had come to his general audience. At the junction of the nave and transepts, he alighted from the throne, walked nimbly up the seven steps to the throne in front of the altar, turned and sat down. He spoke to all, with much eloquent use of his thin, long hands, adorned only with the Fisherman's Ring. He looked a solitary figure in his simple white robes. He spoke first in Italian, then in French, then in English for the benefit of a group of US sailors, soldiers and airmen. He went on in German. He was very much at home in this language, for he had served as a papal nuncio in Germany before the war. He addressed a special message to a thousand pilgrims from Bavaria, who earlier had distinguished themselves by lusty singing. After the Pope had finished, some of them cried out, '*Grüss Gott, Heiliger Vater, aus Bayern*' (Greetings, Holy Father, from Bavaria). The Pope smiled and gave them his blessing. Then he spoke in Spanish to pilgrims from South America, Mexico and Spain. They clapped enthusiastically on hearing their own language. Once he had finished speaking the Pope moved among the pilgrims; many seized his right hand, knelt and kissed it, whilst he talked informally with a large number of the faithful. Others, and I noticed an ample woman from Bavaria well to the fore here, pressed forward to greet him. Pope Pius was a frail man, and his whole body was shaken by the heartiness with which some of them shook him by the hand. He spoke contentedly to them all. He laid his hands on the heads of young children, to whom he presented medallions handed to him from a green velvet purse.

It was a strangely pleasant mingling of the regal with the informal. Once the audience was over, the Pope sat on his portable throne again and was borne out of the cathedral amidst renewed cheering and clapping, followed by his guards, some of whom were bearing presents which the faithful had given him – crimson velvet-embroidered shoes, books and pictures.

It was impressive that the rank and file of this great Church could get so close to the man whom they revere as the Vicar of Christ on earth.

After the audience had ended, we all streamed out of the basilica into the cold March winds. There were tonsured Franciscans from Canada, nuns from Spain wearing their silver insignia, Italian priests in galoshes with umbrellas. I also noticed a gaitered Anglican bishop who had come perhaps more to observe than to take part. I heard an Austrian woman turn to a friend as they walked out through the great door, saying as she touched her ring proudly, 'That ring has been blessed by the Pope.'

A few months later I was to report the death of this

remarkable man. His reign of nearly 19 years had begun shortly before the second World War broke out. He died in the papal summer villa of Castel Gandolfo. It was in the far-off experimental days of Eurovision, the televised link now so much taken for granted. Italy had been scheduled some months earlier to provide television material in what turned out to be a highly dramatic week. I recall staying up all night in Castel Gandolfo to give the latest news from the little piazza, crowded with local wine farmers and hundreds of correspondents from almost every country in the world. Once the funeral was over, the cardinals converged on Rome to meet in conclave and elect the next holder of the keys of St Peter.

Who would it be? There seemed no obvious choice. Popular Roman feeling ran for the Armenian Gregory Agaganian, the bearded head of the missionary organization, the Propaganda College. Indeed, much to his embarrassment, he was greeted during the interregnum by shouts of '*Viva il Papa*' in the streets of Rome. However, the old saying held true: that many go into the conclave as pope and come out as cardinal.

There are many other superstitions. The Romans say that a thin pope is invariably followed by a fat one. Pius XII certainly was thin, Pope John, who eventually followed, was a jolly, corpulent farmer type. He in turn has been followed by Paul VI – a frail, ascetic, lean figure. There is another belief that a pope with an 'R' in his name is followed by one without. Pius XII's name was Pacelli; John XXIII's name Roncalli, and now Paul IV – Montini. It remains to be seen whether this belief will once more be borne out when the next pope comes to be elected.

Some of my colleagues in London, perhaps understandably, seemed to have forgotten exactly what went on during a conclave, otherwise I would not have received instructions from a television producer who said: 'We want you, old man, to go into the conclave, film all the cardinals as they pass and tell us what their chances are.' I gently reminded my colleague in London that the conclave was a very secret affair – in fact that the cardinals were walled up and locked in, hence the name 'conclave', and that their diet was liable to grow more Spartan if they did not come to an early decision. 'Never mind,' he said cheerily, 'I know you'll do your best.'

It was an eye-opener to see how the minor officials of the Vatican work on such an occasion. In those days they were underpaid and, seeing that popes don't die all that often, they were willing, some of them, to allow a 'fee' to be offered before producing the permits and the keys. I was lucky in having an experienced Italian cameraman to guide me through the maze of officialdom, and thus was allowed, shortly before the command '*Extra omnes*' was given, to go to the second floor corridors which lead to the Consistorial Hall and the papal apartments, set up the camera and wait for the cardinals to arrive. I had taken the precaution of availing myself of the friendly help of a papal carabiniere on guard outside the lift who arranged to mouth the name of the cardinal to me before opening the lift door and saluting. Thus, for example, he mouthed 'Spellman', and as the diminutive figure of the Cardinal Archbishop of New York trotted forth I was able, as my cameraman filmed, to give a thumb-nail sketch of the man and his chances in the pontifical stakes.

An American pope? The United States supplied the bulk of the money for the Vatican's coffers, so why not? Yet it did not seem likely. When Spellman himself was asked who would be the next pope, he replied with humour: 'You can rule out at least half the College of Cardinals; they can hardly walk.' A shrewd observation: for the pope requires, among other qualities, considerable physical stamina to endure all those long, demanding ceremonies of which he, in heavy robes, is the central focus.

So they came past: the majestic figure of Wyszinski of Poland, the bluff Gilroy of Australia, the Spanish, the

Portuguese, the German; then the grey-bearded French Cardinal Tisserant, who had officially pronounced Pope Pius XII dead, calling him three times by his Christian name Eugenio, though dispensing for the first time in the long history of the Church with the tradition of tapping the dead pontiff's head with an ivory and silver mallet. The Italians, clever, alert-minded men used to running the Church, which they had come almost to regard as their right to govern, were much in evidence. Among them the genial, corpulent yet brisk figure of Cardinal Angelo Roncalli, the Patriarch of Venice, who laughed and chatted with his fellow cardinals as though at his ease in his club. He was nearly 77, and considered a possible choice if the cardinals thought that a transitional compromise pope was what the Church needed after the long authoritarian rule of Pius.

The experts even looked up the old church fathers' writings to see whether anyone not a cardinal might succeed. They found that this was possible, though it had rarely happened. Archbishop Montini of Milan was the man in people's thoughts. His time, however, was still to come.

All went well for me for the first half-dozen cardinals, whom I knew well enough. Then the carabiniere at the lift, with an unmistakable shrug of his shoulders, signalled to me that the next arrival was unknown to him. I turned to my Italian cameraman, Vittorio.

'*Chi è?*' I asked.

With a gesture of utter despair, Vittorio mumbled, '*Desastro*'.

By this time the little, elderly man, fragile as a piece of toast, all tassels and crimson silk, was approaching our camera. He glared at us as he passed, seeing that we were not shooting a foot of film and inferring, quite correctly as it turned out, that we did not think much of his chances for the papacy. Subsequently I found out that he was a Portuguese cardinal.

However, apart from him, I was able to identify and pro-

vide a few lines of background information on all who passed
our lens. Then, after they had all gone in, I stepped briefly
in front of the camera and said that we all had seen the new
pope, though none of us yet knew who he would be. It was
effective television, and a real guessing game. For weeks I had
worked far into the night dredging up anecdotes and little-
known material on at least half-a-dozen *papabili*.

Having read the pontifical race card, as it were, we made
our way through a series of doors and gates, which were
unlocked for us by various officials who sprang seemingly
from nowhere, out on to the loggia above the right wing of
the massive quadruple Bernini colonnade which embraces
the piazza in front of St Peter's. We set up the camera, with
the Sistine Chapel in the background, and I was about to
launch into a commentary explaining that behind me the
cardinals would soon be in conclave, that the smoke would
tell the news to the world from the tiny chimney on the left,
and then, swinging the camera further to the left, that the
newly elected pontiff would appear on the balcony over the
main portico of St Peter's to be presented and then to give
his first *Urbi et Orbi* blessing to the city of Rome and to the
world. Just as I was about to begin, the Vatican official who,
after much persuasion, had given us permission to do this,
erupted on to the scene and said to my cameraman excitedly:
'I gave you permission to shoot silent film here, I did not give
permission to speak.' There followed a considerable alterca-
tion and much gesticulating. I tried hard to keep in my mind
what I intended saying and when the tumult had subsided
went ahead, fearful of further interruptions. Never was I
more relieved than when I bid a suitable farewell to the
Vatican official concerned, slipping an envelope into his side
pocket as I shook his hand. By this time he was negotiating
with an American film unit complete with a great lorry
equipped with cameras on mobile cranes which, with some
difficulty, had entered the austere courtyard of St Damasus.
The can of film I had already sealed for airfreighting to the

BBC in London, and it was shown that evening. Since that early TV effort I have found time and again that the pre-preparations take far longer than the actual commentary and filming itself.

There were three days of anxious waiting before the announcement was made, and it was during this period that I had one of my most searching tests as a correspondent. Our broadcasting box was on the top left arm of Bernini's colonnade, from where we had an excellent view of the incongruously domestic-looking tin chimney which rose from the stove in the corner of the Sistine Chapel in which the ballot papers were burned – with wet straw if there was no conclusive result, making lots of smoke of a blackish colour, and with dry straw, making wispy white smoke, if the cardinals had reached an agreement.

I had studied the procedure long and carefully and had been assured by all the Vatican experts that the first ballot generally was a courtesy affair, a mark of deference to some elderly and worthy member of the Sacred College, who knew he had no chance of ascending the papal throne, but who yet deserved well of the Church. I was in the box next to the Vatican Radio commentator, a voluble Italian Jesuit, Father Pellegrini. We waited and watched for the first smoke signal. It must be remembered that the conclave was sealed off from the world outside – even the Jesuits had no 'hot line' – and as the great crowds in the piazza below waited with us, all eyes glued to this chimney stack in the far right hand corner, no one knew what to expect.

Suddenly there came a puff of smoke, fairly voluminous and greyish in colour. It turned to near white and I could hear my Vatican colleague shouting into the microphone excitedly: 'It's a miracle, it's a miracle. On the first ballot, the very first vote, the cardinals have elected a successor to Pope Pius XII.'

It was hot, I was tired after weeks of incessant work, and sweating in my cubicle. At the back of my mind I heard the cool, appraising words of Sir William Haley who had said to me, almost as an afterthought, when I started off as a young war correspondent many years back: 'I don't mind if you're late with the news, but for God's sake be right.' I watched the smoke billowing out – it was now an indiscriminate yellowish grey – took my courage in both hands and described the uncertainty it caused in me and said that, even though the Vatican commentator thought a new pope had been elected first time round, I did not. Meanwhile the agencies had flashed round the world that a pope had been elected first go, and special editions were out on the streets before the report was corrected. The BBC, to its credit, backed up my report and did not commit the same blunder.

The Vatican had obviously lost the art of making smoke signals. Subsequently we found out that, for the first time, the Vatican authorities had decided to use chemicals instead of wet and dry straw. One cardinal only was allowed to supervise the burning of the ballot papers, Cardinal Ottaviani, who had very poor eyesight. Apparently what happened after the first ballot, which was a formal, courtesy ballot, as I had presumed it would be, was that the wrong packet of chemicals was put into the stove, creating this peculiar grey-yellowish smoke. Only subsequently was the mistake discovered. For future conclaves I understand there will be direct communication between the Sistine Chapel and the outside world, probably through Vatican radio. So my successor in Rome will not have to go through the agonising few seconds that I had to experience on that hot autumn day in 1958. Nor will the Vatican radio spokesman have to claim a miracle and so innocently mislead the world.

After three days of indecisive balloting and confusing smoke signals, just when it looked as though a long conclave was in store, the puff of whitish smoke went up from the Sistine Chapel where the cardinals were immured, announcing the election of the new pope. Quickly the word went round Rome, and soon the piazza in front of St Peter's started filling to capacity. Out came the tapestry over the balcony above the main entrance to the basilica, with a flourish of trumpets the name of Angelo Giuseppe Roncalli was announced by the quavering voice of the aged Cardinal Canali, and then, as many questioned exactly who and what kind of a man the new Pope John XXIII was, a sturdy figure in white came forward to give his first benediction to the city of Rome and to the world. An old man, a careful and safe man, that was what most thought, as they saw and heard him for the first time. A careful man who would not rock the ship of St Peter.

CHAPTER TEN

Good Pope John

Pope John was soon to propel the Christian barque forward as it had never been driven before, buffeting through the tempests and the currents. He was to call the second Vatican Ecumenical Council, the first such assembly for 100 years. The Roman Catholic Church was never to be the same again.

What sort of man was now at the tiller? Roncalli had been born in the little mountain village in Northern Italy of Sotto il Monte, near Bergamo. His parents were poor farmers; the *polenta* was carefully measured so that each member of the family of seven children had his rightful share. In the carefully written notebooks of his early life, extracts from which were later edited and published in 1965 under the title *Journey of a Soul*, by his devoted secretary, Mgr Loris Capovilla, now Archbishop of Loreto, the future Pope wrote ingenuously: 'I was a good boy, innocent, somewhat timid. I wanted to love God at all costs and my one idea was to become a priest, in the service of simple souls who needed patient and attentive care.' The journals were to continue for 60 years. In various small penny notebooks, on loose leaves of paper, I have seen these notes and observations written in the neat, cursive hand of a man who seemed to have had time for everything. Pope John was never in a hurry; he knew exactly what he wanted to do in the few crowning years of his life, as though he had secretly been preparing for these highest duties throughout his career.

It had not been a startling one. A priest in the seminary at Bergamo, then further studies in Rome where, as he notes in his diary for 29 April 1903, the arrival of King Edward VII on a State visit to Italy impressed him enormously. It contains a hint of the ecumenical trend of thought already developing in his young mind.

Just now Rome is celebrating the arrival of Edward VII, King of England. . . This man is invested with great authority; he is king of one of the greatest nations, and so he deserves to be honoured and respected. The world crowds tumultuously round this man, who attracts them because he is well dressed and surrounded by a magnificent suite, and people believe this to be the summit of greatness and grandeur, and it does not occur to them that from the top of Monte Mario [a hill north of the Tiber overlooking Rome] none of the happenings in the city can be seen or heard. Still less do they think that above Monte Mario, and above all the mountains of this earth, where nothing is known of these trifling events, there is a God who sees and hears all, in whose sight all today's revellers and this man also are like specks of dust; a God who will one day judge them. . . A gorgeous livery, a waving plume are enough to excite men and throw them into ecstasy, and meanwhile no one has a thought to spare for God. . . even serious persons get carried away by all this, like men of the world. . .

Yet this man, a Protestant, did one really good thing while he was in Rome. And it was this; showing himself superior to certain tendentious currents of anti-clericalism here and in other countries; in the height of his power he did not disdain, indeed he considered it an honour to visit and pay homage to another man, a poor persecuted old man, whom he acknowledged to be greater than himself; the Pope, Vicar of Jesus Christ (Leo XIII).

This event today is so solemn as to make a glorious page in the history of the Roman pontificate; a highly significant event this, of a heretical king of Protestant England, which has persecuted the Catholic Church for more than three centuries, going in person to pay his respects to the poor old Pope, held like a prisoner in his own house.

It is a sign of the times that after such a night of storms we see the new dawn rising from the Vatican, a slow but real and sincere return of the nations to the arms of their common Father who has long awaited them, weeping over their foolishness . . .

For this reason King Edward's visit, while it convinces me of the vanity of worldly fame, moves me to thank the good God who holds the keys of men's hearts and who, through all the intrigues of politics, finds a means of making known the glory of his name. . . .

These indeed are prophetic words from the young priest in Rome, not yet 22 years old, standing in the crowds watching the King of England drive across St Peter's piazza with his splendid equipage to call on the dying Pope Leo XIII.

Pope John was to travel a long way before he was to return to take possession of the Vatican. Back to his beloved Bergamo as secretary to Archbishop Radini-Tedeschi, who taught him wisdom, discipline and discretion. Then to Bulgaria as papal nuncio in most difficult circumstances and to other Balkan countries which, at that time, were going through violent anti-clerical phases; to Paris after the liberation in 1944 to deal with the problem of collaborators and the divided French; and finally to Venice where he had hoped to end his days. All this, so it transpired, was the long prelude to the culminating years in the chair of St Peter.

Perhaps he knew it, for all his personal modesty. When told of his election in the painted Sistine chapel and asked if he would accept, he said: 'I am made to tremble and to fear. I bow my head to the chalice of bitterness and my shoulders to the weight of the cross.' And then, asked what name he would take, he said simply, 'John'. There had not been a Pope John for 600 years. The last pope who had called himself John XXIII had in fact been an anti-pope, and is buried in Florence. The new Pope John was led to a side room next to the altar. It is small and austerely furnished – there is a *chaise percée* for the candidate, who probably needs it at that awe-inspiring moment. There the papal tailor had prepared three sets of vestments in varying sizes for the new pope, whoever he would be, and for the first time put on Pope John the large white soutane and the crimson shoes embroidered with a golden cross, a lace surplice, a red and gold stole with the prophetic symbols of the ship of the Church on each side and the white papal skull cap. Then Pope John went out on to the balcony of St Peter's for the first time to give the inaugural pontifical blessing of his reign to the cheering crowds below. Afterwards he said to his neighbouring prelates: 'They all love me except the tailor, for I could not raise my arms high enough to give a proper blessing.'

After the arcane austerities of Pius XII, a new life seemed to surge through the bleak and lofty corridors of the Vatican Palace. Pope John was given to doing the unconventional. He walked about the gardens unannounced. A few days after his election he was taking a turn in the Vatican Gardens when two Swiss guards, their tunics undone because of the hot sun, hastily buttoned their tunics and stared speechless at the Pope.

'What are you staring for?' asked Pope John. 'Look, the conclave wasn't a beauty contest, you know.' His large Jumbo ears and blunt kindly face, his stout physique and peasant's hands were comforting to all except himself. '*Come sono brutto*,' (How ugly I am), he kept muttering to himself as he was shown the colour film of his coronation. He revived the use of the crimson velvet cap trimmed with ermine, not worn by popes for centuries, though often depicted in early portraits; possibly to cover up his great ears, more probably to go back to earlier times. He had a great sense of history.

Pope John was a man about whom stories grew and multiplied. Whole books of them have been published. He was a man whose very character encouraged anecdote, and, though some were not authentic, one felt, rather as in the case of Churchill, that they ought to be. He made it his business, for example, to look into the pay of the more humble Vatican workers. He talked to one who got into his lift with him by mistake. The man seemed transfixed with nervousness until the Pope said: 'Well, which floor are we going to?' And as they got out in the basement which Pope John was exploring, they talked. The Pope asked him about his family, how much he was paid and finally what party he belonged to, though he really was not interested in politics as such – far more in what the man would answer. The man stumbled and replied, probably untruthfully, that he was a Christian Democrat. The Pope looked at him knowingly for a moment, then, prodding the workman's stomach with a stubby forefinger, said: 'You and I both belong to the same party.' Then, pointing to his own generous proportions, he added: 'the party of the middle.' Soon after that all wages and salaries in the Vatican were raised, the first time for years.

Pope John asked correspondents to a special audience a few days after his coronation. He greeted us with these words in the frescoed Clementine Hall where we were all assembled: 'I welcome you all here this morning. First of all I should like to apologise to you for having given you so much trouble in these past few days.' A roar of appreciative laughter went up. We had been sweating for weeks on every angle of the papal story, checking historical details, revising biographies of possible popes during the long drawn-out days of secret conclave, trying to read aright the Vatican smoke signals and then the final work describing the election and elaborate coronation ceremonies in St Peter's. 'I read many of your articles on the conclave,' the Pope continued. 'They were very interesting, imaginative, some rather far-fetched, if you don't mind my saying so. Your talk was very good, but (with a broad smile) I think our silence was better.' A brash young American reporter somewhere in the depths of the throng shouted out: 'Your Holiness, was it a close vote?' This shocked most present, since it was an audience and not a news conference. Pope John replied quietly, without, however, ceasing to smile: 'You are a young man and still have time to learn that there are occasions when it is wiser not to put a question.' He then went on to chat affably about our work, exhorting us always to tell the truth, and saying, as I was to hear him claim so many times afterwards, that St Paul would have been a journalist had he lived in the twentieth century and would have out-written the lot of us. As I went down the broad staircase with my colleagues, we knew that here was a new force in the Vatican, a lovable, outgoing man who had something to give to everyone who knew him or even saw him and, as it was to turn out, to the millions more who never saw him in real life. He was a man who understood the human heart, because his own heart was so full of instinctive compassion for all; he encouraged people to live better, happier lives simply because he was there – a reliable, lovable, universal grandfather.

Wits in Rome dubbed the new pope 'Johnnie Walker', because he preferred to go on foot and see for himself. He went to the nearby prison, to the children's hospital, to all the Vatican offices, its fire brigade, its telephone exchange, its shops and its sick bay.

His visit to Rome's grim Regina Coeli gaol was an unforgettable occasion, and put the security forces very much on their mettle. Here was the Pope of Rome doing an unheard-of thing, going in among the convicted criminals of the capital's main prison. (It was built incidentally by a predecessor of his, and stands on the banks of the Tiber below the Janiculum hill not far from the Vatican itself.) There they waited for him, some behind bars in their striped prison garb. Pope John had comforting words for them all: neither smug, nor condescending, but words full of compassion. One convict broke through the ranks, knelt before Pope John, seized his hand to kiss and, looking up into the kindly, moved face, said: 'Holy Father, I am a murderer, is there any hope for me?' Pope John gently raised him to his feet and as the prison guards and security men looked on amazed, embraced him wordlessly. It was one of the most moving moments I have ever experienced.

He drove round Rome visiting working-class parishes, and finally ended the tradition that the pope should stay almost at all times within his prescribed sphere of the Vatican, or in the summer villa of Castel Gandolfo. He had the natural genius of the common touch, and yet never lost his own dignity.

In spite of all that has been written about this jovial pontiff who seemed to have time for everyone, Pope John was very conscious of the dignity of his high office. No one, not even his closest associates in the Vatican, ever addressed him familiarly as '*tu*'. He himself never used the form except at most to five people, his brothers and sister and to his old friend and teacher, Mgr Rossi. Even his private secretary, Loris Capovilla, told me he always used the rather old-fashioned '*voi*' to him until the very end of his life. Though Capovilla often shared his table, the formalities of conversation were always observed, even at meals. Pope John had no intimate friends, because he was a friend of all mankind. He worked incessantly to break down barriers dividing men of different races and ideologies. Some in his Church have sought to denigrate him since his death for having allegedly encouraged Communism, especially in Italy, through his encyclicals *Mater et Magistra* and, especially, *Pacem in terris*. A short-sighted view. It took Pope John's clear vision to see that East and West would have to learn to live together if they were not to die together under the fateful mushroom cloud. During his pontificate many bitter anti-clericals turned back to the faith they had discarded under Pius XII. Pope John did not live long enough, alas, to complete his work of reconciliation; smaller men are now trying to belittle his influence. Yet he reigned long enough to start a revolutionary process within his own Church, and in man's religious thinking generally.

Once, when driving to a working-class suburb with his secretary, who had prepared a rather severe homily for him to deliver to the predominantly left-wing congregation there, Pope John grew enthusiastic at the welcome he received as he drove along the route to the modern, rather ugly church. During the service he said: 'I had another sermon to preach to you, but instead I want just to tell you this: you are wonderful people, all of you, and I want you to become even better parents, better young men and women, better boys and girls. We, all of us, can improve, and I know we shall all go on trying. Your welcome convinces me that you will.' On the way back to the Vatican Palace, Pope John turned a little shamefacedly to Capovilla sitting opposite him in the great black Vatican limousine with its simple red-lettered registration number, SCV 1, and said: 'I'm sorry I did not deliver the sermon you had so carefully prepared for me; it was a good one; but these thousands of wonderful people, who could have been watching a football match or enjoying one another's company, came to welcome me. And [pointing to the windows from which many were waving to him] tonight every one of these people will be talking about the Papa. Now isn't that a good thing?'

Mgr Loris Capovilla lived until recently in a small flat behind the apse of St Peter's, in a building which was once the Vatican mint. Vatican coins and medals are still struck, but in Rome, on the Italian side of the border. Mgr Capovilla is young for his 50-odd years, a lightly built, volatile Venetian with an all-consuming affection for Pope John. To visit him in his home, as I have done several times, is to come into contact afresh with the great, warm personality of Pope John, as alive as when he trod the earth. Loris Capovilla was left all the Pope's personal documents, and has thousands of his letters, which will occupy historians and theologians for decades to come. He has rows and rows of photograph albums, many of them captioned by the Pope himself, and amongst them pictures of Pope John in St John

Lateran under which the Pope wrote, 'The new Pope takes possession of St John Lateran.' This is a church for which he had a great affection. It existed long before St Peter's, and it is the church in which Pope John wished to be buried. His sense of history saw in the Lateran what a mother church should be. Set at the confluence of the ancient, consular roads leading to Rome, it was more than just a church. It was a university, a school, a library and a hospice, with a hospital to tend the sick – the symbol of the Church's abiding care for her children. All can still be found on the Lateran hill today.

Pope John's last wish, however, was not destined to be carried out. Instead he lies in a chapel in the crypt of St Peter's. His simple white marble tomb, bearing the words 'Johannes XXIII PP', is perpetually decked with flowers. There are always many of the faithful kneeling in prayer before the mortal remains of this great pontiff, who – a saint in his own lifetime – is now on the way towards beatification and canonization.

There were rows of books, which John especially liked, now in Capovilla's library. The closest print, and the most ancient print on greying paper would not daunt him. He would annotate and often put his own comments in front of each volume. Generally he wrote in Latin. One comment reads: 'This book, though a credit to its writer, is certainly no credit to its binder.' It was an old book which had recently been rebound in some haste and the covers were already curling. Adjoining his rooms, Capovilla had his private chapel in which Manzù's bust and death mask of John immediately catch the eye. Manzù was a simple lad from Bergamo, who left school after only a few years of elementary learning to work in the local cemetery helping to carry the coffins to the grave. From that he was allowed to carve inscriptions, then simple motifs for the headstones. He graduated to marble angels and the like, all the time developing his art quietly along his own original lines. Pope John encouraged him, though knowing that he was not a man of formalized religion. Manzù laboured for years on the bronze Door of Death for St Peter's, with its moving portrait of Pope John in prayer, and the even more touching scene, on a frieze at the back of the door, of Pope John receiving the homage of the first negro cardinal of modern times, Cardinal Laurean Rugambwa of Tanzania.

Pope John was already dead when, in 1964, the great doors were finally hung. Manzù refused to be present if any religious ceremony were held. In deference to the sculptor's wishes, Pope Paul agreed to be present early one morning with him to inspect the work, with no formality. The great bronze doors are on the left of the basilica. Especially delightful as a footnote to the great theme of death are the animals at the bottom, added no doubt to soften the starkness of the theme; a fox curled up with its brush protecting its head, an owl, a hedgehog and a tortoise. Manzù knows nothing of politics in the normal sense of the word. Nevertheless, he is exploited by the political forces of the left for his independence of spirit. Pope John saw right through him and recognised a great and dedicated artist.

On the walls of his flat Capovilla had gouaches of Pope John done by Manzù. He did several dozen of them in preparation for his sculptures and medallions, but destroyed all but three of them which Loris Capovilla was allowed to keep. He has also among his treasures a golden chalice recently completed; a simple cup with a lamb trussed by its feet hanging from the stem to illustrate the saying in Isaiah, 'He was brought as a lamb to the slaughter . . . and he opened not his mouth.' Today Manzù is a successful artist of international reputation, with a permanent exhibition near his studio in the country south of Rome.

Capovilla is a quick talker. I begged him to write his memories of Pope John whilst they were still fresh. He had the unique privilege of being with him for the last ten years of his life, and has around him the priceless collection of Johanniana to keep the memories green. Near his desk is a bronze cast of Pope John's right hand, the hand which was raised so often in blessing. On his desk is a double silver frame enclosing two colour photographs of Pope John. In the bookshelves are the lengthening rows of books in many languages that have already appeared on the great pontiff, learned disquisitions on his life and writings, great tomes on the significance of the Vatican Ecumenical Council, a volume or two of jokes about the Pope.

Capovilla never tires of talking about his master. He has many friends in all walks of life who come to talk with him, to catch a pale reflection of the great man who meant and still means so much to millions throughout the world. Once when I was there a young Japanese Carmelite, Father Gabriele, radiant in the freshness of his recent ordination, came to listen. He was a shy man who looked much younger than his 36 years, and who eventually talked of his own ideas. He had brothers and sisters, he said, who, like his parents, were Buddhists. 'We all search for a road,' he said, 'a road towards the goal of truth.' Capovilla told me, when the smiling friar had gone, that Pope John had spoken to the young man once at a general audience in the days when the Japanese was still a seminarist. Since then Fra Gabriele had always returned, each time bringing a present, an exquisite silk painting or book of Japanese reproductions; each time taking back with him some little souvenir of the Vatican. Pope John firmly believed that all religious men, whatever their persuasion, had bonds which linked them and were to be respected. His was not an arrogant, exclusive religion. Privately he condemned many of the overbearing and distressing practices of individual priests, who often, for example, terrified men and women on the point of death with their growling insistence on confession.

At this point in our conversation Capovilla enlarged on the heroic end of his beloved Pope. Pope John knew his days were numbered long before he took to his bed in the summer of 1963. He was serene in mind until the very end. Capovilla, whose face in those sad last days was so well known to television viewers all over the world, could hardly restrain his tears every time he entered the dying Pope's bedroom. 'How now, Don Amleto,' Pope John would say, 'why are you so sad? And Professor Valdoni [the eminent heart specialist], why is he wasting his time staying here? Tell him I am grateful for his company; there is little he can do for my body. Perhaps I can do a little for his soul. Now tell me a *barzaletto* [a joke]; speak slowly, for I think I can last out until you have finished.'

This was Pope John, even in his final agony, thinking of others, trying to cheer them up by asking them to cheer him up. Fighting back his emotions, Capovilla launched on a long story of a young nervous priest called Pifferi and his adventures. Despite the pain and fading strength, Pope John smiled as the tale unfolded. When it had ended he turned his face to one side and was dead.

Pope John was not afraid of death. He was furious, however, about those who thought that unless a man was prepared formally at the end he would linger in purgatory. 'How can this be true,' he said, 'in time of war or in these modern times when so many meet sudden death on the roads every day?' He was equally contemptuous of the worldly greed of man. Shortly before his death, he told his nearest servants and collaborators with whom he always said the rosary in the evening: 'Don't get too attached to money. I know you have your problems, but they are worse if you only think in material terms.' Capovilla said that many did not understand fully what he was saying, but that afterwards they realized that Pope John had never wavered from his own saying: 'I was born poor and I will die poor.' He made several wills. In one of them he wrote: 'I am poor, thank God, and I mean to die poor.' That was in 1950, eight years before he became what his brother Giuseppe described as, 'a prisoner *de luxe* who cannot do all he would like to do.'

CHAPTER ELEVEN

The Measure of the Man

There are many versions of the story of how Pope John came to call a Vatican Ecumenical Council. It is generally agreed that the inspiration came to him whilst talking to his Secretary of State, Cardinal Domenico Tardini. Tardini had served long under Pius XII in this capacity without the title and without the rank of cardinal. Pope John was quick to set this right. Tardini misjudged his new master, however. I remember talking to him shortly after the papal election, and asking him how the new Pope was doing. 'Well, he is new to the job,' said Tardini, 'and we haven't yet trained him in the way he should go. Now with Pope Pius, we had him trained to a hair. We would place documents before him for signature. He would choose his pen carefully, try it on a piece of paper first, use a pen wiper if necessary, pull back his sleeves so that his white cassock would not be sullied, and sign with a flourish. The trouble with Pope John is that he always wants to study each document carefully before signing. But, as I say, he is new, and in time we will have him trained.'

Poor Cardinal Tardini, he never did train Pope John. Like most of his fellow cardinals, Tardini had decided that the new pope would be merely transitional, keeping the machine ticking over, appointing cardinals to replenish the depleted Sacred College, and generally carrying on quietly. Pope John, however, knew he had only a few years of life left. Had he chosen to, he could have sat back and let Tardini and his colleagues do all the Vatican staff work, signing as a formality, without reading very much. Pope John was very different, however, from the man most of his electors believed him to be. He was an avid reader of everything, a staunch believer in the authority of the pope, and had his way. A man of great heart, he was appalled at the divisions of mankind – white against black, East against West, poor against rich, and above all Christian against Christian, to say nothing of Christian against Jew, Moslem, Hindu, Buddhist and non-believer. Pope John opened a window and let the fresh air of human commonsense blow along the corridors of Vatican power. In doing so he heartened the whole world, Christian and non-Christian alike.

One of the first shocks for the Vatican was the Pope's determination to meet unusual people; difficult people, from the protocol point of view. Such a person was the Archbishop of Canterbury. No primate of the Church of England had crossed the Vatican threshold since the Reformation. Yet in 1960 Dr Geoffrey Fisher, then Archbishop of Canterbury, did just that. Vatican officials were scared to death. What was afoot? There must be no publicity – indeed, there is no official pictorial record of this historic occasion. Yet the Archbishop went, without ceremony, wearing his purple cassock, his pectoral cross and his Canterbury cap straight to Pope John. The two men embraced and talked of what united their two churches. They had an easy, frank conversation, two elderly, experienced men who knew that the divisions of Christianity were an offence to God and man and who did what they could to lessen them. Soon afterwards, Dr Fisher retired as Archbishop. Pope John remained.

Early in his reign Pope John received Canon Bernard Pawley – now in Canterbury – who was sent to Rome by the Archbishop of Canterbury as a special envoy to report on the preparations for the Vatican Ecumenical Council. Pawley looks a severe man, yet, to those who know him well, he is the most humorous, kind and erudite of friends. He was the first Anglican to have had a long talk *à deux* with Pope John, for he speaks fluent Italian and is a well-versed Latinist. He told me that he felt completely at ease when, after the formalities were done, Pope John invited him to sit next to him for a talk. 'Are you a theologian?' asked the Pope. Pawley replied that, apart from basic theological training which he had received for ordination, he was not a theologian. 'Good,' said Pope John, 'nor am I. It is these theologians who have got us into the mess, and we have to get ourselves out. Now we can really talk.'

The difficulties surrounding a pope are hard to imagine, however frequent a visitor one may be to the Vatican. He is always in danger of being organized by the permanent officials. Though the head of a great organization, the pope must inevitably delegate much of his day-to-day authority and hope that his wishes are carried out. This does not always happen. Cardinals and other prelates at the central levers of control can hasten, retard or quite simply cause to lapse many such wishes. Pope John knew this well. That is why he evoked the old Christian idea of collegiality, calling in the bishops to assist him in reaching decisions. That is why he was able to intervene successfully in the Council's debates when the diehards were making things difficult, blocking, for example, a key declaration on the Church in the modern world. That is why he called the Council: to put an end in the kindest way possible to the dictatorial powers of the Curia, the central body governing the Church in all its manifold activities throughout the world.

For all his straightforward humanity, Pope John had not been a diplomat for nothing. He could disarm even his most powerful opponents with charming candour. The story is well known of Cardinal Ottaviani, the son of a baker, who had risen to a post of great eminence as head of the Curia, the man who actually crowned the Pope, the man who, as I have related, caused confusion throughout the world by mixing up the chemicals in the burning of the conclave ballot papers, so that the wrong signal was emitted. At the height of one of the early Council debates, Cardinal Ottaviani was heard to observe to a friend: 'At least I hope to die in the fold of the one, true Church.' Pope John heard of this, and invited Ottaviani to his private library for a chat. Ottaviani went fearing the worst. Instead Pope John conversed affably about a number of topics before the Council and then, taking Ottaviani by the arm, moved across to the window overlooking Rome and said: 'Isn't this a wonderful view in the sunset.' That was all; his kindness won through the tough defences of Ottaviani, who has outlived Pope John and who, though now replaced by a Yugoslav, Cardinal Seper, still puts up a skirmish for the conservative cause when he can, but who must know in his heart that the will of Pope John will ultimately prevail.

One of the unanswered riddles of our time is what would have happened had Pope John and President Kennedy lived on for some years longer. Would there have been an East-West *rapprochement*? Many think there would.

I can recall the unusual interest which the visit of Alexei Adzubei, Mr Khruschev's son-in-law and editor of *Izvestia*, caused when he came to Rome with his wife Rada in 1963. Adzubei was lionized by the Communists and the pro-Russian organizations of Italy. It was rumoured that Pope John wanted to see the Russian couple, but that Vatican protocol did not want the visit to be formal. In order to get round the difficulty, the Adzubeis were asked to come together with the committee of the Foreign Press Association and of the Italian Press Federation. Accordingly we went to the Vatican Palace. Adzubei wore a dark suit and a tie (rather rare for him) and his wife wore the veil required on these papal occasions. (Afterwards she told me it was an old Russian custom for women to wear a veil!)

There we sat in one of the throne rooms, about 50 people in all. Pope John came into the room through our ranks and was applauded. Making himself comfortable on his throne, he put on his spectacles and was handed his speech by his private secretary, Loris Capovilla, who sat modestly on a stool at the side of the throne. Two members of the Noble

Guard flanked the Pontiff as he read his speech, never once glancing at the Russian guests. It was the usual admonition to us journalists to tell the truth as we knew it, never deliberately to falsify or twist the news for this or that advantage – and the customary words about St Paul being one of the first journalists. At the end some of us were presented to the Pope. I went up after the Italians and the Pope, speaking to me in Italian, held on to my hand as he asked from where I came. He had a firm and comforting handshake, his eyes were a kindly blue, and his whole face was that of a kindly elderly grandfather, to whom one could confide anything.

When I told him I came from England he smiled and said: 'What a wonderful and rich language yours is. It is like the sound of the sea beating against the rocks, a very rich language. I can read it and I have read the writings of Newman and Faber [who, I afterwards discovered, was one of the Pope's favourite English ecumenical writers and whose well-thumbed volumes, translated into Italian, were never very far from his bedside]. But alas, I'm too old to talk to you, or to learn enough to conduct a real conversation with you in your own tongue, *scusi tanto* [please excuse me].' And he smilingly lifted up his hands in a typical Italian gesture of resignation.

For a brief few seconds Pope John had entirely concentrated on me; his was the great man's gift of making you feel that you alone were the person he had been waiting to talk to. Others followed me, but not Alexei and Rada Adzubei. Pope John seemingly had not noticed them. However, as we were leaving, I observed that they had been taken by a Vatican official on a 'special tour' of the Vatican Palace. In fact they had been shown into the Pope's private library.

It is now known that Mr Khruschev was putting out feelers for a meeting with President Kennedy in the hope of easing tension in the world, and that the visit of his daughter and son-in-law to Pope John seemed a suitable occasion to further these efforts. It was to come to nothing because of the slowness and suspicion on both sides.

Pope John was the despair of his entourage, for he would always over-run his time. He loved talking to people. He would show them the great globe presented to him by the faithful in Chicago – as high as a man – which stood beside his desk and which he could spin by touching a switch. The world was his home, and its people his family. He prayed for everyone when he said his nightly rosary with his nearest collaborators. In another audience he told us how he prayed for all the children in the world that had been born that day. He would often depart from his written notes and talk on, easily and at length, about his thoughts at that given moment. He used to be a writer in a humble way himself, and told me that when, as a young man, he saw his first article in print, he felt like a mother having produced her first child. At this he looked down at his ample stomach and chuckled. There was often laughter at his audiences. He taught something which many Christians had apparently forgotten, that religion can be a happy thing of laughter and joy, not merely of puritanical gloom, as so many make it. His thoughts were neither involved nor difficult. They went straight to the heart, because Pope John was a 'natural' who could communicate with everyone, even from the window of his study high up in the Vatican – a tiny white figure to the thousands in St Peter's piazza below. I remember once, on a warm evening, many had brought their children with them to see the kindly Pope – 'Jovial John', as he had also been dubbed in the English-speaking world.

'How kind of you to come and wish an old man good things on his birthday,' he said over the loudspeakers which carried his words echoing through the piazza. 'I will not keep you long, but before we say our prayers together I want you, when you go home, to kiss your children and say to them, that is a kiss from the *Papa*.' Simple, almost banal words, but the sincerity which lay behind them caused many round me to weep, as I did, as they listened.

This innocent simplicity shines out above all in his *Journal of a Soul*, which can be undervalued by cursory readers because of its seeming naiveté. It was not intended for publication, and indeed Pope John had great misgivings about it ever being read by eyes other than his own. Who of us who has ever kept a personal notebook would not be embarrassed by our views and attitudes expressed with such fervour in our youth? Yet some of the remarks recorded in his journal are worth studying carefully, if one is to have the full measure of the man. 'To be gentle and humble,' he wrote, 'is not the same as being weak and easy-going.' 'My poor life, now such a long one,' Pope John wrote again in 1960, 'has unwound itself as easily as a ball of string. . . I neither fear to die nor refuse to live. Above all one must always be ready for the Lord's surprise moves.'

Thus he was prepared when voting in the conclave raised him to the papal throne. He wrote that he never did anything to swing the voting, but that he accepted God's will. He confided in a letter to his brother Severo:

Because of this choice the name Roncalli has become known, loved and respected all over the world. You are very wise to keep yourselves humble, as I too try to do, and not let yourselves be influenced by the insinuations and tittle-tattle of the world. All the world wants is to make money, enjoy life and impose its will at all costs, even with violence, if this should unhappily be necessary. . .

I am well aware that you have to bear certain mortifications from people who like to talk nonsense. To have a pope in the family, a pope regarded with respect by the whole world, who yet permits his relations to go on living so modestly, in the same social condition as before! But many know that the pope, the son of humble but respected parents, never forgets anyone; he has, and shows, a great affection for his nearest kin; moreover, his own condition is the same as that of most of his recent predecessors; and a pope does not honour himself by enriching his relations but only by affectionately coming to their aid, according to their needs and the conditions of each one.

This is and will be one of the finest and most admired merits of Pope John and his Roncallis. At my death I shall not lack the praise which did so much honour the saintly Pius X. 'He was born and died poor.'

Pope John's wishes were faithfully carried out. His brothers still tend their vines in Sotto il Monte, but even they cannot prevent the birthplace of their brother becoming a place of pilgrimage for men and women, many of them not even Christian, who come to see the humble surroundings from which this direct and great-hearted man sprang. His share of the property is still in the hands of his brother Giuseppino, who has always worked the fields. To each of his brothers he bequeathed 10,000 lire (at the time a little over five pounds sterling) and a choice of some modest piece of his household furniture as a remembrance.

Long after his death, Pope John is still being accused of having furthered the cause of revolution, of having undermined the authority of the Church. Such a premise can be argued quite convincingly. Even Pope Paul seems to listen at times to those who have put this point of view. Yet Pope John from his pinnacle had a lofty vision. He saw all mankind and its burning problems. He felt he belonged to all mankind, and had a duty to try to help all, irrespective of creed, regardless of their politics. All had souls, all were made in the likeness of the Creator, all had the right to be helped. If this or that local persuasion gained a temporary advantage, no matter, the long view was the right one. Hence his memorable encyclical *Mater et Magistra*, on the social rights and duties of mankind; hence *Pacem in Terris*, the plea for a reasonable understanding to bring about peace in the world.

Not that Pope John was consciously a political pope. Politics naturally form part of the pattern of human life, and cannot remain unaffected by a man who was determined to end the professional clerical club atmosphere of his Church, a man willing to see the needs of individuals who make up the masses, each in his own light.

CHAPTER TWELVE

Rome and Canterbury

When Dr Geoffrey Fisher decided to call on Pope John on his way back from Jerusalem, the first visit of any Archbishop of Canterbury since the fourteenth century, he took the Vatican almost unawares. This normally so self-confident body seemed extremely nervous about it. Cardinals in the Curia sought to play down the whole meeting (in contrast to what was to happen when Dr Ramsey came five years later) and strong pressures were brought to bear on the Archbishop not to make any statement in Rome. In the end, apart from a sermon at evensong in All Saints Anglican Church in the via Babuino, Dr Fisher had to content himself with briefing a few British correspondents in the British Embassy.

The Vatican, though not Pope John, wondered what lay behind such a move. Apart from visiting the Holy Land, Dr Fisher had called on the Orthodox Patriarch Athenagoras in Istanbul, and thought it natural to follow this up with a visit to the 'Patriarch of the West', to give the Pope one of his many titles. In his sermon, the Archbishop was careful to point out that he was calling on Pope John neither to boast nor to complain, but only to greet him in courtesy of Christian brotherhood. Such a visit, he went on, could only happen because the Pope, on his side, had made it clear that he would receive him in a similar spirit. Dr Fisher added these memorable words: 'Here is indeed a day, simple, unspectacular, hardly to be observed, a whisper of the still small voice of the Holy Spirit.'

Seldom had a visit, however, attracted so much public attention, in spite of the Vatican's attempt to minimise the occasion. The two men, both in their seventies (Pope John was 79 and Archbishop Fisher 73) immediately took to each other. Pope John was at the threshold of his private library to greet the Primate of All England. He welcomed him with an embrace and spoke in Italian. I asked Dr Fisher what in fact Pope John's opening words were, and the Archbishop replied smilingly: 'I don't know exactly what he said, but I suppose the gist of his greeting was, "Dr Livingstone, I presume." ' They remained closeted together for more than an hour. A first move had been made towards breaking the ice of mistrust formed over the centuries. There was neither embarrassment nor hesitation in their conversation, translated expertly by the then archbishop, now Cardinal Samorè, of the Vatican secretariat (the Vatican Foreign Affairs department). Dr Fisher was highly delighted by the meeting, and told the Pope that they were making history, to which the Pope agreed. Before leaving Rome Dr Fisher also had a long talk with another of the Vatican's great men, the eminent German biblical scholar Cardinal Bea, also in his seventies, who, behind the scenes as well as in front, had done so much to promote better understanding between the various Christian denominations. It was a wonderful, climactic moment for Dr Fisher to announce that he was relinquishing his post as Primate.

Five years later his successor, Dr Ramsey, called on Pope John's successor, Pope Paul. What a difference the Vatican Council, which had just ended, had made! This time the Archbishop was given the maximum honours due to the head of the Anglican communion in the world. He was the Vatican's official guest, and enchanted the 70 or so young Roman Catholic seminarists at the Venerable English College where he was lodged. He also immediately captured the hearts of the Romans. They perhaps were reminded of Pope John. The same massive build and kindly smile, the same dedication and quiet modesty of a man who knew clearly what he wanted, the same Christian forbearance and friendliness, which struck a harmonious chord with the more reserved Pope Paul. The meeting five years before of Pope John and Dr Fisher had obviously borne fruit. As a result, a permanent body of representatives of the two churches was established to discuss in a frank and friendly way the things which united and the issues which divided the two denominations.

I was present in the Sistine Chapel at the first meeting of these two Christian leaders. Before entering – side by side – they had a brief personal meeting in the Hall of the Vestments. Then, followed by their retinues, they moved slowly through the grill gates into the magnificent frescoed chapel where popes have been elected in secret conclave down the ages. The bluff, rugged Archbishop and the almost fragile-looking Pope Paul sat on two crimson and gilt chairs placed in front of the altar beneath the awe-inspiring picture of Michelangelo's 'Last Judgment'. All round me were diplomats, selected clergy and students, laymen. I saw no women present at this ceremony, and in fact one American woman journalist was turned away, though properly accredited, while Dr Ramsey's wife, out of deference to the Roman tradition of celibacy, did not travel with her husband to Rome. Speaking in almost Trollopian English, Dr Ramsey spoke first, greeting the Pope as a dear brother in Christ. 'All Christendom gives thanks for what was done in the service of unity by the greatly loving and greatly loved Pope John XXIII. It is in the same divine inspiration that Your Holiness works and prays for unity.' Dr Ramsey added: 'On the road to unity there are formidable difficulties of doctrine.' At this the Pope nodded his head in a comprehending gesture, whilst some of his curia cardinals sitting at the side of the chapel looked straight ahead grimly. 'All the more, therefore, it is my hope, and that of Your Holiness too, that there may be increasing dialogue between theologians, Roman Catholic and Anglican and of other traditions, so as to explore together the divine revelation. On the road to unity there are also difficult practical matters about which the conscience and feelings of Christian people can be hurt,' the Archbishop continued. (He was alluding primarily to the Roman Catholic Church's unbending, some might say arrogant, attitude towards the question of mixed marriages.) 'All the more, therefore, must such matters be discussed together in patience and charity.'

The Archbishop ended his address – probably the first time that English had been spoken officially in the Sistine Chapel – with these memorable words: 'It is only as the world sees us Christians growing visibly in unity that it will accept through us the divine message of peace. I would join my voice to the voice of Your Holiness in pleading that the nations agree to abandon weapons of destruction, to settle their problems without war, and to find a sovereignty greater than the sovereignty of each separate State. So may the song of the angels be echoed in the wills and actions of men. *Gloria in excelsis Deo et in terra pax.*' A moment of silence, and then applause.

Pope Paul replied in Latin, and said that the visit of Dr Ramsey filled him with joy and hope. He recalled how Archbishop Fisher had visited his predecessor, and said that the present visit was repairing a bridge which for centuries had lain fallen between the Church of Rome and the Church of Canterbury; it was a bridge of respect, of esteem and of charity. It was being rebuilt by spontaneous initiative and wise confidence. 'May God bless this courage and piety. From now on charity can and must make itself felt and demonstrate its great power. Where there is charity and love, there is God.'

As the Pope ended his address the congregation of cardinals, diplomats and representatives of all the separate churches – Anglican, Greek Orthodox, Protestant, Lutheran, Presbyterian, Methodist, Baptist and Italian Waldensian, and the erect figure of the Salvation Army leader in Italy, burst into renewed applause. The two leaders rose and embraced each other with the kiss of peace as the clapping soared up to the vaulted frescoed roof, where the vigorous sybils and prophets flanked Michelangelo's 'Creation'. It was indeed a dramatic, moving occasion, and both men showed their deep emotion as they made their way slowly out of the Sistine Chapel.

Altogether, Dr Ramsey had three meetings with the Pope. At the final joint service in the great abbey of St Paul without the Walls, both men ceremonially signed a joint declaration inaugurating a series of dialogues between the two churches, with the aim that they might lead to unity. As Pope Paul escorted the Archbishop into the sunlit courtyard at the entrance of the great basilica, in an impulsive gesture of farewell, he suddenly took off the ring he was wearing, a great emerald crossed with diamonds, and slipped it on the Archbishop's finger. And almost unobtrusively amidst the applause which followed this gesture, Mgr Capovilla, the private secretary to the late Pope John, gave Dr Ramsey his beloved Pope's breviary, a fitting relic of the man who, seven years previously, had glimpsed this vision of Christian unity.

These then were the great public moments of this important meeting. But there were significant moments behind the scenes as well. No young seminarist of the Venerable English College at that time is likely to forget the presence of their illustrious guest. His frank and open way of discussing problems with them and above all his very Englishness caught their imagination as few previous guests had done. I recall interviewing him the night before he left Rome to return to Lambeth Palace. He got through the television business with great ease and forthrightness, and then went upstairs to the students' common room to give a farewell address. I stayed behind to talk over a drink with the quiet and wise rector of the college, Mgr Leo Alston. The *'Venerable,'* as it is known, is one of the most hospitable places in Rome. Suddenly we heard a burst of applause as the Archbishop finished his talk to the students. Then the young men broke into singing *'Vivat ad multos annos'* – a rare tribute, normally reserved for a newly appointed bishop of their own Church.

The following morning, when the Archbishop was due to take his leave, he told them that he would have loved to have studied at the college. 'Things may not happen in my lifetime,' he said, 'but for you, my goodness, the prospects of closer collaboration in Christian brotherhood are thrilling and exciting indeed.' To the joyful amazement of the students in the courtyard he then threw his Canterbury Cap high into the air and caught it as cheers rolled round the place. Then the students knelt as he gave them a farewell blessing, and entered his car to drive to the airport. An Archbishop of Canterbury had done much to bridge the gap of centuries of misunderstanding and mutual suspicion.

The English College, which started in the Middle Ages as a hospice for pilgrims, became the training centre for English Roman Catholic priests after Henry VIII's break with Rome. In a way, it might uncharitably be described as a one-time Quisling establishment aimed at the overthrow of Elizabeth with the connivance of Charles V of Spain in the sixteenth century. To this day its students still pray for the re-conversion of Britain to the 'true faith', but much of the ghetto mentality of British Roman Catholics has passed. The Archbishop's visit gave them all a feeling of belonging to the wider Christian body of Britain.

However, no one should be under any illusion about the Roman Catholic attitude towards ecumenism. The Vatican still sees this in terms of wayward Christians of other denominations returning to the fold, rather than adapting their ancient hierarchical system to accommodate others. Some, rather cynically, believe that the Vatican, seeing that Christianity everywhere is on the decline, now judges it opportune to gather support for its waning appeal from other churches. The Roman Catholics, for all their monolithic façade, in which more than a few cracks have appeared over the past decade, face exactly the same problem as other

Christian denominations – indeed, one might say of most other religions – namely the decline of vocations and priestly authority, and the growing indifference of the laity, many of whom are far better educated than of old, when the Church had virtually a monopoly of schooling at all levels. In a word, organised 'churchy' Christianity now seems largely irrelevant. While various sectors of it are striving with might and main to keep themselves in office, there are many young Roman Catholic priests who chafe at the Vatican's authority and its inability to give a strong and clear lead in solving the problems of our day – such problems as war and peace, birth control and priestly celibacy, quite apart from the question-able ethics of being a great financial power in the temporal world.

CHAPTER THIRTEEN

The Vatican Council

So many books have already been written on the Second Vatican Council and its influence on the Christian world that it is difficult to recall what a stir the announcement of its impending assembly evoked in 1959. The Vatican had been used to one-man rule under Pius XII, who allowed the Sacred College of Cardinals to dwindle in number and, to some, appeared to become more of a solo act with every year that passed. When I came to Rome in 1958 he was an aloof actor on an uncrowded stage, ascetic, authoritative, given to making speeches to all and sundry on every conceivable topic from astronomy to hotel-keeping, a pontiff from whom the words flowed in unceasing tide, all of which are now neatly bound in dozens of volumes in the present Pope's private library. In those days, correspondents were kept at arm's length by the Vatican. A favoured few who cultivated the editor and assistants of the Vatican's newspaper *L'Osservatore Romano*, and whom the Vatican could rely on to spread the right kind of news, were given an occasional slight insight into events, but even then only briefly. Most of us discreetly cultivated prelates of various countries who gave us their viewpoint and what information they had been able to glean from their particular sector of the Vatican's multifarious activities.

It was therefore something of an event when, in October 1959, the Vatican actually summoned correspondents to a news conference – an unheard-of occasion. The Cardinal Secretary of State, Cardinal Tardini, who spent most of his spare time running a boys' orphanage, raising funds for its maintenance from anyone who came within hailing distance, called us to his orphanage on a hillside north of Rome, to explain what the Vatican Council, which Pope John, to the cardinal's utter surprise, had just announced, was all about. The cardinal deliberately played a slow game, sending out questionnaires to bishops, papal nuncios, prelates and heads of religious congregations throughout the world, collating their replies and then sending them further questions. He calculated that there would be several years of study before the Vatican Council could actually be convened. In fact the Council opened almost three years to the day after this conference was held by this alert-minded and cheery-looking prelate. Cardinal Tardini started off by reminding us that the last Council, at which the dogma of papal infallibility had been proclaimed, had been called nearly a century earlier in 1869. This papal infallibility, the Cardinal was at some pains to explain, was a divine gift, though rarely, if ever, invoked. It preserved the pontiff from error in matters of faith and morals in exercising his supreme authority in both the legislative and executive fields of the Roman Church.

Then the cardinal added – surprisingly, when one looks at what really came out of the Council – that the whole conception of this unique assembly was not one of any compromise with Christians outside the ranks of the Roman Catholic Church, to whom, however they looked with charity and cordiality. The Council would deal with internal affairs of the Church, and he did not expect it to last for long. In the event, it lasted three years and could have gone on longer still. By 1965 Pope Paul, who had inherited the explosive legacy of Pope John, thought that enough was enough.

Changes came over the Vatican's antiquated information service. Up to 1959 the Holy See's idea of news was to record what had happened in *L'Osservatore Romano*, a remarkable specimen of journalism, with a baroque style all its own. It still thinks nothing of having columns of Latin on its front page. Its editorials are sybilline. They have to be read extremely carefully several times before the real points emerge. Even then they are so hedged about that it is easy for their author to deny any particular interpretation of his comments if he chooses. With the announcement of the Vatican Council an entirely different situation arose. Hundreds of newsmen from all parts of the world converged on Rome to report its first session. Among them were some formidable forces, journalists who were priests, journalists who had been priests and had given up their priesthood to write instead about religious affairs, journalists who wanted to become priests, as well as lay correspondents, many not belonging to the Roman persuasion, some not even nominally Christian.

The Vatican was slow to meet the new requirements. A good start was made, however, by at least allowing us in to the opening ceremony in St Peter's, after having issued us with handsome slim leather-bound passes. My vanity is still tickled when I recall that my *tessera* was 'No 1', one of the few press passes I have kept as a souvenir.

We had been led to expect a kind of parliament, with the cut and thrust of debate in Latin. Nothing could have been further from reality. Cardinals and bishops had to hand in their speeches well beforehand, and deliver them when one of the four moderators, or chairmen, called on them to do so. However, as a tribute to the need for Christian unity in an increasingly indifferent world, a number of delegates from outside the Roman fold were invited as observers – Anglicans, Lutherans, Presbyterians, Evangelicals, Methodists, Congregationalists, Quakers, Copts, Armenians and Orthodox, including in their ranks some of the greatest living non-Catholic theologians. They particularly wanted to see whether Vatican theology was still anchored to the teachings of Thomas Aquinas, which, as one of them remarked to me, would be like studying astronomy before the days of Copernicus. They did not have to wonder for long. Some theologians within the Roman fold, such as Hans Küng, Rahner and others, were to prove very stormy petrels long before the end.

Altogether some 2500 Council fathers took part in the memorable opening ceremony. They included a number from Communist countries in Eastern Europe – though the redoubtable primate of Hungary, Cardinal Mindszenty, was a notable absentee. He only reached Rome in 1971 in time for the third synod. Well over 1200 of the assembled bishops were guests of the Pope. They came from parts of the world whose people were too poor to finance their journeys and their protracted stay in Rome.

The brilliantly lit nave of St Peter's had been transformed into a vast conference hall. Tiered stands ranged on either side, with reasonably comfortable green upholstered tip-up seats, folding desks and kneeling stools. The Council fathers could sit whilst listening to the addresses, stand when speaking themselves and pray during the Mass preceding each day's session. The cardinals were accommodated in rather more roomy seats covered with crimson velvet. The moderators, or presiding chairmen, had their places at a table just in front of the high altar, on whose steps a throne was placed for the Pope, whenever he chose to be present. When he was not there – apart from the opening ceremony he came but rarely – he could, if he wished, follow the proceedings on a closed television circuit, which he frequently did.

The whole Council area was curtained off from the side aisles of the huge basilica by rich hangings of crimson damask fringed with gold. Precious Flemish tapestries were draped between the pillars, depicting Raphael's masterpieces woven by patient and pious fingers centuries ago. Behind the Council fathers were special galleries for the *periti*, the experts who accompanied their bishops and who did much of the 'devilling' for them between sessions. In a place of honour, near the Pope's throne and the high altar, were the non-Roman Catholic observers, together with one or two Vatican advisers to identify speakers, interpret and generally help them follow the proceedings more closely.

Pope John XXIII inaugurated this solemn assembly on 11 October 1962. Speaking in sonorous Latin, he said that the present Council would take into account the errors, the needs and the opportunities of our times. 'By bringing herself up-to-date where required, the Church will make men, families and peoples really turn their minds to heavenly things.' In characteristic vein, Pope John, an ample and benign figure whose warm-hearted personality could not be concealed even by the heavy ceremonial vestments and triple crown he was wearing, spoke of the need to make use of the medicine of mercy rather than that of severity. The unity of the Christian and human family must be promoted. Unfortunately such an ideal had not yet been attained, he observed, and it was therefore the duty of the Roman Catholic Church to work actively for it.

It was the greatest gathering the Roman Church had ever seen. As the bells pealed out after the inauguration, the dignified procession of abbots, bishops, patriarchs and cardinals in their gorgeously embroidered copes and mitres – some prelates of the Eastern rites wearing jewelled crowns – made its way out into the sunshine. Though less sumptuously apparelled for the day-to-day sessions it was always a remarkable sight during the Council to see the great stream of prelates spill out of the basilica shortly after noon each day, for all the world like a great magenta-coloured waterfall in slow motion, seeping down the broad steps debouching on the graceful, vast piazza.

During that first difficult session Pope John did what he could to assuage the general dissatisfaction at the lack of a constant stream of information and background. The old guard was fighting a determined and skilful rearguard action to maintain the age-old secrecy and unquestioned authority of the Vatican. The idea of those in control was only to release information on what they deemed was useful, and to hush up differences of opinion whenever they could. They did not succeed, thanks in no small measure to some courageous prelates, who saw to it that we were given a fuller picture of what was being talked about in the daily sessions of the Council.

Just a few hours after he had opened the Vatican Council, Pope John received some 800 journalists in the Sistine Chapel. He looked understandably tired after the long opening ceremony, but walked briskly enough in his white and crimson robes to the throne which had been set up in front of the altar. It was in this chapel that he had received the very first homage due to him as pope immediately after his election in 1958, when all the canopies over the conclave cardinals' chairs, save his, had been lowered. He spoke to us affably in French, uttered with a fluent southern accent. He warned us that any distortion of the truth for sensational purposes could cause incalculable harm. 'But, gentlemen,' he went on, 'I didn't mean to talk to you about any little failings you may have.' Laughter rippled round the crowded chapel. Pope John was a master in eliciting happiness from his hearers, even when gently reproving them. The sensationalism which he deplored was often caused by the Vatican authorities' deliberate policy of mystification. (Someone once said that almost everything in the Vatican is a mystery but very little a secret.) Pope John went on: 'Deep-rooted prejudices can exist, serving to keep alive in men's hearts pockets of resistance, of suspicion and of misunderstanding, the consequences of which are regrettable for the advancement of harmony between men and nations. These prejudices most often rest on inaccurate or incomplete information.' I have rarely heard a better case for an efficient Vatican information service. Alas, it has even now, years after the Vatican Council, not yet come about, though things are slowly improving.

Perhaps in the nature of things this is not easy. The pope is an absolute authority. Few, if any, are privy to his inmost thoughts and intentions. At the same time the pope is trying to democratize and internationalize the organization of his

Church. He obviously cannot ride these two horses together, so the mystery, if not the secret, of what really goes on in the labyrinths of the Vatican continues. Journalists have their sources, men who with dedication give their version of what they think is afoot. They are often proved wrong, and the journalist, relying on the information they give, is castigated accordingly. But what else can be done, if the pope, unlike the president of the United States, has no real confidante who is both an experienced public relations man and someone whose word correspondents can trust?

Besides the grave issues which were to be reviewed by this great gathering, there were many fascinating sidelights to the descent on Rome of nearly 3000 Roman Catholic prelates and their retinues. Some, like the Americans, smoked long cigars, stayed in the best hotels, and liked their midday whisky. The Vatican Council had two coffee bars on either side of the nave of St Peter's, known as 'Bar Jonas' and 'Bar Abbas', where non-alcoholic drinks, as well as buns and biscuits, were dispensed free. They were well patronized; monks used their cowls to deposit their prayerbooks and papers in, the better to have both hands free to help themselves. There was, however, a brisk trade in the little bar near the sacristy, where normally priests go to refresh themselves after celebrating Mass. Here stronger drink could be obtained at a moderate price. The Anglo-Saxon clergy in particular were regular clients.

It was interesting to see how some of the United States clergy, arriving in Rome in their soberly cut suits, made for the nearest ecclesiastical tailors to buy flowing cloaks and round beaver hats. They then went in full rig to the Council to discuss whether priests should wear these more elaborate habits instead of soberly cut suits. In the event the sober suiters won the day, to the chagrin of the tailors. I once asked Cardinal Rugambwa, the first African to receive the red hat, at least in modern times (St Augustine of Hippo and St Cyprian were of course coloured men), whether he had

had many messages on his elevation to the purple. He told me the first half-dozen cables he received from Rome were all from ecclesiastical outfitters offering to fit him out at a special price. It costs several hundred pounds to do this, the long watered silk scarlet train and the ermine trimmed vestments being among the most costly items. The ring is generally the gift of the pope. The Indian prelates, I noticed, were those who wore the simplest attire, their pectoral crosses often being of wood. Yet men love dressing up, and most clergymen are certainly no exception.

The clerical outfitters of Rome were in their heyday with so many distinguished prelates in the city for weeks on end. In the heart of Rome, their shop windows were ablaze with vestments – chasubles, surplices of fine lace, copes and white mitres – all of which every Council father had to wear on certain occasions. The bishops also were busy stocking themselves up with other items: shoes with silver buckles (now abolished); purple socks; flowing cloaks and lightweight mackintoshes reaching to the ankles; glossy flat-crowned, broad-brimmed beaver hats with special hat bands of twisted green, red or gold cord, according to rank; girdles with tassels and fringes; capes for the cardinals, and so on. It is not easy for a layman to penetrate these shops, still less to find out from the proprietors the prices of the goods on offer. In fact the clergy get good value for money. On the shelves of the main outfitters great bolts of brocades and silks and satins are stacked, whilst in the back rooms men and women are bent over their tables tailoring, stitching and embroidering. Some of the finest work is done by nuns in the tranquil, undistracted atmosphere of the cloister. Indeed, a book could well be written on how these handmaidens of the Lord serve the priests on earth, not only praying for them, but even in the more mundane tasks of cooking, cleaning and generally keeping house for them.

Italy, in any case, has a long and proud artisan tradition. And the clergy stick to their own tailors throughout their career. A small and exclusive shop, Gammarelli's, which is just behind the Pantheon and is where most English priests go, was the tailor Pope John used in his youth. When he became pope the shop proudly displayed a white skullcap, as worn only by popes, in its window. I passed there shortly after Pope John's election, and saw a young English seminarist studying it intently. Perhaps he was dreaming that he too might one day step into the shoes of the fisherman, to become the first English pope since Nicholas Breakspeare in the thirteenth century, Pope Hadrian IV, who lies buried in St Peter's crypt with the Stuart exiles not far away. Queen Elizabeth, the Queen Mother, paid a generous tribute to her Scots ancestors in paying for these tombs to be restored, when she visited Rome in the early '60s.

Since the Council ended there has been a swing away from 'triumphalism', the term used for all this gorgeous panoply. Like their Protestant counterparts, some clergy have taken to wearing dark suits, collars and ties instead of the cassock and dog collar when walking about the streets, though in church they don the traditional vestments, which their congregations expect them to wear. Pope Paul has set the tone in more simple, yet elegant, ecclesiastical garb.

The arrival of so many clerics from every part of the globe for the Vatican Council and the synods which followed was naturally good for business. Tailors, hotelkeepers and shopowners all did well out of it. Some airlines and car-hire firms went so far as to issue brochures in Latin. *Automobiles novissimae locantur* – new cars for hire – with *securitatem amplius* – fully insured – *apertis condicionibus* – on the best terms. The advertisement did not say whether the chauffeurs spoke Latin also, but it added that cars could be hired 'without a driver' (*sine raedario*).

Once the majestic opening ceremonies of the Council were over, the fathers got down to business in a way which surprised the Curia. Many sinister motives have been imputed to this hardworking body, which, like any central administration, is a necessary but not particularly popular organization. At the first plenary session all the fathers of the Council were handed a handsome white plastic folder embossed in gold letters, in which they found, among other useful information (including the Latin brochures for air travel and car hire firms), a list of candidates suggested for the ten commissions to be set up to work out the compromise formulas after each vote had been taken following speeches from the council chamber. It was, therefore, a surprise on the first working day to see the fathers stream out of St Peter's less than an hour after they had entered, especially since the sessions always began with the enthronement of the book of the gospels and the celebration of Mass, which took the best part of an hour. Many of the Council fathers had objected to having the ready-made list of candidates thrust upon them. They wanted to propose new candidates, so they decided to cut their first session short. It was a healthy sign that the bishops were quick to realize their own independent rights. To be fair, however, one must admit there had not been a Council for almost a century; as one official put it, the machine required running in before it could work smoothly and efficiently. Pope John wisely stayed aloof from this initial episcopal gear-crashing. He was to intervene dramatically later on when matters had reached serious deadlock, but for the moment was content to bide his time.

One curious aspect, in retrospect, was that the sessions were supposed to be secret. However, many bishops, who wanted good publicity at home 'leaked' news to correspondents. We all had our sources, although those of us who were at home in several languages found it particularly exhausting rushing from one briefing to the next and trying, at the end of each day, to piece together the varying reports on the day's deliberations. To some speeches there were political overtones. Pope John himself, for example, set the cat among the pigeons early on by referring to the western territories of

Poland, much to the annoyance of the West Germans, who had not finally accepted the Oder–Neisse line as the definite frontier. Cardinal Montini, as Pope Paul then was, had a brush with the Spanish authorities when he wrote asking General Franco to show clemency to certain members of the Spanish opposition who had been given heavy prison sentences. French bishops were not slow to canvas members to make a pronouncement on nuclear disarmament, peace, Communism and other pressing world problems. The Africans started propaganda for services in the vernacular instead of Latin, and for the rules to be changed so that married deacons could help celibate priests in their uphill work of converting the heathen.

To avoid starting on controversial issues it was decided to begin with a debate on the liturgy, a seemingly safe topic (though it turned out otherwise). This was to give the back-room boys, or *periti*, more time to digest the many ideas which came pouring out of the assembly, aimed at giving the Church a new look – exactly as Pope John, in calling for an *aggiornamento*, wanted it to do.

The first session of the Vatican Council met 36 times in all. Nearly half those present rose to speak or submitted their views in writing. The Council fathers, by the end, had put forward projects on the liturgy, on the sources of revelation, at which there were some sharply divided views on how far the tradition of the Church should be accepted as of equal importance as that of the holy scriptures; on modern communications and entertainment – a weak and hastily conceived project, this; on Christian unity, about which there was enthusiasm in some quarters and marked coolness in others; and on the nature of the Church itself. They were only proposals and were handed to the commissions for drafting and review. They had nine months in which to do this before the Council was to meet again. Most prelates were relieved that no new declarations on doctrine had been suggested.

From the working of the first session it was clear that the more forward-looking opinions had gained the ascendancy over the die-hard traditional outlook. This progressive trend was without doubt encouraged by the presence of so many distinguished non-Roman Catholic observers, who, although they had not the right to take a direct part in the Council's discussions in St Peter's, were active in promoting contacts outside with the Council Fathers, many of whom sought their guidance on theological and other matters to help formulate their own ideas. This was perhaps a miracle in itself when one considers how, until the death of Pius XII, the Roman Church appeared almost arrogantly self-assured in its conviction that it was right and all other churches were wrong. This idea of *Extra Ecclesiam Nulla Salus* persists, but it is gradually making way for a more flexible attitude towards other Christians, even though basic Roman Catholic doctrine seeks to remain as firm as ever.

Pope John had certainly let in the fresh air of open discussion with a vengeance. In the words of one of the most active Swiss theologians, Professor Hans Küng, 'We all went back home different men as a result of it.' Most of the younger men – and Küng was then barely 40 – looked to the future and its promise rather than fearing progressive ideas as a threat to all the past traditions of the Church.

In the closing ceremony of the first session Pope John spoke of 'a good beginning'. 'It is necessary for brothers gathered together from afar round a common hearth to make each other's acquaintance, to look at each other squarely, and to reflect on the conditions of the apostolate under the most varied climates and circumstances, in order that there should be a thoughtful and profitable interchange of views on pastoral matters. The fruits of the present Council are still to come.' It was obvious that Pope John thought it could end its work by the second session. He was then 81, with only a few more months to live. Already, however, he had given new heart, not only to Christians in and outside his

Church, but to many of other faiths, to those of little faith or none at all. He was dead before the second session of this 'great and glorious enterprise', as he called it, opened nine months later. He was and still is mourned by millions who had never even seen him, but who somehow felt in their hearts, more than knew in their minds, that a great and good man had gone from their midst, and that the world of 1963 was thus a lonelier and more frightening place in which to live.

It was a foregone conclusion that Cardinal Giovanni Battista Montini, the Archbishop of Milan, would be elected as Pope John's successor, and it was as Pope Paul VI that he inherited the difficult legacy of his predecessor. Before his election he made it abundantly clear that he would carry on in the spirit of Pope John and this, together with all the other advantages he possessed, including an exceptionally fine style in writing clear and succinct Italian to express some of the subtlest concepts of religious thought, made his election certain. There was no serious rival.

Six days before the second session was due to open in September 1963 with a debate on the nature of the Roman Catholic Church, the draft decree of which had been worked out by a special commission during the intervening nine months, Pope Paul gave a first taste of his quality. He assembled the Curia and told its august members that their body was suffering from 'venerable age', and needed to be simplified, decentralized and reformed to meet the needs of the present day. Pope Paul had himself worked for 30 years in the Curia. He knew what he was talking about. What the Pope had foremost in mind was the creation of an episcopal senate, or synod. Bishops from all parts of the world would meet regularly in synod in Rome and advise the pope – a bishop like themselves – on the Church's policy in a rapidly changing world.

The old saying that popes come and go but the Curia remains would thus no longer be entirely true. In fact, however, it was only five years later, in March 1968, that the major curial reforms began seriously to take effect. The congregations or ministries were reduced from twelve to nine, regular 'cabinet' meetings were instituted, and it was laid down that no one should hold office for more than five years and that all such offices should lapse on the death of the pope. At the same time Pope Paul started the slow process of replacing some, but not all, of the predominantly Italian cardinals, as they reached the retiring age of 75, with some of the best men from the five continents, thus giving the Curia a more international composition, and reflecting more exactly the distribution of Roman Catholics throughout the world.

In the past the Curia had managed the popes, and, even after this bombshell the old guard, led by the self-styled 'Vatican policeman', the Trastevere baker's son Cardinal Alfredo Ottaviani, for many years head of the Holy Office – now the Congregation for the Doctrine of the Faith – put up stout rear-guard action.

One of those who had a great influence on the new Pope in the early days of his reign was the Dutch Cardinal, Bernard Alfrink, who insisted that the Church was founded by St Peter *with* the apostles. He wanted to convey the point that the pope as the successor of St Peter was to be regarded as *primus inter pares* rather than a supreme single authority taking lofty decisions on his own. Italian cardinals, on the other hand, argued that it was the *primacy* of Peter which mattered most, indicating that they would prefer the old system of an infallible pope (he was almost always Italian anyway) with supreme power. One of the great dilemmas still facing the Roman Catholic Church is the incompatibility of these two doctrines.

Looking beyond this problem as he girded himself for what he knew would be a Vatican Ecumenical Council which would need far more than the two sessions for which Pope John had bargained, Pope Paul had his eye on the wider and more distant horizon of Christian unity. He was not to be hurried over this. He said in his opening address to the Council fathers, reassembled for their second session: 'Serious and complicated questions remain to be studied and resolved in the field of Christian unity. Many conditions are required before satisfactory solutions can be reached, conditions which are, as yet, premature. We are not afraid to await patiently the blessed hour of perfect reconciliation.'

The second session showed that the Council machine had by this time been run in. The bishops were enjoying their newly-found authority. They were not afraid to stand up and criticize the rigid authority of the Curia as it then existed – in fact, Pope Paul himself had given them the lead. There was a heartening vitality about this second round of discussion and one moment of drama when the German Cardinal Frings of Cologne clashed with Cardinal Ottaviani, who left the nave in a huff and did not return for twelve days. It was encouraging for many in and outside the Council to hear cardinal contradicting cardinal, archbishop disputing with archbishop, and to follow the sweep and countersweep of argument from all parts of the world.

The Roman Catholic Church in these debates showed clearly that it was not the fossilized institution many had held it to be. The turning point of the second session was 30 October 1963. It was on that day that an overwhelming majority of Council fathers voted for a far greater degree of authority for bishops in their national conferences – a more direct sharing with the pope of responsibility for governing the Church. But as the second session ended it became clear that much still remained to be reviewed and pondered. Of the seventeen draft decrees before it, the Council had so far approved only two. The first allowed the vernacular to replace Latin in the administration of sacraments and in the Mass. This was a victory, not only for the Africans and others in the newly established Christian churches in the mission fields, with their problems of tribal dialects and languages, but also for the clergy in Communist countries, where religious instruction was largely forbidden. It meant that the priests, in church at any rate, could devote more time to talking to the faithful in their own language. The second decree approved the use of mass communications for the common good. The direct televising of the Council in some of its aspects had created enormous interest in the Roman Catholic Church throughout the world. Yet the Vatican still remained extremely nervous of correspondents.

I myself was censored at the beginning of the second session when I was about to do a short, quite inoffensive, introductory talk in front of the camera in St Peter's piazza to outline what the Council was likely to discuss. A curial Monsignor objected. Just before I was due to begin, a plain-clothes papal gendarme came and told me that this Monsignor in the Vatican had deleted from my script references I was about to make to the Pope's ideas on having new and closer relations with his bishops, and on the possibility of replacing Latin by modern languages in the liturgy. I was astounded at this, since both points, I knew, had already been agreed. The papal gendarme looked rather embarrassed when I asked what would happen if I mentioned these things nonetheless. He told me he would have to confiscate the film. Already a motor-cyclist was waiting to take it to Rome airport for showing in London that night. So reluctantly I accepted the censorship, and did a shorter 'stand-upper' (as these efforts are known in television jargon) and it was duly air-freighted to London for broadcast.

An hour afterwards the Vatican held a news conference, presided over by the American Archbishop Martin O'Connor, president of the Social Communications Commission. 'We want to help you all we can,' he assured the six or seven hundred of us. 'We know that during the first session things were not as good as they might have been. This time we hope to give you greater help for free and full reporting of the Council.'

Hopeful words indeed. Afterwards, not wishing to spoil the promising atmosphere, I went privately to the Archbishop and told him what had happened to me an hour earlier, commenting that his good intentions had not so far percolated down to his subordinates. His reply astounded me: 'We are not censoring you, Patrick, we are only trying to convince you.'

Naturally from the freedom of Italy I was able to broadcast all of this, much to the annoyance of the Vatican, or more specifically the Curia. They never tried to censor me, or as far as I know anyone else, again. Incidentally, the Monsignor who made the gaffe became a good and helpful friend.

The Council still had many controversial subjects to discuss: the Roman Catholic attitude to the Jews, the burning question of religious liberty, the issues of war and peace, the problems of world hunger and the imminent population explosion. And there was the need to turn passive Christians, as the Belgian Cardinal Leo Suenens put it, into active Christians to fight growing materialism, indifference and downright atheism in the modern world.

Yet under the guidance of Pope Paul the second session saw a slowing down of the pace of things. Pope John, when he decided to call the Vatican Council, said he wanted to let in some fresh air. The winds of change blew with gale force for a while along the corridors of the Vatican, and no one knew whither they were blowing. The second session proceeded more cautiously. The reaction of the Curia was strong, as though they had been given the task of shoring up some of the storm defences blown down by Pope John's whirlwind reign. To them, Pope Paul seemed to symbolize the calm after the tempest. He was, in fact, playing himself in gently, and seemed to have every intention of carrying on the work of his far-sighted predecessor.

If anyone hoped in September 1964, at the outset of the third session, that it would turn into a discussion of abstruse theological points and other issues concerned mainly with a clerical club of esoteric exclusiveness, the debates which followed quickly disabused them. The Council really caught fire on the issue of religious liberty. In the past the Roman Catholic religion had not been so keen on religious liberty for others, but only for itself when persecuted. One of the most courageous speeches on this explosive question came from the Archbishop of Westminster, Cardinal Heenan. He held up Britain as an example of a land where religious freedom really was put into practice. He recalled the bitter fight between Protestant and Catholic in the sixteenth century, and reminded the Council that a Catholic Queen Mary had dealt no less ferociously with Protestants than a Protestant Queen Elizabeth with Catholics. Both sides had their martyrs. But all that was past history. 'For the sake of the common good in a dwindling world, freedom of religion must flourish in every nation all over the world.' Many outside the Roman Catholic Church, he concluded, did not think it believed in religious freedom. 'Let us declare to the whole world once and for all our heartfelt belief as Catholics in the full liberty of all the sons of God.'

It was a stirring speech and warmly applauded. It came from a man who at the outset of the Council had not started off with such liberal views, who still retained something of the 'ghetto' attitude common among many British Roman Catholics, but whom the Council had changed, making him look beyond narrow national perspectives.

Although votes were not taken on this draft during the second session, there was a similar broadening of mind towards the problem of the Jews. Down the centuries the Christian Church has certainly done its share to promote anti-Semitism. Now the Council was making amends, and a majority of fathers wanted to exonerate the Jews from the age-old charge of deicide. Cardinal Heenan summed up what many felt on this issue. 'The Council must proclaim the Jews not guilty. It would be equally unjust for all Christians in Europe to be judged guilty of the deaths of millions of Jews in Germany and Poland. It was no less unjust to condemn the whole Jewish people for the death of Christ.'

The third session in fact surpassed most hopes. The monumental decree on the nature of the Church was given an overwhelming vote of approval, and was solemnly promulgated by Pope Paul. It laid down the principle of episcopal collegiality. The bishops of the world, together with the pope, but never without him, now had supreme authority over the Church. In their national episcopal conferences the bishops would in future wield far greater power, and not have to refer to Rome each and every decision concerning their local work. The corollary to this was the curtailment of the powers of the dominating Curia. It was to take some years before this powerful body would submit to the reforms upon which the Council had decided, but by the spring of 1968 the whole structure of the central administration had been changed.

Time, however, seems to be of far less consequence in the Vatican than elsewhere. Harold Macmillan put it well in his autobiography *The Blast of War* when he described his audience with Pope Pius XII towards the end of 1944. '. . . The chief impression on my mind was . . . a sense of timelessness. . . Centuries come and go, but this is like living in a fourth dimension. And at the centre of it all, past the papal guards, and the Noble Guards, and the monsignori and the bishops and the cardinals and all the show of ages – sits the little saintly man, rather worried, obviously quite selfless and holy – at once a pathetic and a tremendous figure. . .'

The bishops had shown their power by throwing out a draft decree on missionary work, a draft which Pope Paul had personally asked them to approve. They were, however, far from content with its proposals, and wanted more time to amend it. The Pope, to remind them perhaps that collegiality should not be taken too far, and that he had not forgotten his supreme powers, personally changed some particulars in the decree on ecumenism. This ecumenical decree set in train vast and promising movements between the Christian churches towards unity, and showed a welcome, if only slight change in the hitherto exclusive attitude of the Roman Church.

The declaration exonerating the Jews from the traditional charges of deicide was also given overwhelming approval in the dying days of the session, but the controversial draft on religious liberty almost led to a revolt. Led by two American cardinals, 800 bishops petitioned the Pope for a vote to be taken, after the moderators had decided against this. The Pope prudently upheld the chairmen's decision, and the vote was postponed, not however without much head-shaking, for the bishops who had petitioned wanted a statement of man's inalienable freedom to follow the dictates of his own conscience on religious matters. Behind all this, of course, was the desperate struggle of the curial die-hards and their associates, who saw the levers of control slipping from their grasp.

The third session was also remarkable for the admission for the first time of woman observers to the Council, and for the invitation to certain laymen to address this ecclesiastical assembly. The Church was getting a new look with a vengeance.

When the bishops came together for the fourth time, in September 1965, Pope Paul made it clear that this would be the last session of the Council. For one thing, though this was not mentioned publicly, the cost of this great gathering was very heavy. Even the seating, which had been hired temporarily in the expectation of a short council, had proved to be a costly item.

The mood of the fathers was thus one of austere determination to press on with the heavy agenda before them. Pope Paul, in another of his dramatic announcements, told the assembly at the outset that he intended to fly to New York to make an appeal for peace at the General Assembly of the United Nations – he was becoming a political pope indeed. He still seems to revel in these wider actions, possibly as a relief from the more rarefied problems of his Church. They certainly give the Vatican greater prestige and influence in the conduct of world affairs.

Journalists were not usually allowed to attend the working sessions of the Vatican Council. In fact, well ahead of the day on which he hoped to attend, a cardinal had to vouch in writing, and in Latin at that, that one was a responsible person worthy of such a privilege. I was lucky to have such a privilege through the kindness of Cardinal Heenan.

The Vatican Council always got down to work early. Bishops began to arrive from about 8.30 a.m., and to take their places in the tiered seats ranged on either side of the nave of St Peter's. The statue of St Peter, whose toes have been worn away down the centuries by the kisses of the faithful, was robed and crowned, and symbolically watched the cardinals, who were ranged immediately opposite this venerated bronze figure in their own scarlet robes. It was a scene rich in colour and dignity.

Though the vastness of the basilica dwarfs all human beings there was nothing stiff or forced about the behaviour of the Council fathers. There was a relaxed House of Commons kind of atmosphere with the members chatting as though waiting for Mr Speaker to make his entrance – in the Council's case, one of its four chairmen or moderators. When I was there, it was the iron-grey-haired German, Cardinal Doepfner, who presided. First as always came the Mass, with soaring music sung on that particular day by 44 choir-boys of Regensburg cathedral. They were complimented afterwards by the secretary-general of the council, Archbishop Felice, later created Cardinal, who is as at home in Latin as in his native Italian. '*Optime*,' he said, '*Optime*,' and the Council fathers applauded as the fresh-faced boys in their scarlet cassocks and freshly laundered cottas walked as seriously as they could past the cardinals and out into the vestry for coffee and buns.

Next came the enthronement of the Book of the Gospels, its richly illuminated pages gleaming in the candle-light of the flanking acolytes, followed by Mass. Then the council began its daily working session. The first speaker was a Belgian bishop. Orotund Latin phrases echoed along the gilded vaulting and round Michelangelo's dome under which I was sitting among priests and monks from a dozen different countries. In a place of honour near the moderators' table was the special box for the non-Roman Catholic observers. They sat in groups, each with a translator to help in following the statement of the Bishop de Smedt of Bruges on religious liberty, who spoke his Latin with a fine oratorical flourish.

The sun slanted down through the windows. On occasion the Council fathers riffled through their papers; at one point there was a burst of seemly laughter and applause at some delicately turned phrase of the speaker. To me his lapidary Latin sentences conjured up visions of Roman senators in their togas, expounding the law in the Forum situated not so far away. As the hands of the ornate clock at the end of the nave crept towards eleven, and the two bars in the basilica made ready to open their doors, the odour of incense used at the Mass was subtly superseded by the fragrant aroma of coffee. It was bad luck on any speaker on his feet just then, for the bishops tended to leave their seats *en masse* and make for the two bars on either side of the nave. One Indian bishop said publicly in the Council that the real work was done in these bars. Conversation there was certainly animated, as bishops helped themselves liberally to cakes and coffee. They smoked as they discussed points with their fellow Council members. An English bishop was in earnest conversation with a French abbot, an American archbishop was talking to a bearded and hooded Armenian prelate. In spite of the robes and bejewelled crosses and chains it was all very natural and human, though perhaps it was slightly incongruous to see a well-manicured hand with a large episcopal ring delicately, almost ceremonially, drawing a glass of Coca-Cola from a tap. A small group of bishops who needed something stronger than coffee were in the special bar. A notice in five languages reminded the bishops to put out their pipes and cigarettes before returning to the aula. One by one they drifted back to their seats after refreshment.

In the aisles and chapels flanking the nave many of the famous and lesser-known figures of the Council could be seen talking. I noticed cardinals, priests, nuns and lay observers, both men and women, and in the background the Vatican firemen, ushers and first-aid attendants unobtrusively on duty. I was back in my place just in time to hear the closing speeches and the final prayers. And then we all streamed out of St Peter's into the warm noonday October sunshine.

The fourth session left many decisions still in abeyance – notably, on the Pope's personal insistence, that of birth control – but it had achieved much. Certainly old clerical attitudes towards the laity had been buried for ever. This great gathering which had become so much a way of life for for those taking part was suffused with sadness towards the end. A sense of anticlimax stole over the closing sessions, which all the magnificence of the ritual could not quite conceal. At the centre of it all was the slight figure of Pope Paul; 'a walking question mark', as one American described him.

The Vatican Council had condemned nuclear warfare, it had declared war on poverty and ignorance, it had championed religious liberty, it had set forth a more open-minded attitude to other Christian churches, to Jews and other religions as well as to non-believers. It had renewed the emphasis to be placed on the Bible as the supreme source of divine revelation – this particularly pleased the Protestants, who felt that the Reformation was at last bearing fruit where it was most needed – and it brought a fresh approach to religious education and missionary work.

Pope Paul must have heaved a sigh of relief when it was formally over. With his far-sightedness, however, he knew that the post-conciliar phase would be the supreme test of his pontificate. Up to now he had largely been carrying on the work of Pope John. Many had drawn an unfavourable comparison between him and his genial predecessor. He was a sensitive man, and he knew and suffered under the comparison. It was hard indeed to follow such a man. Even when Pope Paul suggested that both Pope John and Pope Pius be considered for the long process of beatification and eventual canonization, there was misgiving. The young Swiss theologian Hans Küng said to me that Pope John was anyway too obviously good to require the official imprimatur of canonization. About Pope Pius he said nothing. About Pope Paul there is still much to be said.

CHAPTER FOURTEEN

A Church on the Move

The idea of the pope as a prisoner of the Vatican had already been weakened considerably by Pope John. In his brief pontificate he left Rome a number of times, visiting parishes outside Rome and travelling further afield to Loreto and Assisi, the first pope to use the vast marble Vatican railway station in decades.

It was left to Pope Paul to become the globe-trotter. It is now an accepted fact that the Pope flies all over the world, but I remember the stir when he announced, less than a year after his election, that he intended to visit the Holy Land, there to meet the Orthodox Patriarch Athenagoras. I accompanied Pope Paul on that first momentous journey, and saw what calm nerves he had when hemmed in by great crowds. To the Arabs of Jordan he was in any case a holy man, a follower of a much revered prophet. They streamed in their thousands to Jerusalem to see him pass along the via Dolorosa. I had placed myself, armed with a tape recorder, at the fifth station of the cross, where, as the New Testament relates, Simon of Cyrene was ordered to bear the cross of Christ on his way to Calvary. It was a corner at which the road turns roughly at a right angle and ascends to the church of the Holy Sepulchre, the last of the fourteen stations.

It was a warm January day. The Arab shops, which sell olive wood rosaries and boxes, inlaid chests, medals and souvenirs of every kind, were open. Each shopkeeper had at least half-a-dozen members of his family crowding to watch the papal procession. The cafés bordering the narrow street were open too, and old men sat puffing philosophically at their hubble-bubbles. I stood next to a television camera platform, and fondly thought I would have an unimpeded view of the Pope as he came through the Damascus Gate, pausing at various shrines along the way, where monks and nuns were waiting to greet him and to pray with him.

What actually happened was an unedifying scramble, a pushing and shoving without compare. My recording apparatus was knocked to the ground, while Arab legionnaires beat about them to clear a path for the Pope, who throughout remained calm, if pale-faced and tense. Had he missed his footing at any point he would have been crushed to death. As it was, all I could see was his white skull-cap floating like a leaf along the stream of people's heads. Some cardinals and others of his retinue, old men, looked pale with fright, and one at least sought refuge in a coffee shop until all was over. How different from the orderly, spacious ceremonies of St Peter's! Pope Paul would have been well advised to have taken some of his burly Swiss bodyguards with him to control the surging crowds.

As the Pope passed near where I was precariously standing, an Arab legionnaire was about to hit me on the head with his cane; then, seeing my press lapel badge bearing the photographs of King Hussein and the Pope, he smiled broadly, said, 'Welcome,' and whacked the person next to me instead. A near miss. Jerome Caminada of *The Times*, behind me and considerably taller than I, had a slightly better view and escaped a similar blow.

When Pope Paul finally reached the Church of the Holy Sepulchre, the Moslem gate-keeper opened the massive doors of this much fought-over Holy place. It is a sad comment on the divisions within the Christian church that by tradition only a Moslem family can be entrusted with controlling who goes in and out. The sepulchre itself is divided into sections, with the Greek Orthodox, the Coptic and the Latin (i.e. the Roman Catholic) Church each claiming their part and erecting their altars in front of their respective portions of the tomb. The Copts, for instance, allow you to touch their segment of the holy tomb, spray your hand with rosewater as you do so, and expect an oblation in return.

There have been undignified scenes in this old church, with Franciscan monks coming to blows with Orthodox priests about their precise territorial rights. However, on this occasion the local leaders buried the hatchet, and allowed Pope Paul to move round the entire church before praying at the Latin altar where he celebrated Mass. The ancient electrical system of the church was obviously over-taxed by the needs of television lighting. During the service the wires began to burn, causing near-panic. Pope Paul, however, oblivious of the danger, or perhaps in cool-headed courage, continued his prayers and by his steady example recalled the congregation to a state of calm. The fire was hastily put out, and the Mass ended peacefully. It had been a long and tiring day, but Pope Paul seemed strangely uplifted by the throng. The words of the gospel, that they pressed forward to touch the hem of His garment, took on a direct meaning for me as I struggled to keep up with the procession.

The great Jordanian crowds were for the most part driven there by respect rather than piety. This was certainly coupled with a feeling of flattery that so august a person had visited their country, the cockpit of one of the oldest and most bitter antagonisms in the world.

By the same token the Jews in Israel were impressed by the Pope's visit to their side of Jerusalem and to Nazareth. Their attitude was more one of curiosity than of belief, since the Pope, for them, is the representative of a false Messiah, though, as head of the tiny Vatican State, he is worthy of the highest honours.

We correspondents were allowed to cross over the Mandel-baum Gate, the heavily guarded boundary of the divid-ed city of those days, as many times as we chose. Some of us found that it was quicker to file our stories from the Jewish side than from Jordan, though the greatest tact was necessary to avoid giving offence to the sensitive Arabs.

For their part the Israelis were only too delighted to help.

It was a journey which left Pope Paul with little time for rest. He always gives the impression that he is a pope in a hurry, rushing through his pilgrimages, as though he does not want to leave the Vatican in the hands of his advisers for long. Paradoxically, however, the Pope is at his happiest and most relaxed when working through the strenuous schedule of a pilgrimage, where every minute is carefully measured. Like American presidents, he is a great man for 'the press of the flesh'. So of course was Pope John, but, with his affability and complete lack of a sense of time, the latter could never have carried out such pilgrimages according to a tight time-table – nor would he have wished to have done so.

Outstanding among the meetings Pope Paul had in Jerusalem was that with the Orthodox Patriarch Athenagoras, a tall, bearded prelate like some Old Testament prophet, who flew to the Holy City from Rhodes. It was the first meeting between the heads of the two churches since Constantinople broke away from Rome over nine centuries ago – after hurling anathemas at each other – the great schism which came about when the Orthodox church leadership said that it was not prepared to accept the primacy of Rome over Constantinople. It was an historical moment – a 'fraternal gesture of two pilgrims with their eyes fixed on Christ', as the official communiqué put it.

There can be no doubt that Rome places the highest priority on a reunion with the Eastern Orthodox churches, for in spite of the schism and the anathema, which have been mutually withdrawn, Rome has never ceased to recognise Orthodox orders and sacraments as valid. This is not the case with other churches, much to the chagrin of some Anglicans. Pope Paul nevertheless took the occasion to meet the Anglican bishop in Jerusalem as well as the heads of other eastern churches, including the patriarchs of the Coptic and Armenian churches, whose history goes back to the earliest Christian times.

The Pope's return to Rome was a tumultuous occasion. Thousands of Romans, in spite of the late hour, welcomed him back with an imposing torchlight procession round St Peter's square. For the Romans like their bishop to be seen among them, and they were extremely proud of the first historic pilgrimage he had made.

Roughly the same pattern was followed when Pope Paul visited the United Nations, when he went to Bombay, to Fatima and Bogotá, to the Far East and elsewhere. They were all lightning visits, and he was never out of the Vatican for very long, yet every time was the occasion for a great welcome home.

No one took exception to his journey to New York, where he made an impassioned plea for an end to war in the world. The delegates listened respectfully, but, alas, soon resumed internecine hostilities in the Middle and Far East and in Africa.

The visit to Bombay caused dissatisfaction among the Portuguese, who were still smarting over the loss of Goa – in fact the Portuguese press was not allowed to report on the papal visit to India. That was perhaps why the Pope thought it prudent to put Portugal next on the list of his pilgrimages. He flew to Fatima on 13 May 1967, and after eight hours on Portuguese soil flew home again. His appearance at the celebrations, which marked the fiftieth anniversary of the apparition of the Madonna, had an electrifying effect on the million and more faithful, in many cases simple peasants, who had camped in the surrounding woods in the pouring rain for days to catch a glimpse of him.

I flew with him in his specially chartered Portuguese plane. In spite of the heavy programme ahead he seemed euphorically relaxed about it all. He came aft for a word with each of us, followed by the stewardesses – chosen to fly on this privileged occasion for their seniority rather than their beauty. He even answered our question whether he thought the age of miracles was over with a thoughtful, 'No, I don't think it is.'

The miracle of Fatima, where according to pious belief the Virgin Mary appeared six times to three shepherd children in 1917 on a bleak hillside, is still a matter of embarrassing controversy, even to devout Roman Catholics. Some believe that not only did the Madonna appear perched on a holm oak and deliver prophecies, but that the sun revolved strangely and rushed towards the earth – a phenomenon which Pope Pius, years later, also claimed to have seen, together with a vision of the Blessed Virgin. Two of the three witnesses died shortly after the Fatima apparition, and are buried in the basilica erected on the spot. The third, Sister Lucia, who met the Pope on this fiftieth anniversary, has been in an enclosed order of Carmelites for most of her life.

The fervent adoration at the shrine, with men and women shuffling in prayer on their knees, was unforgettable and to me rather frightening. After it was all over and the Pope was winging his way back to Rome, the faithful were still coming up to the crimson and gilt throne on which he had sat to touch it with their rosaries, a form of religious fetishism strange to behold.

The prophecy of Fatima has long been respected by many devout Catholics. It is kept in a sealed envelope in the secret Vatican archives, its contents known only to the pope and a few of his closest advisers. Two prophecies, one declaring the imminence of the end of the first world war, the second speaking of an eventual reconversion of Russia to Christianity, have been allowed to leak out to the public over the years. The third is thought too terrible ever to see the light of day. Yet I have spoken to serious men who claim to have read the third prophecy of Fatima. It declares, they claim, that the devil will insinuate himself into the very highest ranks of the Roman Catholic Church, which will finally fall apart, and that the world thereafter will come to an end.

Certainly the Roman Catholic Church knows that

Christians as such have their backs to the wall. From my many talks with Roman Catholics, priests and lay, it is clear that they are finding this a severely testing time. Some priests and monks of my acquaintance now have considerable doubts about heaven and hell, a dogma they had taught without question until the recent Vatican Council. Some have secret doubts about their entire religion, as the pressures of the outside world and its expanding knowledge grow ever more persistent.

On the one hand, there are the pious monks, often with no pretensions to profound scholarship, but who are prayerful, reciting their offices and fulfilling their religious duties as a matter of course because it all has a deep traditional significance. One said to me vehemently: 'The trouble today with these young priests is that they don't pray enough. They are too caught up with the world about them, trying to be "with it" instead of thinking about the long-term verities of life.'

I also ran across experienced priests, hard-working and eager when they took up their duties, but who over the years have become assailed with a gnawing doubt about the wisdom of some Vatican decisions. They are in a cruel dilemma, for they are highly professional men, well briefed in the arguments of the Church, sometimes inclined to be more like church lawyers than simple men of God. Nevertheless, they soldier on, knowing that, unlike doctors and lawyers, they cannot abandon their profession without causing scandal. Few are prepared to face the unpleasant consequences of such a desperate step. Their number is, however, on the increase, just as the number of vocations among young men and women is on the decline.

One young student, I remember, told me how he had almost completed his seven arduous years of study, he had already been ordained deacon, and then decided that he could not go through with his mission. It was not, as the hierarchies so often make out, simply that he found celibacy too severe a rule of life. It was rather his conviction that such a sacrifice was not worth while if he thought the Church which he hoped to serve was not going in the right direction.

There was also a young nun I knew who had willingly served her order for fifteen years, renouncing a comfortable life which she would undoubtedly have had in her rich and devout family. The Vatican Council filled her with hope and pride that at last Christians of all denominations were drawing closer together. I used to see her often during the Vatican Council, and was impressed by her joy and serenity in her work with Christians of many other communities, to whom she gave an outstanding example of the Roman Catholic Church at its best. When the Council was over, her order transferred her to the United States, where she found the local clergy doing their best to carry on as though the great inspiration of the Vatican Ecumenical Council had never happened, some even going so far as to allege that Pope John had done irreparable harm to the hitherto mono-lithic structure of his Church. So, with a heavy heart, she decided to revoke her vows and left the order. In both these cases – and they are by no means uncommon – the superiors involved showed great understanding to cover their disappointment.

The young man is now a teacher. The former nun returned to Rome and found fulfilment in marrying and having two children. I often saw her and her Protestant husband after she had made her tremendous decision. She is not a whit less religious than when she was a nun – perhaps less narrowly Roman Catholic, though no less a Christian. She certainly did not leave her order to get married, but she has found fulfilment in taking this step and continues in friendly harmony with her old order in their ecumenical work.

One aspect of this rule of celibacy is rarely mentioned. Aside from the religious connotation of personal sacrifice, it is an eminently practical and economic rule when the running of a great international organization is in question. Single men and women are easier to move about when they have no close family ties, and, of course, it costs less. The whole idea of celibacy is now coming under far closer scrutiny as vocations dwindle, though Pope Paul remains adamant. Yet, he, the successor of St Peter, cannot but remember that this apostle was himself a married man. And, for a Church which accords almost divine worship to the Virgin Mary, it is odd that women have such a subservient place in its everyday affairs.

On the highest level the Vatican can still be hard and seemingly uncharitable. There was more than a little jealousy shown when the outspoken Belgian Cardinal, Leo Josef Suenens, appeared at the side of Pope Paul at the outset of the Council. He seemed to be the Pope's favourite some years back, but fell from grace because of his liberal views on ecumenism. He welcomes the reformation under way with his Church. He is a striking prelate, with an angular countenance, and twinkling, humorous eyes. When I called on him at the Belgian College at the corner of the via Quattro Fontane he told me that he saw good in all denominations. He does not hold the traditionalist view that the only way to salvation is through union, on the 'return to the fold, all is forgiven' principle. If I understand him aright, he thinks rather in terms of the people of God, no longer divided into exclusive groups, but each seeking their salvation in a tolerant and co-operative manner. It was humiliating for this great man to be warned against giving news conferences in the official Vatican press centre, where journalists were invited to listen to many far less eminent. He was not to be beaten, and met us in the basement room of a modest hotel to tell us with a resigned smile that, during the Vatican Council, he had had the impression of being in a lift. 'When you look down, you see that we have risen a floor or two; but when you look up, you realize just how many floors there are still to go before you get anywhere near the top.' He once wrote an authoritative book on the place of nuns in the world, a book highly commended by Pope Paul. In it he says, 'In this world our human ant-hill is astir in all directions. The old ideals are being replaced by new ones – frankness, efficiency, sincerity and sobriety. . .'

Cardinal Suenens is a great yet humble man, alert to the menace of irreligion and indifference in the world, where material well-being can absorb all man's energies and becomes an end in itself. 'The world is a paradox; we must love it,' he says, 'yet defend ourselves against it; collaborate with its enthusiasm, yet direct it; admire it, yet set limits to it; encourage it along every path that can lead to good, yet warn it of the pitfalls and precipices that flank the way. The Christian life,' he adds, 'will always be a paradox. But, in our times especially, being a Christian demands a greater maturity and clear-sightedness, as well as a deep sense of responsibility if God is to mean anything in this world of ours. . .'

CHAPTER FIFTEEN

Roman Knights

It did not take me long to realize that there were two diplomatic corps, one accredited to the Italian Republic, the other to the Vatican, but it was some time before I stumbled on the fact that there was a third, and much smaller diplomatic corps accredited to the Sovereign and Military Order of Malta. The Order is the remnant of the once glorious Knights of St John who succoured the pilgrims and fighting men at the time of the Crusades. They were driven from the Holy Land and settled first on the island of Rhodes. Driven from there, they moved to Malta (they are generally known today as the Knights of Malta) and this period when they built Valletta (so named after their Grand Master de la Vallette) and withstood the terrible siege of the Turks, was their finest hour. Subsequently they degenerated, and were finally thrown out by Napoleon before he in turn was defeated and Malta became a British possession for more than a century and a half until its recent independence. The rump of the Order moved to Rome, where it still occupies a *palazzo* in the central via Condotti, easily identified by its graceful courtyard with the white Maltese Cross above a fountain and a villa on the Aventine Hill overlooking the Circus Maximus. The entrance to this villa is well known, for through the keyhole of the main entrance door one spies the great dome of St Peter at the end of a long avenue. The villa has a chapel by Piranesi, one of the few buildings this great artist ever built, most of his designs remaining on the drawing-board to delight countless lovers of ancient Rome down the generations. There is also a museum, incorporating models of galleys used by the knights when they were a naval as well as military force to be reckoned with, and many pictures and documents illustrating the chequered history of this ancient order of chivalry.

For a number of years before I arrived in Rome a bitter dispute had been raging between the Order and the Vatican. Nominally under the authority of the Vatican, the Order jealously guarded what was left of its independence and resisted what in effect was a take-over bid. At one point the struggle was so acute that the Vatican permitted the founding of a rival, the Order of the Holy Sepulchre, in an attempt to eclipse the Knights of Malta. But they clung to their rights and privileges with quiet tenacity, though, as a religious order, they ran the risk of excommunication. At one stage a knight of the Order, whose name has since been expunged from the lists, divulged confidential information about the dispute to the French writer Roger Peyrefitte. This cynic, who had already aroused Vatican displeasure with his *Keys of St Peter*, wrote a swingeing account of Vatican machinations to gain control of the Order. At that time the knights were very much an exclusive club. Its upper echelons were filled by men whose nobility had been proved at least for two centuries, and who could boast sixteen quarterings on their coats of arms. They formed the top two classes of the Order, the Knights of Justice and the Knights of Honour and Devotion. A smaller group, known as Knights and Dames of Magistral Grace, formed the third category, designed for those of less noble origin. Today the Order has changed its character, and these ancient, almost archaic requirements are no longer strictly observed.

Although the last Grand Master in Malta, von Hompesch, did not put up even a token struggle before fleeing Napoleon's occupation, the Order has never given up its claims to certain palaces on the island: notably the Grand Master's palace; the residence of the Governor-General and the *auberges*, once the hostels of the knights of differing *langues*, or language groups, used today as government offices; the armoury and library and the great co-cathedral of St John – all in Valletta – which was once the conventual church of the Order. I accompanied the present Grand Master when he made a State visit to Malta some years ago, where he laid a wreath on the tomb of the great de la Vallette.

When Pope John became pope he did his best to heal the rift between the Order and the Vatican. He approved a new constitution for the Order, guaranteeing afresh its sovereignty and independence. Shortly afterwards, 29 knights met in secret conclave to elect their new Grand Master – the office having remained unfilled for some years. First they attended Mass in their chapel, which is hung with the banners of the Order. After a frugal breakfast they returned, some of the electors, professed knights – those who had taken the vows of poverty, chastity and obedience – in black robes, the others in splendid uniforms of scarlet and gold. After invoking the guidance of the Holy Spirit they proceeded to the villa, their standard bearer at their head carrying the scarlet flag emblazoned with the white Maltese Cross. Before entering, those armed handed over their swords to a custodian. They took their places in a tapestried hall on either side of a long table beneath the portraits of the previous 76 princes and Grand Masters.

The electors bore some of the most illustrious names in the world, but on a card before each chair the only title given was the humble one of 'brother'. Each elector was handed a wooden ball, with a hole into which he slid his ballot paper. The name receiving most votes was then put to a second vote, this time the electors using a white ball to signify assent and a black ball to show disapproval. The 77th Grand Master elected, with the subsequent approval of the Pope, was a quiet lawyer of modest stature, Angelo de Mojana di Cologna. Aged 56 at the time of his election, he has an impeccable aristocratic pedigree, his family claiming noble lineage back to well before the Middle Ages. He became a Knight of Honour and Devotion in 1940, took his first vows ten years later, and in 1957 took the final solemn vows as a professed member at a time when the dispute with the Vatican was at its height. His election came as something of a surprise, but no doubt his experience as an administrative lawyer and his markedly serene talent for compromise swayed the electors, who saw in him a sovereign who would pilot the Order into calmer waters after the stormy past. His title is 'His most Eminent Highness Fra Angelo', and devout ladies curtsey to him whilst the men give him the courtesies due to a cardinal.

This election and the subsequent appointment of a new Grand Chancellor, a Canadian of Welsh origin, Quintin Jeremy Gwyn, breathed new life into this ancient organization. More emphasis was laid on charitable and hospital work, for the Order is in essence a Hospitaller Order, and less on the conferring of decorations on important Roman Catholics throughout the world. (The Order, by the way, boasts some of the most beautiful decorations in existence, as befits such an ancient institution.) It works in leper colonies in Africa, has hospitals in Latin America and Europe, sends medical teams to war-stricken areas, and in France organizes road ambulance services, among other things.

In Britain it has a hospital in St John's Wood. Much of the property it once held was lost after the reign of Henry VIII. Some of it was taken over in the reign of Queen Victoria by the Order of St John of Jerusalem, popularly known as the St John Ambulance Brigade. It is a sign of the ecumenical times that the Soveign Order, though not recognized by the British government, has very amicable relations with its Protestant counterpart. The Grand Prior and other dignitaries are always honoured guests when the British Association of the Order hold their rare dinners in the city. These are held in the Merchant Taylors' Hall, since this company has special links with the Order. In former times it made the jerkins which the knights wore under their armour, and even today the two institutions share the same patron saint, St

John the Baptist. In some ways both the Order and the St John Ambulance Brigade foreshadowed the Red Cross and many other similar organizations.

Quintin Gwyn does not lay claim to sixteen quarterings, though he believes that one of the Welsh martyrs was a distant ancestor. He brings to the Order the experience of a lifetime in business, and is an untiring traveller on the affairs of the Order in every part of the world. In his work he is helped by his graceful and devoted wife Barbara, one of the few ladies ever to have lived in the hitherto monastic Palazzo di Malta.

On its ground floor is the *ambulatorio*, where the public can come at any hour for medical treatment. Across the court-yard is the small hand mint where coins of the Order are still struck for the numismatic collector. The Order also has its own stamps. These cannot be put to postal use, but are eagerly collected by numerous philatelists. These stamps are on sale at the Order's post office on the upper floor of the *palazzo* – a strange place where stamps are bought but letters never posted.

The Order hopes one day that it will be possible to acquire territory of its own again, perhaps the tip of Malta or some other island in the Mediterranean. Then it will not only be able to use its stamps and its money, but – and this is a distant dream – may be able to revive some of its past sea-going glories by having its own flag on the oceans.

This may appear to some to be something of a Never-Never Land, but ruling this mini-State are men of good heart out to help humanity. They enjoy their work and the picturesque ceremony that attends it, but those who have seen the sick and bed-ridden pilgrims cared for on their journeys to and from Lourdes, as well as at the shrine itself can testify to the practical sense behind these uniforms em-blazoned with the Maltese Cross.

Compared with the large British Embassy to Italy, the British Legation to the Holy See is a modest establishment.

It must be one of the few British legations left in the world, for most missions have long since been inflated to embassy status. One of the reasons for this modesty is the fact that the Queen is nominal head of the Church of England, and religious as well as national susceptibilities might be hurt if the minister in charge were elevated to the rank of ambassador. Every successive British government shelves the question of up-grading the mission, in spite of continued Roman Catholic pressure to do so. In consequence, the Vatican does not have a nuncio at the Court of St James, who would automatically become doyen of the diplomatic corps, but has to content itself with an Apostolic Delegate accredited to the Roman Catholic hierarchy in Britain.

To head the British Legation to the Holy See calls for particular qualities, for the minister has to convey to the pope and his advisers the attitude of the British government on questions of the day – no easy task in these times of Irish violence and unrest. The present minister, the urbane Mr Desmond Crawley, narrowly missed death early in 1972 when a bomb was thrown through his sitting-room window late one night.

In 1958 the British Minister was an extremely colourful character, Sir Marcus Cheke. In years past, when he was vice-marshal of the diplomatic corps, he had compiled a confidential handbook for young British diplomats proceed-ing abroad for the first time in their careers. It eventually leaked to the press, and I had a copy by my bedside for years and relished its flavour of old-world courtesy and shrewdness. The mythical young diplomats were called Mr and Mrs John Bull and were sent *en poste* to the mission headed by a Sir Henry Sealingwax. There were delicious notes on how to behave when invited by the *chef de mission* and his wife Lady Sealingwax. One gem I remember dealt with the occasion when the ambassador gave the young third secretary and his wife a lift home after a reception to which they had all been invited. The correct procedure, according to the booklet, was to thank them for the lift and then to wait at the kerbside and wave until the ambassadorial Rolls had driven from sight. One may laugh at such courtesies in this brasher age, as also about the problems of dropping cards, signing books and *placement*, but there was a lot of commonsense in the advice given. For instance: always refer to your colleagues by their Christian names, so that you give the impression that your mission is a devoted and happy family, even if it is seething with internal intrigue. Again, never stay with your wife at a cocktail party, but mingle separately and compare notes afterwards in case there should be anything to report to the ambassador. By the same token, never avoid talking to a bore, for he may be important. Another hint was to go to any funeral requiring official British presence: 'many a useful contact is made by a handshake over the open grave.' There was good advice too on how to deal with the government of the country in which the mission operated: 'Do your business efficiently and note the attitude of the government official with whom you are dealing. As you leave, cast a quick glance over your shoulder; you may find that the official has relaxed and after putting on a stern front is actually smiling – or the converse could also happen. On the other hand, if a government official should call on you, escort him to the door and close it behind him after you have completed your business before relaxing in any way.'

Having read and appreciated this little masterpiece some years earlier I was naturally more than usually interested to see its author. I expected to find a snowy-haired old diplomat. Instead I found a spruce and dapper man in his early fifties. I told him that I had read and admired his booklet. 'You shouldn't have read that. How did you get hold of it?' I told him it had become common knowledge years ago, a fact of which he was seemingly unaware. We turned to talk of the Vatican, and here Cheke showed himself to be very well informed. It was obvious that he enjoyed all the pomp and circumstance of the papal court, and he told me that the Vatican and the Court of St James's watched each other closely on matters of ceremonial, since both laid great store on doing things in the proper way. Marcus Cheke had had plenty of opportunity to see how matters were conducted in Buckingham Palace when he had to escort new ambassadors to present their letter of credence to the Queen. So the grandeur of St Peter's and the Vatican palaces was something which he took in his stride.

He told me, at that first meeting, that he had established good personal relations with Pope Pius XII. In fact he had just been to see him following his return from leave in Britain. 'Whilst I was there I thought I would present the Pope with a copy of the *Shorter Oxford Dictionary*, knowing how keen a student of English he is,' said Cheke, warming to his subject. 'I paid for it out of my own pocket, the Foreign Office would not pay for such a thing. Then I thought, shall I give him the ordinary linen bound edition, or a leatherbound one? Well, I decided that the linen bound one would be right, for the Italians bind books so well themselves. However, as I looked at it, it seemed rather a modest gift, so I added a copy of *Burke's Peerage* as well.'

Then he took out a copy of *Harper's Magazine* from his desk and handed it to me. 'It is a very good article and can tell you more than I can.' All through our talk there was a twinkle in his eye as though he was shrewdly summing me up before deciding what to tell me. He had more than a touch of the stage about him, and was one of the few diplomats who delighted in getting into his formal dress complete with sword, a cape thrown over his shoulders, and attending the interminable ceremonies of the Vatican. To see him walking down the nave of St Peter's or through the screen of the Sistine Chapel to take his place near the altar was delightful. The ceremonial and protocol for him had an inner meaning. Nor did he mind being a mere minister, having to allow ambassadors of newly independent countries to take precedence. He was dignity and serenity itself, and I have rarely found a man happier or more suited for this delicate assignment. It was an inspired appointment of a man who had a natural courtesy and a deep sense of religion combined with a whimsical sense of humour.

When Pope John succeeded Pope Pius, Cheke was soon on equally friendly terms with that remarkable pontiff. The zenith of his career came when Queen Elizabeth the Queen Mother, accompanied by Princess Margaret, came on an official visit to Rome, and paid a courtesy call at the Vatican.

This was in the spring of 1959. Marcus Cheke had those correspondents interested in the story round to his house on the via Camilluccia, a graceful villa with a lovely garden now hemmed in, alas, by ugly blocks of flats. He was clearly excited at the prospect of having the Queen Mother and her daughter to dinner. He explained in minute detail what arrangements had been made, down to the flowers which would decorate the table. He also gave us a perfect example of his patient courtesy. Launched well into the account of the preparations for this forthcoming occasion, he was interrupted by the late arrival of an elderly American woman journalist. I must confess that I was inwardly annoyed at the interruption, just as he was getting into the flow of his account, and I dare say others were too, for the correspondent concerned was not popular with her colleagues, and known for her irascible manners. However, Marcus Cheke offered her a chair, and said, 'I do apologize for living so far out. You must have found it rather difficult to find my house. Now I am sure your colleagues won't mind if I just repeat for your benefit what I have already said.' It was a gallant gesture of kindness, and I felt ashamed at my hard feelings at the late arrival. Cheke explained that he had invited two cardinals, who apparently had to sit together. The difficulty was that he had laid on a splendid meal though one of the cardinals was known to eat only toast and the other only apples. In those days cardinals were always received by two servants carrying candles when they made their entrance. Cheke showed us the long candlesticks made of white-painted wood on which four candles bound together were set.

'Well, I know that is the tradition,' he went on, 'but I felt that we had to do something special for the Queen Mother. Accordingly I have arranged for my servants to escort her in with silver candelabra and then, when she and the princess have arrived in the drawing room and have received the other guests, they have instructions to nip smartly round the back and replace the candelabra on the dining table.' He was in his element as he described all these plans; he had his house hung with ancient banners for the occasion – which passed off splendidly.

Apart from this love of grandeur, Marcus Cheke had another side to his character. He would go for long walks in the Alban Hills with students of the English College, starting at sunrise and tramping with them all day, to return with them to their summer residence overlooking Lake Albano. When he held the Queen's birthday party, at which many cardinals and other high Vatican dignitaries were present, round the corner from the main garden was a grove for the students complete with a barrel of beer and a darts board.

I shall never forget the last such occasion. Already a dying man, he received his guests sitting in a chair with his devoted and anxious wife Constance standing at his side. 'Have you seen my cardinals, Patrick?' he asked proudly. 'There are 22 of them here.' A short while afterwards he was taken to a clinic and Pope John paid him the ultimate honour of visiting him. It was an unusual thing for a pope to visit a Protestant diplomat, but Pope John, with his ecumenical vision and his undoubted affection for this distinguished British diplomat, stayed by his bedside for some time.

'Is there anything I can do for you, my son?' Pope John asked. Very feebly, Marcus Cheke smiled and said, 'I would like you to say the Lord's Prayer with me.' The Pope took him by the hand, and together they said, each in his own language, the 'Our Father'.

The next day Marcus Cheke died. He left instructions that he should be buried in England. He could have been buried in the so-called Protestant cemetery where Keats was laid to rest and where Shelley's heart was buried, but he knew that even this was a complicated procedure which would give his colleague, the British Ambassador to Italy, much labour. To the last Cheke was a very perfect gentle knight. He was one of the last of the mild eccentrics which have down the generations served their country well. In his earlier career when in Portugal he once startled his hosts at a garden party by arriving on the back of a donkey, whose hooves he had spent hours polishing. My friend the late David Walker, who was there at the time in Lisbon, said that by the time Cheke arrived the reception was well under way and great quantities of food and drink had already been consumed, so that very few present thought his arrival unusual. But knowing Marcus Cheke, I don't suppose he minded all that much.

He, and a number of ministers both before and after him, were aided and counselled by another character, Jim Utley, an honorary attaché and a devout Roman Catholic. He was a mine of Vatican information, though his contacts were almost entirely with the traditionalists. He was devoted to Marcus Cheke and his successors until his death.

James Utley was an elderly confirmed bachelor when I first got to know him, well experienced in the ways of the Vatican, from which he received several honours. Originally he had come to Rome as a tutor to one of the princely families and had over the years attached himself in an honorary capacity to the British Legation to the Holy See. One of his brothers was a Dominican monk, and the Vatican was his life. Utley was a traditionalist not only in thought but in dress, appearance and manners. Of medium height, rather portly and a of a cheerful countenance, he sported a monocle for added panache and always seemed most at ease when in formal attire. For years he contributed a Christmas story to the *Tablet* – enchanting vignettes of life in nineteenth-century Rome as related by a cardinal to his nephew. Like his imaginary cardinal, he was a connoisseur of good living. He helped a young waiter set up a restaurant round the corner from the legation, and a table was always reserved for him. He had the strange habit of putting sliced lemon into his red wine. He said it tasted better that way. He advised on the décor and lighting of the restaurant, which was truly Roman in its way – not garishly fashionable, but a place where you could be sure to find a decently cooked meal with reasonably priced wine to go with it.

He died in the legation he had served so long and where he lived in his last years. On the very night he was due to retire – he was well into his seventies – he dined as usual at his restaurant and returned at his usual hour. The next morning the porter found him dead in his room in a pool of blood. The circumstances of his unexpected death were never satisfactorily explained. It was a tragic end for a man who had devoted his life to the delicate operations of an important, and often under-estimated British diplomatic mission.

CHAPTER SIXTEEN

Special Occasions

Anyone living in Rome, whatever his job, soon experiences the joy and sometimes the burden of a constant stream of visitors. The pleasure of such occasions generally outweighed the fatigue, though some callers obviously found it difficult to understand that one had work to do, and could not show them round all the time. One friend of mine hit on the splendid idea of sending her less loved visitors round Rome on the *circolare* tram, where they could have a ride of two and a half hours for a modest 50 lire. The more understanding of our callers, however, found their own way to what they wished to see, and dropped in for an occasional meal or a drink. I once said to my wife, 'The word must have got round all right: call on the Smiths – lovely view, good cooking, knowledgeable information, all for the price of a bunch of flowers.' And my wife replied, 'Well, that's not a bad reputation to have, and they don't all bring flowers, anyway.'

Sir Hugh Greene tended to bring his tribute in bottled form. We had worked together in the early war days in the German Section of the BBC, and between bulletins would put the typist in a huge waste-paper basket, and then indulge in a little fielding practice with a cricket ball, until it was safe for her to emerge again and get on with the next batch of news. Hugh Greene is extremely tall, with searching pale blue eyes, and what wispy hair he has reminds one more of a new-born baby than anything else. An inveterate journalist, it was comforting to know that this former foreign correspondent was at the apex of affairs at the BBC. He told me that he took tremendous delight in the hurly-burly of his post, and during his term broke down the 'Auntie' image of the Corporation, by encouraging irreverent shows such as *That was the Week that Was*. I feel sure it reminded him of his pre-war days in Berlin, where tartly scurrilous cabarets were all the rage. He was never a man to stand on ceremony, could drink endlessly – mostly beer – without its having much apparent effect, and could at times be disconcertingly iconoclastic in the eyes of his closest collaborators.

Perhaps he was incensed by the high-handed treatment I had once received at the hands of the Vatican censors, for he decided to accept an invitation to address a meeting of Vatican officials and chose as his theme the evils of censorship. He arrived on a cold February day in 1965. Rome was about to have its first real fall of snow for 200 years. When one's chief comes on such a visitation there is a mass of detailed planning beforehand for the local man. I had accordingly arranged a round of meetings and meals as well as an audience of Pope Paul. He was the guest of the embassy and the legation, and there was a copious dinner at George's restaurant just off the via Veneto in honour of the top brass of the Italian radio and television organization, the RAI, which went on well into the early hours. Early on the following morning I drove through the snow to take him to his lecture appointment. He looked a bit pale in his vast room in the Grand Hotel. He had certainly not expected snow and was aghast when he looked out of his window on waking to find everything white. At first he thought that it was the result of a hangover, and his alarm increased when he saw a large tree in the piazza beneath his window quietly subside, like a ballerina taking her final curtain call, under the unwonted weight of the snow on its branches.

As we drove to the lecture hall, I saw for the first and only time the Romans driving slowly. The municipal authorities, who had no idea how to deal with this unusual fall – there were not even shovels to cope – had the mad idea of trying to hose the streets down, which made matters worse. When we arrived at the hall, which was already fairly full of clerics and other Vatican officials, together with a sprinkling of RAI representatives, the interpreters had gone on strike about something or other – I never discovered what was their grievance. We waited, and I brought a *caffé corretto* (strong coffee laced with brandy) for us both to help clear our heads after the carousing of the previous night. The interpreters were pacified, and the chairman of the meeting introduced Greene. As he began his lecture, all the lights went out. There was a pause while candles were hastily brought from a nearby church, and Sir Hugh went on with his lecture, highly amused by the mysterious circumstances – interjecting that perhaps he had better sing *Lead Kindly Light* in the hope of getting the lights back. The current, however, remained cut, so the aggrieved interpreters could not translate anyway and I doubt whether very many understood the burden of Sir Hugh's remarks on the futility of censorship. However, I managed to get scripts printed and distributed before he reached the end of his address, during the course of which he made a brief reference to the fairness and balance of my despatches on the Vatican Council, which still had its final session to run.

The following day I accompanied him to the Vatican, together with the BBC's Roman Catholic adviser, Father Agnellus Andrew, for the private audience with Pope Paul. The former stringent rules about ceremonial dress which had obtained when I had first come to Rome had been swept away by the earlier sessions of the Council, and we were permitted to go to this personal meeting in sober lounge suits instead of formal dress – though Fr Andrew wore his monk's habit, the only time I ever saw him in it. We were escorted with grave ceremony by Swiss guards and damask-liveried *bussolanti* – the Pope's personal retainers – through the great frescoed Clementine hall, then round three sides of the quadrangular palace, passing through chambers of growing magnificence until we reached the small throne room. Gone was all the baroque crimson and gilt of Pope

John's days. Everything had been redecorated in grey and gold in the subdued good taste of the present pontiff, who had removed many of the florid ornaments of his predecessor, including the Murano chandeliers of incredible garishness.

We were kept waiting for well over half an hour before the Pope's personal secretary motioned us towards the private library, the door of which had been opened. As we entered, the slight figure of Pope Paul rose from his desk with a smile to greet each of us with a warm handshake, holding our out-stretched hand in both of his, as is his invariable custom, at the same time looking straight into our eyes. We sat on three high-backed chairs arranged in front of the Pope's desk, where the Pope resumed his seat. His English was slow and carefully phrased. After the customary courtesies were accomplished he turned to Sir Hugh and said, 'You have a very famous name – how is your brother Graham? [he pronounced it 'Grarm', in a gravelly voice]. Why does he not come to see me? He has promised, but he never comes.' Greene told the Pope that his brother was well, and that he would be pleased to pass on Pope Paul's message. 'When I was Archbishop of Milan,' the Pope continued, 'I had time to read his books, but now [he waved despairingly at the papers on his desk] I have very little time. He is a great writer in the cause of goodness and truth. Please tell him that I would like to see him very much.'

The Pope then switched to French, in which he is far more at his ease. He complimented Sir Hugh on his lecture and went on to say how pleased he was that the BBC had a permanent correspondent in Rome. With the hint almost of a winking smile the Pope added, 'he has done much "propaganda" for us, both in Rome and on our travels.' At this point Fr Andrew broke in proudly to say that many millions in Britain watched or listened to religious broadcasts from the BBC. Pope Paul beamed as the Franciscan enumerated these facts. Perhaps I was a little firm, but I interrupted my colleague to make clear to the Pope that the broadcasts were not exclusively Roman Catholic, since the majority of the British were Anglican and Protestant. The Pope, who is a good listener, turned to Sir Hugh and said, 'I hope you are happy with the Catholics in the BBC and that they give a good account of themselves.' There followed a concise explanation by Sir Hugh of the activities of the BBC, in which some emphasis was placed on its services round the world in many languages as well as in English. The clock of St Peter's had long since struck noon. The audience was drawing to its close. Pope Paul, rising from his desk, said, 'I hope you will accept a souvenir of your visit to Rome,' and then handed us medallions marking the second year of his pontificate. He ended, as he began, in English: 'I bless you, your family and friends, your colleagues and all who work in the BBC.' Then, pressing a button on his desk, he added, 'This is an age of publicity. Perhaps you would like a photograph?'

Felici, the tubby papal photographer, dressed in formal clothes, came in, took one flash picture and withdrew backwards. We took our leave of this solitary, frail-looking figure, for whom our visit had been a momentary interruption of his other, far more arduous tasks. It had all been simple and dignified. None of us spoke as we made our way back from the Pope's study through the throne rooms and ante-chambers, past the Noble Guard in their gleaming helmets, past the Gentlemen of Cape and Sword, past the Swiss Guard and the papal flunkeys.

Nothing can possibly be grander than Italian grand opera, and if you want to see and hear it at its full-throated, luxurious best, you cannot do better than get tickets for *Aida*, performed during the summer in the ruins of the Baths of Caracalla. It seats some 5000, and has an enormous stage set between two massive ruined pillars of these ancient Roman baths. The dapper and energetic stage director for many years was a Signor Cruciani, and he showed me round on the morning of the performance of this highly successful opera which Verdi originally composed for the opening of the Suez Canal. As we walked across the broad stage, scene-shifters stripped to the waist with hammers in their belts were putting up gigantic papier-mâché Pharaohs and sphinxes and – adjusting great columns with lotus leaf capitals in faithful replica of the temple of Karnak. It takes 150 scene-shifters to cope with this opera, and in the triumphal scene there are almost a thousand on the stage at the same time – contingents of victorious warriors with shields, lances, swords and banners, trumpeters on the temple walls, choirs on and off stage, the hero Rhadames riding in on a chariot drawn by four spirited horses, while other horsemen gallop across the stage at intervals to the tumultuous applause of the huge audience. Even greater applause is reserved for the third act, which takes place by the banks of the Nile. As the curtains sweep back, the waters of the river shimmer in the silvery moonlight and a camel lopes disdainfully across the stage to the delight of the audience. Yet musically the opera is not just an excuse for showmanship. The acoustics of the arena are perfect, and the humid night air puts no special strain on the singers whose voices float out clearly to the farthermost corners of the auditorium. Not for nothing was St Cecilia born not far away.

Santa Cecilia, the patron saint of music, was a Roman girl. She belonged to the patrician family, the Gens Caecilia, and was put to death during the persecutions of Marcus Aurelius. It was a slow death. She was placed in a *calidarium*, a deep pit, where they tried to boil her, but she emerged unscathed, singing. Then she was beheaded. One of the most touching statues in the world is by Maderna, done in the sixteenth century, when they found her body, according to legend, still in the state it was in when freshly buried. It shows a young woman seemingly asleep with a veil over her head and a deep gash in her neck. The artist had been present when her body was discovered, and was clearly moved and inspired by what he had seen.

She lies buried in the lovely old church in Trastevere which bears her name – one of the most peaceful places in that noisy area of Rome, with a fountain playing in the courtyard before the graceful portico of African marble. As someone who has always loved and admired the tradition of English church music, I like to think that there is a special link between Santa Cecilia and England, for near the church door is the tomb of an Englishman, Cardinal Adam Easton of Hertford, who was held prisoner by Pope Urban VI. Richard II managed to intercede for Easton's release, after the unfortunate cardinal had managed to smuggle a letter from his jail to the English Benedictines describing his calamitous fate. Urban did release him, but stripped him of his princely rank. Easton led an obscure life as a monk for eight years until a new pope was elected, Boniface IX, who restored him to his former dignities. I like to think of him presiding with Santa Cecilia over all the choirs in England who maintain the tradition of singing unto the Lord Sunday by Sunday.

The saint is certainly evoked by the Academy of Saint Cecilia in Rome, founded by the great Palestrina, and still in the second half of the twentieth century a great centre of music under its gifted leader Professor Renato Fasano and his Virtuosi di Roma, one of the foremost string quartets in the world. Yet Rome and indeed Italy is most noted for opera – and every Italian enjoys going to his favourite Verdi or Puccini, his Rossini and Donizetti – and many other composers' operas besides. The Rome opera house disputes with Milan and Naples for the operatic palm. It is a remarkable building, with its great painted dome showing what could be the triumph scene from *Aida*. Above its lofty proscenium there is still an inscription to 'Mussolini Dux' (another case where the Italians have seen fit to let sleeping memorials lie) and immediately below it an illuminated digital clock. I recall the first time I visited the opera, shortly after the liberation of Rome. They were performing *Tosca*, and Gigli and Maria Caniglia sang the principal roles. There had been some malicious gossip that Gigli had been a Fascist sympathiser, and this was his first appearance. The atmosphere was tense. He came on, without the usual ripple of applause reserved for great artistes even before they opened their mouths, and sang Cavaradossi's aria while painting in church. He hung on to the penultimate note until he was almost about to burst. Then someone in the gallery shouted '*Bravo!*' and the whole house was drowned in deafening applause. Whatever the allegations, he had sung his way back into the hearts of the Italians, and the whole opera was a personal triumph for a man who had one of the loveliest voices the world has heard.

The Romans are notorious late-comers to every kind of spectacle. When Sir John Barbirolli came to conduct he would begin punctually as the clock's figures flipped to nine, and many richly dressed patrons had to wait fuming in the foyer until the first scene had ended. 'Glorious John', as Vaughan Williams dubbed him, was a favourite with Roman musicians and public alike. He was dapper and small and once, after I had dined with him – he ate sparingly before a performance – we walked together from the Hotel Quirinale through the door which leads straight into the opera house. He was wearing a wide-brimmed, black Borsalino hat which he told me proudly had been given him after he had completed a Verdi recording. 'And,' he added, 'do you know I have exactly the same size as Verdi, who wore a hat exactly like this?' He took my arm as we walked slowly to the artistes' entrance. He was already a sick man, and his hands trembled. Yet when he took up his extra lightweight baton, made specially for him by an artisan in the United States (who had made them for Toscanini, whom Barbirolli had succeeded), his hand was as steady as a rock. 'You know, Patrick,' he once said to me, 'I have conducted some of the best orchestras in the world and some of the worst. And some of the best can be the worst on their off days. They know their conductors. They are like horses. When you come into rehearsal they size you up and within the first few minutes know whether you are a good jockey or not. If you're not, they'll have you off.'

The Rome Opera orchestra responded to Barbirolli as I have never heard them for anyone else. They loved his Venetian wisecracks at rehearsal, and he communicated to them his devoted enthusiasm to the work being performed. I had known him down the years ever since he had first brought the Hallé Orchestra to Vienna shortly after the war. I had seen him again in Berlin where he had conducted the Berlin Symphony Orchestra in the bare Titania Palast and received a standing ovation. He conducted every kind of music with a particular passion, but his heart was in Italian music, which enabled him to soar to lofty pinnacles of the sublime. Yet he was a modest man off the concert platform, for ever worrying over scores and how they should be bowed —he was a cellist in his early years. Supported by his devoted wife Evelyn Rothwell, the gifted oboist, he had his diaries full of engagements for years ahead. He could not imagine ever taking a holiday, and even after several collapses went on with his music-making. His last concert in Rome shortly before his death was in the Basilica of Maxentius.

His fund of anecdotes was unending. One of his favourites told how a British sergeant came to his dressing-room after a performance of a Verdi opera. He thanked John for a wonderful evening. 'Do you really like Italian opera?' inquired John. 'Yes sir, very much, except . . . well, it seems to me to be all prick and daggers, doesn't it?' John also told me that the British were great music lovers. He had once been in a taxi coming down Saint Martin's Lane when it was held up because a dray carrying blocks of ice from the firm of Carlo Gatti and Stevens had broken down in front, causing a traffic jam. The driver, an enormous man with waxed mustachio, in a leather apron, was scratching the side of his chin looking at the wheel which had come off. He took his time. The taxi-driver hooted, leant out of his driving seat and shouted, 'Hey you Pagliacci, on with the f—— motley!' 'You see what I mean?' said John with a twinkle. He was good company, whether talking music, cooking or eating at one of the many *trattorie* he used to patronize near the Opera House.

Like all great conductors he never tried to stand between you and the music. It was never 'Barbirolli's *Requiem*' or 'Barbirolli's *Lied von der Erde*' – it was as near what Verdi or Mahler intended as he could make it. On that last open-air concert in the ruins of Rome he opened with a graceful and zestful Rossini overture. Then, going off, he tripped over the spike of a double bass, fell flat on his face and injured his temple. However, he insisted on carrying on. Only those of us in the front rows noticed. He came back, undaunted, to conduct Stravinsky, and in the interval murmured to me, 'I rather liked that *Firebird*,' as though it was none of his doing. He had plans for Japan, for every capital in Europe, recordings and recitals of every kind. A few months later he collapsed over his desk while conducting a recording. It was the way he always wanted to go, surrounded by his beloved music he had served so well. I like to think that Santa Cecilia was waiting for him on the other side.

Two biographies have been written since his death, both giving detailed accounts of his life and work, but neither has managed to capture the man as I knew him, a perfectionist of his art, a man who never forgot his countless friends, and who inspired a devoted band of Mancunians to follow him across the world wherever he performed. For all his frail frame and tiny stature, he was a musical giant, and, more than that, a great human being. He enriched the lives of thousands who never knew him personally, yet who felt they did when he mounted the rostrum and cast an imperious, quelling glance over his shoulder at the audience to bid

them be silent, before raising his baton – a magic wand
which opened the gates of Elysium, and gave a glimpse of
the infinite.

CHAPTER SEVENTEEN

Arrivederci Roma

By the time 1970 came round I realized I had completed 30 years' reporting for the BBC in various parts of the world. Rome had changed in the thirteen years I had been there. Overpopulated, noisy, badly administered – for who can run a capital with a deficit of a thousand million pounds? – yet incomparable, eternal. I never minded leaving Rome on an assignment. I was not one of those expatriates who felt there was nowhere else I could live happily. Everywhere was home for me; and we had put down a few really deep roots in Switzerland, where we had always had a small house in the mountains, a refuge from the hurly-burly of the world. It beckoned ever more insistently as the years ticked by. Some of my despatches dealt with problems which cropped up in one form or another over and over again. Who would be the next pope? Would a non-Italian take over after more than four centuries? Would the Communists come to power in Italy? What would happen to the remaining monarchies of the Arab world? Would Malta become a Russian base? Would war break out again between Israel and Egypt after the uneasy truce? Was there any sign of Russia loosening its grip on Eastern Europe? Would the United Nations really tackle the problems of the developing world and narrow the gap between rich and poor before it was too late? Would more countries accept family planning as a sensible way of controlling population growth? Who would take over when Franco goes? What about Portugal? Would Roman Catholic priests be allowed to marry? What chances were there of Christian unity? Would Turkey, under its military regime, solve her pressing social and economic problems?

What about the Greece of the colonels? Would King Constantine ever return from exile?

I rushed round reporting on these and other questions. Suddenly I wondered why I had been doing it for so long. When I started out on my travels as a young man, I was imbued with the idea that the public had the right to know. I still believe it. The task of the correspondent is not easy. He has to comfort the afflicted, and, in doing so, often afflicts the comfortable, as often as not in his own organization and in his own country, as elsewhere. Could I ever think of doing anything else? The BBC had become a way of life. I held it in affection and respect, yet I knew that Rome could not go on for ever. Where next? No correspondent likes to return to an earlier post. I was too old for the New World, and I had served in most of the other places abroad. I had always gone where I was sent. Now it was time to bow out gracefully, which I did.

It was fun while it lasted. I felt that, of all my many fascinating assignments, the Italian one was certainly the finest. All roads had led to and from Rome. I took the road to Switzerland without too much regret, knowing that Rome is always there, in its heart immutable and welcoming in its rather off-hand way. I go back there often, and its warm-hearted casual attitude is reassuring. In Switzerland I would not see the *cupola* of St Peter's rising out of the morning haze as I took breakfast in my ancient tower home. Instead I could see the mountains rising majestically out of the mist. I did not hear the noonday cannon fire from the Janiculum any longer. Instead, there was the song of many birds, which, apart from swifts and pigeons, are noticeably absent from most great Italian cities. I would no longer have every weekend disrupted by sudden news stories breaking. I was free at last from the tyranny of the telephone call from London.

I miss it all, of course, for a natural vanity in being asked for the latest news is well satisfied when you are a correspondent and expect a ringside seat at every occasion of public interest. I had been a one man band most of my life. It was time to let someone else put on the harness and trumpet out his discoveries. I still cannot make up my mind whether I am sorry or not, for I continue to write. One cannot break the habit of a lifetime. Yet now I can do it when I feel like it. Perhaps the whole species of foreign correspondents, such as I was trained to be, is a dying one. Jet flight and satellites demand the instant story; though valiant efforts are made, in-depth treatment is not what the public wants. Journalism has always been largely allied to the show world. I was lucky to have had my time in the BBC when I did, before television changed the habits of the masses, who now want to see rather than hear. Rome sweet Rome, it will always remain. A reminder of the more than a quarter of a century of newsgathering and trying to understand why things happen and why people act the way they do. Rome is a good place for such observations. You never say good-bye to Rome. Once you have lived there you always belong. It does have a special touch of eternity, for you never really leave it for good. It is always *arrivederci Roma*.

Gordevio, 1974

Index

Index

Adzubei, Alexei, 173-4
Adzubei, Rada, 173-4
Agnes, church of St, 38
Agnus Dei, 28
Albano, Lake, 21, 109-10
Alfieri, Vittorio, 57
Alfrink, Cardinal Bernard, 199
Alston, Mgr Leo, 183
Andrew, Fr Agnellus, 234-5
Annunciation, broadcasting journal, 23
Assisi, 22
Athenagoras, Patriarch, 179, 210, 213

Babuino, via del, 90
Badoglio government, 35
Baglin, Bill, 53
Balcon, Jill, 88
Barbirolli, Sir John, 239-42
Bartlett, Vernon, 51, 83-5
Bartoli, Domenico, 64
Barzini, Luigi, 54-60, 131
Battistoni, shop of, 17
BBC, 11, 21, 53, 80, 106-7, 156, 236, 244
Bea, Cardinal Augustin, 180
Bedford, Duke of, 39
Belice, 60
Bethany, Ladies of, 38
Blessings, papal, 28
Bolton, Glorney, 75
Borelli, Fr, 92-3
Borromee, islands of, 45
Burns, Fr Charles, 117-18
Burton, Richard, 98-100

Cacciatore, Vera, 87-9

Caffarelli, Duke of, 17
Caminada, Jerome, 211
Canali, Cardinal, 137
Caniglia, Maria, 239
Capitol, 31
Capovilla, Archbishop Loris, 158, 164-8, 173, 183
Caracalla, baths of, 236
Cardinale, Claudia, 101
Cassian, St, 24
Cauzique, Louis, 14
Cecilia, St, 237-8
Cheke, Sir Marcus, 225-30
Chigi, Palazzo, 36
Christina, Queen of Sweden, 45
Churchill, Sir Winston, 80, 162
Cinecittà, 98
Clare, St, 22
Clemente, St, church of, 17, 134
Collegio Romano, 32
Coghill, Neville, 99
Condotti, via, 17
Convento Pozzuolo, 21
Corriere della Sera, 48
Crawley, Desmond, 225
Croce, Santa, church of, 42
Cupertino, St Joseph of, 24
Cyril, St, 18
Czestechowa, Madonna of, 23

Daily American, 68
Damiano, St, 22
Davies, Sir Walford, 80
Daubeny, Peter, 101
Devil's Advocate, 25
Dimbleby, Richard, 66
Dodd, Fr Romuald, 17-20
Dolci, Danilo, 93-4, 96
Doria, Andrea, 39

249

Index